History of the Mongols

Based on Eastern and Western Accounts of the Thirteenth and Fourteenth Centuries

by
BERTOLD SPULER

Translated from the German by
Helga and Stuart Drummond

DORSET PRESS
New York

N. 25962

89 B 1308

*DS
19
.S56 13
1988*

This edition published by Dorset Press,
a division of Marboro Books Corporation,
by arrangement with
University of California Press
1988 Dorset Press

ISBN 0-88029-271-7
(formerly ISBN 0-520-01960-1)

Printed in the United States of America
M 9 8 7 6 5 4 3 2

CONTENTS

I. THE FOUNDING OF THE EMPIRE: CHINGGIZ KHAN AND HIS IMMEDIATE SUCCESSORS

II. THE MONGOLS IN THE EYES OF THE EUROPEANS (REPORTS OF ENVOYS)

III. THE ILKHAN DYNASTY IN PERSIA
(1256–1335/54)

A. THE DEVELOPMENT UP TO THE CONVERSION OF THE DYNASTY TO ISLAM

IV. THE MONGOL KHANS IN CHINA

A.   FROM AN ORIENTAL SOURCE

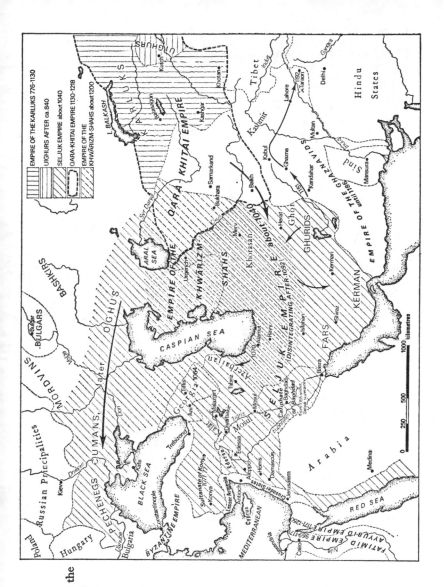

Map 1. States established by the Turks in the East (11th–12th century)

Map 2. Chinggiz Khan 1155 (1167?)–1227 and the Mongol States of the 13th century

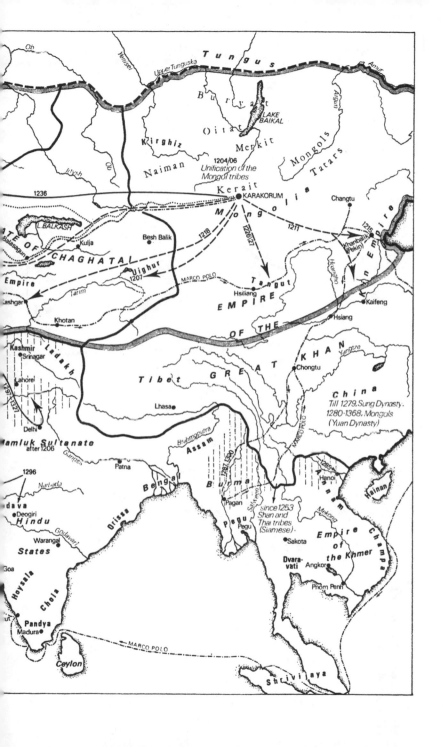

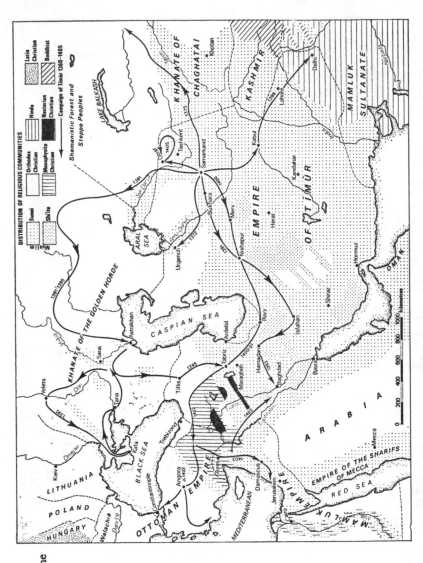

Map 3. Western Asia at the time of Timūr (about 1400)

DISTRIBUTION OF RELIGIOUS COMMUNITIES

Sunni
Shī'ite
Orthodox Christian
Monophysite Christian
Hindu
Nestorian Christian
Latin Christian
Buddhist

Shamanistic Forest and Steppe Peoples

Campaign of Timūr 1360–1405

KHANATE OF CHAGHATAI

KASHMIR

MAMLUK SULTANATE

EMPIRE OF TIMŪR

O M A N

KHANATE OF THE GOLDEN HORDE

ARAL SEA

CASPIAN SEA

LITHUANIA

POLAND

HUNGARY

Walachia

BLACK SEA

OTTOMAN EMPIRE

MEDITERRANEAN

ARABIA

MAMLUK EMPIRE

EMPIRE OF THE SHARIFS OF MECCA

RED SEA

LAKE BALKASH

Kiev

Yelets

Sarai

Astrakhan

Tana

Kafa

Tiflis

Trebizond

Angora × 1402

Constantinople

Damascus

Jerusalem

Mecca

Baghdad

Basra

Hormuz

Shiraz

Isfahan

Hamadan

Maragheh

Tabriz

Ardebil

Merv

Nishapur

Heat

Bukhara

Samarkand

Tashkent

Otrar

Urgench

Kabul

Kandahar

Lahore

Delhi

Kashgar

Khotan

0 200 400 600 800 1000 kilometres

INTRODUCTION

The Mongol invasion was as much a great divide in the national history of the Near East as in that of Eastern Europe. In both regions a continuous development, which had occurred over centuries and which had led to their being deeply imbued with a religious culture, seemed to have been brought to a sudden end. Even in the West, which had been only fleetingly exposed at its eastern extreme to the Mongol danger, and which had attributed the sudden eastward retreat of the Mongols in 1241 to the slaughter on the battlefield of Liegnitz and in the Mohi plain of Hungary, there began a new era. It was generally believed in Europe that there had at last been found in the Mongols allies against the Muslims. They were expected to crush the relentless and centuries-old enemy by means of an attack from the rear, to save the tottering crusader states on the Syrian coast, and to give new life to the desire to free once and for all the Holy Land.

The Muslims, the Christians both in East and West, and the Chinese who were equally concerned, all had good reason to study the new Lords, the 'Tartars' escaped from Tartarus. Confronted by the Mongols, they had either to increase awareness of their own special characteristics or to accept some *modus vivendi* with them. This complex situation impelled everybody concerned first of all to acquire the best possible understanding of the strangers so that they could base any further actions on adequate information. This soon led to the accumulation of a vast number of the most varying reports from which the extracts printed in this book are taken—a wealth of sources comparable with that produced at the beginning of the modern period by the Turkish threat. As a result, the historian has the material for a thorough description of the Mongol invasion of the thirteenth century. This introduction, which should be read in conjunction with the maps, is intended to provide a brief account of the Mongol advance from the East and so create a framework within which the following texts may be placed, to ensure a better understanding.

Within the various Turkish and Mongol tribes who for centuries had populated Eastern and Central Asia, there had already arisen in previous periods leading figures who had become the founders of vast empires. In the West a vivid memory of these remained, personified in the shape of Attila. Later on, the invasion of the Danubian plain by the Hungarians in 895 was a warning of possible dangers from the East. Toward the close of the twelfth century Temujin, although he was the son of a small Mongol chief and thus began without the benefit of any significant dynastic power, had once again succeeded in uniting these eastern tribes. Amongst them were adherents both of Nestorian Christianity and of Shamanism. After various struggles which are described in a Mongol text, the 'Secret History' (see below, pp. 17–29 and 41–57), and which around 1300 was painstakingly recorded once more by the Persian writer Rashīd ad-Dīn, Temujin was recognized as supreme Lord of the Mongols at a great meeting, a *quriltai*, in 1206 and given the title Chinggiz Khan (Čingiz Ḫān). With the aid of his relatives and his friends he was able to build up a strictly disciplined army which, given the fact that the Mongols thought of themselves as destined by divine will to be the rulers of the world (below, pp. 26ff), was soon to become an instrument for extensive conquests.

The first blow after 1215 fell on northern China which had been ruled for almost a century by the 'Golden Kings' (Altan Khans; in Chinese, Kin; hence *China*) originating from the Jurchens, one of the Tungus peoples. Many of their officials went over to serve the Mongols. The next attack was directed against the western part of Central Asia (Transoxiana) and northern Persia. The local ruler, the Khwārizm-Shāh Muhammad II (who had reigned since 1200), had Chinggiz Khan's envoys executed at Otrār on the Jaxartes river; it may well be that they were in fact spies, as he claimed. According to Mongol custom this resulted in a thoroughgoing retribution. The army of Muhammad II, whose Turkish mercenaries went over to the enemy in large numbers, succumbed without a fight on the battlefield. A number of fortified cities surrendered without a struggle; others fell only after heroic resistance which ended in the horrifying bloodbaths described in many different versions by Islamic writers in the thirteenth century (below, pp. 29, 32). The present Afghanistan, northern Persia, and the Caucasian border area lay at the feet of Chinggiz Khan's troops. The Khwārizm-Shāh died in flight. For eleven years his son Jālāl od-Dīn Mängübirdi led a glorious, but in the end unsuccessful, guerilla war against the invaders until, in 1231, he was murdered by a robber.

After a victory over the Russians and the Cumans on the river Kalka in 1223, Chinggiz Khan gave up any further advances toward the West. He died in 1227 during the siege of the capital of the Tanguts who for two centuries had been a powerful people in the border area between Tibet and China (see below, p. 43). His empire did not break up. His sons, of whom the eldest, Jochi, had died shortly before him, remained united and recognized Ögädäi as their overlord (see below, p. 45). Ögädäi achieved the internal consolidation of the state. He encouraged the first steps toward the settling down of at least some of his people and made Karakorum (Qara Qorum) the temporary capital of the new state (see p. 108). At his side Ögädäi's brother Chaghatai (Čaghatay) acted as the guardian of the laws, the *yasa* (see below, p. 39) which had been made at Chinggiz Khan's command.

Now, envoys from the King of France and from the Pope who had clearly become aware both of the danger and of the promise of the Mongol invasion rushed to Karakorum. The danger was exemplified in the campaign of 1241, when the vanguard of the Mongol armies, after having overrun the settlement area of the East Slavs, had appeared on the threshold of Central Europe, but then had retreated again, at the same time withdrawing from Poland and Hungary. The promise resulted from the belief growing throughout the West, that this new army, the Mongols, partly Nestorian Christian as they were, represented the vanguard of Prester John. The existence of this legendary prince in Central Asia had been assumed, since the Seljuks had been defeated in 1141 by a non-Muslim army, which in fact was not Christian either. This prince was now to deal the mortal blow to the Muslims and thus guarantee the rule of the cross over the Holy Land.[1]

---

[1] Jean Richard, 'L'Extrême-Orient légendaire au Moyen-Age: Roi David et Prêtre Jean,' in *Annales d'Ethiopie*, Vol. II (Paris, 1957), pp. 225–42 (q.v. for all details).

As in the seventh and eighth centuries, when the Islamic conquests had united vast areas hitherto under separate rulers and hostile to one another and thus made possible new trade links, so the Mongol conquests made vast areas accessible and connected regions that up to then had hardly known of each other's existence. Only then did it become possible for Europeans to proceed from the ports of the eastern coast of the Mediterranean through the present Ukraine and also through Iran to Central Asia and on to Karakorum. In this way they got to know endless plains, towering mountains, mighty rivers and immense lakes. They came into contact with many different peoples and religions, amongst whom the Nestorians particularly interested them. They naturally concerned themselves chiefly with the Mongols and their way of life, their military efficiency, their religious and moral convictions, their food, their clothes and their dwellings. In short, these travel accounts are the most important sources on the culture and civilization of the Mongols which are available to us from the middle of the thirteenth century. They are more important than the Islamic reports which became available later, more important even than the descriptions in the 'Secret History', since—in contrast with the latter—they are observations made by strangers and, as is always and everywhere the case, they saw things more clearly than the local population. Thus, the descriptions from the two most important travel accounts will take up a great deal of space in what follows (pp. 71–88).

From the reports of these envoys, Europeans, as well as Muslims and Oriental Christians, were able to learn how Ögädäi's son Göyük was elected to be his successor (1246), and how the office of Great Khan passed to the successors of Chinggiz Khan's youngest son Toluy. Toluy himself had not played any significant role when, in 1251, in the face of competition from various other candidates, Möngkä came to power (see below, pp. 64, 87). Under his rule, the Mongols set out for a third attack on the West. Hülägü (Hūlāgū), one of the new ruler's brothers, began to advance on Persia in 1256, after his troops had been strengthened by an accession from the Golden Horde. He destroyed the last castle of the Ismailis (Assassins), those dangerous enemies of the Crusaders and the Sunni, took Baghdad in 1258 and abolished the Caliphate (see below, pp. 115–21). His army was then defeated in 1260, however, at the Spring of Goliath ('Ain Jālūt) in Palestine by the mounted army of the Mamluks which was also organized according to Turkish-nomad principles. Ten years earlier the Mamluks had seized Egypt and created on the Nile a kind of Turkish suzerainty over an Arab-speaking population. In the Near East the Mamluks were to be for decades the enemies of the Mongol rulers of Iran and of Mesopotamia, the Ilkhan dynasty, who in those days were mainly Buddhist. At the same time, however, they were the allies of the rulers of the Golden Horde, who for religious reasons, but probably also for reasons of power politics, had in the meantime become deadly enemies of the Ilkhans. Thus the Ilkhans were confined to the area which in the periods before and after them, was in one way or another under the control of Persian rulers. In this way they became a kind of national dynasty of the Persians whose interests it was to their own advantage to defend. Now and then, however, they were persuaded by greedy viziers to intro-duce economically ruinous measures. Although the Ilkhans did not understand the mechanism of supply and demand, they thought they could copy the Chinese and introduce paper money (cf. below, pp. 139–41). They became victims of drunkenness (cf. below, pp. 122ff). Finally, being zealous Buddhists (especially Arghūn, 1284–91), they clashed with and antagonized their pre-dominantly Muslim subjects. Their opponents, the Christians of the Near East, experienced in contrast what might be termed a final flowering during which it was even possible to maintain occasional contacts with the West, unsupervised by the state (see below, pp. 141ff). When the young Ilkhan, Ghāzān, acceded to the throne, however, he immediately embraced the Sunna form of Islam. Islamic historians regard this, of course, as a result of divine guidance (see below, pp. 144–6). The same Ilkhan (1295–1304), on the advice of his minister Rashīd ad-Dīn, who has himself given a detailed description of the measures, attempted to impose a set of radical reforms. In doing so, the minister also provides detailed descriptions of the state of affairs which made reform necessary. Thus, we gain an insight into situations which were highly typical of the Ilkhan Empire toward the end of the thirteenth century (see below, pp. 146ff). Ghāzān's early death pre-vented these reforms from being carried further. His brother and successor, Öljäitü, changed from one main branch of Islam, the

Sunna, to the other, the Shi'a Twelvers, and built a new capital, Solṭānīyä, not far from Kazvin, but otherwise returned to the old ways of administration. It was not surprising, therefore, that under his son Abū Saʿīd (1316–35), who had become the (nominal) ruler at a very early age, the empire of the Ilkhan began to crumble. Abū Saʿīd was moreover the first Sultan to have solely an Islamic name, and he again reverted to Sunna. Over the eighteen years from 1335 to 1353 the empire endured an agony characterized by power struggles between emirs, palace intrigues, and the breaking away of large parts of the empire, and finally degenerated into full-scale anarchy. The empire of the Mongol Ilkhan in Iran had thus come to an end. In the second half of the fourteenth century, however, it came to life once more under Tīmūr—this time under the auspices of Sunni orthodoxy. It would go beyond the scope of this volume to deal with Tīmūr and his successors, the Tīmūrids, who during their hundred-year rule, split into various branches, helped Persian culture to flourish once again, and so, in a way, made reparation for the horrible destruction their ancestor had brought about. Later on, in 1525, a descendant of Tīmūr, Bābur, carried the name of the Mongols to India and founded there the powerful empire of the Great Moguls, which lasted in some form up to 1857.

In addition to these descriptions of the Ilkhan dynasty, we have fairly thorough reports by foreign writers on the Golden Horde in Eastern Europe. In contrast, however, with the position in Persia and China, no native historical accounts are available. Russian chroniclers, furthermore, confine themselves almost exclusively to reporting warlike events and to the attempt to shake off the overlordship of the Mongols on the part of the Russian princes, the seat of whose power was in (Old and New) Sarai on the lower Volga. In these writings, there are to be found no extensive descriptions of the Mongol culture. This may well have been due to the long-standing antagonism between the Russians and their oppressors, and to the fact that the Russians were not really capable of observing, let alone appreciating, a culture or religion different from their own. They obviously knew nothing of the relations, both friendly and hostile, which their Lords had with the south. There is no mention of the trade via the Genoese colonies in the Crimea, and none, either of the difference between the Horde and the Ilkhan rulers, or of the cooperation with the Mamluks on the Nile which resulted. Part of our knowledge about the Golden Horde derives from the historians of the Byzantine Empire which, after the recapture of its capital Constantinople in 1261, was obliged to steer carefully between the two Mongol states (and the Latins). Even more can be gathered from the writings of the Egyptian historians. One of their reports about an exchange of ambassadors is included (pp. 181ff).

In contrast with the Ilkhan rulers who eventually adopted the religion of the great majority of their subjects, the rulers of the Golden Horde did not turn to the Orthodox faith of their Russian subjects, but—hesitatingly—adopted the Sunna form of Islam. The conversion of Khan Özbek, in 1313, finally established it. Özbek was the ruler whom the Arab traveler, Ibn Baṭṭūṭa, met around 1333 when he arrived on the river Volga during the course of his decade-long journeys of exploration. From him, we have memorable descriptions of life at the court, of the ruler's relations with Byzantium, and of the movements of the people between North and South following the rhythm of the seasons (see pp. 182ff). It is therefore a record of the last stage of the nomadic life of the Mongols of the Golden Horde. In the meantime they had merged with Turkish tribes, some of whom had arrived there with them, while others had come before, to form the Turkish-speaking Sunni Muslim people of the 'Tatars'.

Shortly afterwards, the Tatars became settled here, just as their subjects in Persia or China already were, and they would probably have merged into the Russian national culture if they had not been prevented by their Islamic faith which has kept them separate to this day. Although the rule of the Tatars in Eastern Europe disintegrated after 1357 with a series of civil wars, it did not mean that the Russians under their yoke were able to gain their liberty or have the chance of pursuing independent policies. Indeed, the existence of the Tatars prevented them for more than another century from exercising any influence on the politics of Central Europe or the Near East. As a result, these two regions were able for centuries to maintain independent policies and to assure their cultural development, without any interference from the East or the North. This effect of Tatar rule over Eastern Europe has a significance it is scarcely possible to exaggerate.

Only in 1480, or perhaps 1502, when the Tatar overlordship over the Grand Dukes of Moscow finally came to an end, could Russia embark on the policy of expansion in Europe and Asia which it has followed from then until the present.

We possess far less information about the two Mongol states of Central Asia than we do in the case of the Ilkhan dynasty and that of the rulers of the Golden Horde. Here, the descendants of the brothers Ögädäi and Chaghatai fought each other for decades, until, in 1309, the former had to withdraw from the struggle and seek asylum in China. On the other hand, descendants of Chaghatai continued to live in Central Asia for centuries, far beyond the time of Tīmūr (who died in 1405), although the form of the state changed frequently and there were numerous fights between the different branches. Their political and cultural importance was, however, small.

After the death of Möngkä in 1259, the Great Khans, who were nominally the overlords of all the Mongol states, had had their sphere in China, which was then united in 1279/80 by Qubilai, the brother of the dead Khan, when he supplanted the native Sung dynasty (in the area south of the Yangtze Kiang). Waṣṣāf provides a portrait of him full of courtly praise (p. 165). The Mongol Yüan dynasty now reached out toward Korea, Southeast Asia and Indonesia (below, p. 168); an attempted attack on Japan failed. Within the ambit of Qubilai's court there lived for decades the Italian to whom the West is indebted for the first report on the Middle Kingdom, its power, its religion and its sophisticated culture, Marco Polo (cf. p. 170). Qubilai's descendants (he died in 1294) were, however, no longer recognized as Great Khans in the other Mongol states. Thus the Mongol dynasty in China, too, became identified with a nation state. Their rule here came to an end in 1369. In that year, the last Mongol Emperor of China had to flee from Peking into Mongolia. There he became the founder of a national Mongol dynasty in the area from where, a century and a half before, the Mongols had started on their world conquest. But although the Mongol rulers remained in power there for centuries, they never again achieved more than regional political importance. Later, from 1575 onward, their subjects adopted increasingly the Lamaist Buddhism which had been the faith of their ancestors in China and at one time of their subjects in Persia.

The texts printed on the following pages should be viewed in the framework of the developments that have been briefly outlined and which I have described in a number of more extensive works. Understandably, they can offer no more than a scant selection from the wealth of material that we use to shape our picture of the history of the Mongol Empires. Any selection must be arbitrary, and other scholars might well include different extracts. It is difficult to argue about this in detail. The attempt was made, at any rate, to offer fairly lengthy continuous paragraphs that to some extent show the reader the various authors' styles and whose contents appear interesting, particularly to the cultural and social historian, although not at the expense of military affairs. What was to be avoided was an accumulation of individual notes, for example, on political and military history, which are certainly indispensable in a description of the Mongol Empires, but which were not combined by the individual authors into more coherent passages. The texts were translated in such a way as to be readable to the nonspecialist. The stylistic peculiarities of the original were to be visible, but were not to be overemphasized and certain cuts have therefore been made in places. Notably, interspersed verses that are of purely stylistic importance without adding anything essential to the content were left out, since the purpose of the collection lies in the field of cultural, not literary, history. As far as the selected passages are concerned, since they are mainly of interest as examples of their type, certain names could be left out which in such a context are of no importance and might even be confusing.

The transliteration was chosen in such a way as to be readily comprehensible even without any knowledge of Oriental languages. Only distinctions that are important in the languages with which we are here concerned were retained and are rendered as follows: that between the voiced and unvoiced s (rendered here as z and s, respectively) and that between the velar and palatal k (rendered here as q and k, respectively). Thus q must never be pronounced as qu in English. A stroke above a vowel signifies length. Many words like khan, sultan and others that have become part of the English language, are spelled in the usual English way. In Persian and Turkish words, w is pronounced v; in Arabic words w is pronounced w. The letter i so written is an i pronounced very far back in the mouth, as in many Turkish words; the diphthong *ai* is pronounced like the *i* in child.

A number of texts have been taken from English translations already in existence. In these cases the transliteration has, where necessary, been automatically adjusted to that used elsewhere in this work. It seemed unnecessary and even pedantic to confuse the reader by using different transliterations side by side.

For permission to reprint translations already in existence, I wish to express my gratitude to Professor John Andrew Boyle and to Manchester University Press for selections from *The History of the World-Conqueror* by ʻAlāad-Din ʻAta-Malik Juvaini; to Sir Hamilton Gibb and Cambridge University Press on behalf of The Hakluyt Society for selections from *The Travels of Ibn Baṭṭūṭa*; and to Routledge & Kegan Paul Ltd for selections from *Marco Polo* by A. C. Moule and Paul Pelliot.

The three maps, edited by me, are based on Georg Westermann's *Atlas zur Weltgeschichte*, 1956.

BERTOLD SPULER

Hamburg, September, 1970

SOURCES AND EDITIONS

Mongolian

HAENISCH, ERICH, *Manghol un Niuca Toba'an: Die Geheime Geschichte der Mongolen*, Leipzig, 1937. Restored from the Chinese transcription to the original Mongolian.

KOZIN, S. A., *Sokrovennoe Skazanie. Mongol'skaja chronika 1240 g:* Vol. I, *Introduction to the Study of the Document, Text, Translation, Index of Words*, Trudy Instituta Vostokovedenija XXXIV, Leningrad, 1941.

HAENISCH, ERICH, *Die Geheime Geschichte der Mongolen: Aus einer mongolischen Niederschrift des Jahres 1240 von der Insel Kode'e im Keluren-Fluss* (translated and annotated for the first time), Leipzig, 1941 (hereafter quoted from this edition); 2nd ed., Leipzig, 1948.

Persian

JOWAINĪ 'ALĀ' OD-DĪN 'AṬĀ MALEK, *Ta'rīkh-i Jahān gushā* (*History of the World Conqueror*), ed. Mīrzā Moḥammäd Ebn 'Abd ol-Wahhāb-e Qazwīnī: 3 vols., Gibb Memorial Series, XVI, 1, 2, 3. Leiden and London, 1912, 1916, 1937.

English translation: 'Ata-Malik Juvaini, *The History of the World-Conqueror*, trans. John Andrew Boyle, 2 vols. Manchester, 1958 (hereafter quoted in this edition).

Italian translation: Boyle's version has been translated by G. Scarcia, *Juvaini: Gengiskhan, il conquistatore del mondo*, Milan, 1962.

RASHĪD OD-DĪN FAḌL OLLĀH, [*Jāmi' ot-tawārīkh*] *Sbornik Letopisej: Istorija Mongolov* (*The Collector of Stories: History of the Mongols*), ed. Il'ja Nikolaevič Berezin. Trudy Vostočnago Otdělenija Imperatorskago Archaeologisčeskago Obščestva V, VII, XIII, XV. St. Petersburg, 1858, 1861, 1888. [On the early period of the

Mongols and Chingghiz Khan, until 1227. This edition is very rare and Vol. XV is especially difficult to come by.]

Russian translation: Rashīd ad-Dīn, *Sbornik Letopisej*, trans. from the Persian: Vol. I/1 by L. A. Chetagurov (Moscow and Leningrad, 1952); Vol. I/2 by Olga I. Smirnova (same, 1952); Vol. II by Ju. P. Verkhovsky (same, 1960). [In addition to the text covered by Berezin, deals also with the Great Khans and Chinese emperors, to Qubilai's grandson Tīmūr Qā'ān, 1294–1307. The translation of ch. 1, sec. 22, 'Ögädäi's Building Activities', follows this version.]

English translation: J. A. Boyle is preparing a translation and commentary of that part of Rashid ad-Din's *Jami at-Tawarikh—Universal History* which deals with Mongol tribes and with Chinggiz Kahn's wars of unification in Mongolia before his foreign conquests.

Histoire des Mongols de la Perse écrite en persan par Raschideldin, ed. Marc Etienne Quatremère: Vol. I (only one published), 'Collection Orientale: Histoire des Mongols I', Paris, 1836. [On Hülägü, 1256–65.]

Ta'rīh-i mubārak-i Gāzānī des Rašid al-Dīn Fadl Allāh Abī-l-Hair: Geschichte der Īlhāne Abāġā bis Gaihātū (1265–1295), critical ed. Karl Jahn. Abhandlungen der Deutschen Gesellschaft der Wissenschaften und Künste in Prag. Phil.-Hist. Abt., no. 1, Prague, 1941; reprinted, The Hague, 1957.

RAŠĪD AL-DĪN. *Geschichte Ġāzān-Hāns...*, ed. Karl Jahn, Gibb Memorial Series, n.s., XIV, Leiden, 1940. [There was, moreover, at my disposal, a 'slightly shortened translation' by Walther Hinz who had undertaken a German translation from the Persian of Ghazan's legislative work for the series The Mongolian World Empire (Verlag Harrassowitz, Leipzig) which, however, was never published.]

FAZLULLACH RASHĪD-AD-DIN, *Džami-at-tavarich (Sbornik letopisej)*, Vol. III, ed. and trans. 'Abd ül-Kerīm 'Alī Oġly 'Alī-zāde and A. K. Arends. Akademija Nauk SSSR. Institut Vostokovednija: Akademija Azerbadjdzanskoj SSR. Institut Istorii, Baku, 1957. [On Hülägü to Ghazan.]

WAṢṢĀF (pseudonym for 'Abd Ollāh ebn Fadl Ollāh os-Sīrāzī), *Ketāb-e mostatāb-e Waṣṣāf* (The Elegant Book of Waṣṣāf), 5 vols. including a Persian vocabulary index. Bombay, 1852–53 (1269

A.H.). Lithographed. For the title, cf. *Geschichte Wassafs*, ed. Hammer (next entry), German part, p. 22 n. 1, and W. Barthold, *Turkestan down to the Mongol Invasion*, 2nd ed., London, 1958, p. 48, n. 3.

(Waṣṣāf), *Geschichte Wassafs*, ed. in Persian and trans. into German by Josef von Hammer-Purgstall. Vol. I (the only one published), Vienna, 1856. Cf. C. A. Storey, *Persian Literature: A Bio-Bibliographical Survey*, Section II, fasc. 2, London, 1936, pp. 267–70, no. 344.

IBN AL-ATĪR (Ibn al-Athīr), *Chronicon, quod perfectissimum inscribitur*, ed. Karl Johann Tornberg, Leiden, 1851–76; new printing, Beirut, 1966. Vol. XII (the last: 1189/90 to 1230/31).

Arabic

TIESENHAUSEN, WOLDEMAR (Vladímir Gustávovic), *Sbornik materialov otnosjaščikhsya k istorii Zolotoi Ordy* (Collection of Material for the History of the Golden Horde), Vol. I (Arabic material), St. Petersburg, 1884.

The somewhat modified Turkish version: Ismail Hakkı İzmirli, *Altınordu devleti tarihine ait metinler*, Türk Tarihi Kaynakları, Constantinople, 1941. [The envoy's report of Ibn 'Abd aẕ-Ẕāhir (bottom, p. 181) was taken from this source.]

IBN BAṬṬŪṬA, *Voyages*, ed. and trans. Charles Defrémery and Benjamin Raphael Sanguinetti. Vols. II and III, 2nd ed., Paris. 1877. English translation: *The Travels of Ibn Baṭṭūṭa, A.D. 1325–1354*, translated (with revisions and notes from the Arabic text edited by C. Defrémery and B. R. Sanguinetti) by Sir Hamilton Gibb, 2 vols., The Hakluyt Society, 2nd series, Vols. CX, CXVII, Cambridge, 1958, 1962.

Syrian

BAR HEBRAEUS, GREGORIUS, *Maktĕbanūẕ zabnĕ—Chronicon Syriacum*, ed. Paul Bedjan, Paris, 1890.

Latin

WYNGAERT, ANASTASIUS VAN DEN, *Itinera et relationes fratrum minorum saeculi XII et XIV*, Sinica Franciscana, I, Quaracchi (near

Florence), 1929. Pp. 3–130, John of Plano Carpini; pp. 147–332, William of Rubruck.

PLANO CARPINI, JOHN OF, *Geschichte der Mongolen und Reisebericht 1245–1247*, trans. Friedrich Risch. Veröffentlichungen des Forschungsinstituts für vergleichende Religionsgeschichte an der Universität Leipzig, Series 2, no. 11. Leipzig, 1930. From this source were taken the chapters on pp. 71–88.

ROCKHILL, WILLIAM WOODVILLE, *The Journey of William Rubruck*, London, 1909. From this source was excerpted the chapter on pp. 88–113.

MONNERET DE VILLARD, UGO, *Il libro della peregrinazione nelle parti d'Oriente di Frate Ricoldo da Montecroce*, Istituto Storico Domenicano, Dissertationes Historicae XIII, Rome, 1948.

French

MARCO POLO, *The Description of the World*, restored text in English translation, ed. Arthur Christopher Moule and Paul Pelliot, Vol. I, London, 1938.

LITERATURE REFERENCES

SPULER, BERTOLD, *Die Mongolen in Iran: Politik, Verwaltung und Kultur der Ilchanzeit 1220–1350*, 3rd ed., Berlin, 1968.

SPULER, BERTOLD, *Die Goldene Horde: Die Mongolen in Russland 1223 bis 1502*, 2nd ed., Wiesbaden, 1965. [In both these works it was attempted to list all relevant source materials as well as secondary literature.]

GREKOV, BORIS DMITRIEVIC, and JAKUBOVSKY, ALEKSANDR JUR'EVIC, *Zolotaja Orda i eë padenie* (*The Golden Horde and Its Decline*), Moscow and Leningrad, 1950.

VERNADSKY, GEORGE, *The Mongols and Russia*, New Haven, 1953. (*A History of Russia*, ed. G. V. Karpovich and Michael Karpovich.)

SPULER, BERTOLD, *Geschichte Mittelasiens seit dem Aufkommen der Türken*, Handbuch der Orientalistik V/5, Leiden, 1966.

SPULER, BERTOLD, *Geschichte der islamischen Länder II: Die Mongolenzeit*, Handbuch der Orientalistik VI/2, Leiden, 1953.

SPULER, BERTOLD, *Les Mongols dans l'histoire*, Paris, 1961.

BARTHOLD, WILHELM, *12 Vorlesungen über die Geschichte der Türken Mittelasiens*, German rev. trans. Theodor Menzel, Berlin, 1935.

OLSCHKI, LEONARDO, *L'Asia di Marco Polo*, Civiltà Veneziana, Studi 2, Venice and Rome, 1959.

GROUSSET, RENÉ, *L'Empire Mongol*, 1ʳᵉ *phase*, Histoire du Monde, VIII/3, ed. E. de Boccard, Paris, 1941.

BOUVAT, LUCIEN, *L'Empire Mongol*, 2ᵉ *phase*, Histoire du Monde, VIII/3, ed. E. de Boccard, Paris, 1927.

VLADIMIRTSOV, BORIS YAKOVLEVITCH, *La Structure sociale des Mongols*, trans. from Russian, Paris, 1948.

ALINGE, KURT, *Mongolische Gesetze*, Leipziger Rechtswissenschaftliche Studien, no. 87, Leipzig, 1934.

JAHN, KARL, 'Das iranische Papiergeld', *Archiv Orientální* (Prague), X (1938), 308–40.

FRANKE, HERBERT, 'Beiträge zur Kulturgeschichte Chinas unter der Mongolenherrschaft', Kölner Habilitationsschrift, 1949. Not published.

FRANKE, HERBERT, *Geld und Wirtschaft unter der Mongolenherrschaft* (in China), Das Mongolische Weltreich, III, Leipzig, 1949.

VLADIMIRTSOV, B. YA., *The Life of Jinghiz Khan*, trans. from Russian, London, 1930. French trans., Paris, 1947.

DAUVILLIER, JEAN, 'Les provinces Chaldéennes «de l'Exterieur» au Moyen-Age', in *Mélanges Cavalléra*, Toulouse, 1948, 259–316. [On the expansion of the Nestorians.]

SORANZO, GIOVANNI, *Il papato, l'Europa Cristiana e i Tartari*, Pubblicazione dell'Università Cattolica del Sacro Cuore, 5th series, Vol. XII, Milan, 1930.

PELLIOT, PAUL, 'Les Mongols et la Papauté', in *Revue de l'Orient Chrétien*, 3rd ser., XXIII (1922–3), 1–30; XXIV (1924), 225–35; XXVIII (1931–2), 3–84.

SKELTON, R. A., MARSTON, THOMAS E., PAINTER, GEORGE O., *The Vinland Map and the Tartar Relation*, New Haven, 1965.

I

THE FOUNDING OF THE EMPIRE: CHINGGIZ KHAN AND HIS IMMEDIATE SUCCESSORS

1. The Youth of Chinggiz Khan

(10) When Temujin[1] was nine years old,[2] Yesugai ba'atur[3] took him with him on a journey with the purpose of asking his uncles ... for a bride for him from among his mother's people, the Torgut tribe. As they rode along they met at a point between two hills ... a member ... of the tribe of Unggirat.

He said: 'Brother-in-law Yesugai, whom have you come to see?' Yesugai ba'atur replied: 'I have come in order to see ... the uncles of this my son, to ask for a bride for him.' The other man said; 'Your son is a boy with fire in his eyes and radiance in his face. Brother-in-law Yesugai, I had a dream last night: a white falcon came flying toward me with the two heavenly bodies, the sun and the moon, in its talons, and came to rest upon my hand. I spoke to the people about this dream and said: The sun and the moon have always been there to be seen. But now this falcon has brought them in its talons and come to rest with them upon my hand. The white one has come down. What a magnificent omen he has brought me. Surely, brother-in-law Yesugai, this dream of mine heralded your approach with your son at your side. I have had a good dream. What will prove to be the meaning of this dream? It signifies that you Kiyat people[4] have come as messengers of good luck! From the earliest times we Unggirat people have never, I insist, tried to use the attractions (11) of our nieces and

---

[1] Later known as Chinggiz Khan.
[2] The year of his birth is not known precisely: 1155, 1162, or 1167.
[3] His father.
[4] Kiyat, singular 'Kiyan', the name of Chinggiz Khan's family.

the beauty of our daughters to gain more people, but, whenever you had a new ruler, we placed our soft-cheeked daughters on a . . . cart which, drawn by a black camel, took them speedily to join him on his royal throne. We certainly have never striven for land and people, but we have raised our pretty girls and then placed them on a cart, with a dark-gray camel harnessed to it, and let them go to sit by your side on the high throne. It has been the custom with us Unggirat people for ages. Our women form together with you a special marriage community, our daughters are available for you to choose from. The nieces are valued according to their beauty, just as the daughters by their attractiveness. When our sons get married we emphasize property, in the case of our daughters, beauty. Brother-in-law Yesugai, let us go into my yurt.[5] My daughter is still young. Brother-in-law, take a look at her.' Having said this he led the other man into his yurt and asked him to be seated. When Yesugai saw the daughter, he saw a girl with radiance in her face and fire in her eyes, and in his heart he took a liking to her. She was ten years old, one year older than Temujin, and her name was Borte. On the next morning, after he had spent the night there, he asked for the daughter's hand, and the other man said: 'If I give her to you, having made you plead a lot, she will be valued too highly. If I give her to you and do not make you plead enough, she will be valued too lightly. This is the fate of a girl: she is born in the yurt, but she does not grow old in the yurt. I shall give you my daughter. When you go away, leave your son behind as my son-in-law.' After they had made the agreement, Yesugai ba'atur said: 'Very well, I shall leave my son here as your son-in-law. But my son was afraid of the dog. Brother-in-law, do not let the dog frighten my son!' Having said this, he rode away, having given one of his horses as a token, and he left Temujin behind as son-in-law. On his way Yesugai ba'atur met the Tatar people who had assembled on the Yellow Steppe . . . for (12) a feast. Since he was thirsty, he got down from his horse near the assembly. Those Tatars, however, recognized him. The word went round: Yesugai the Kiyan has arrived. Desiring to revenge themselves for having been robbed, they secretly mixed poison in his food to kill him. As he rode on he felt sick, and his sickness had become still worse when he arrived at his yurt three days later.

[5] The tent used by the Mongols as a dwelling.

And Yesugai ba'atur said: 'I feel sick inside me. Who is that with me?' When Munglik . . . said: 'I am with you,' he made him come nearer and said: 'Munglik, my friend, I have small children. On my way home, after having given my son Temujin as a son-in-law, I was secretly poisoned by the Tatar people. I feel very sick inside me. I am worried about the little ones, about those I leave behind, about my younger brothers, my widow and my sisters-in-law. I want you to know this! But hurry, Munglik, my friend, and bring back my son Temujin!' Having spoken these words he died.

The following section tells of Chinggiz Khan's war adventures in his youth, of how he brought his wife Borte home and of her abduction by his enemies.

(25) So they held council, after which Temujin with two others . . . made his way to To'oril, Ong Khan[6] (prince) of the Kereit, who lived in the Black Forest by the Tula river, to say to him: 'Suddenly we were surprised by the three Merkit[7] and robbed of our wives and children. We come with the plea: Oh my royal Father,[8] restore to us our wives and children!' Replying to these words, To'oril Ong Khan said: 'Did I not make it clear to you recently? When you brought me the sable fur, you said that during the life of your father I had become his friend, and so I was to you now as a father. I replied to that, as the fur was put round my shoulders: "In gratitude for the sable fur I shall reunite your scattered people. In gratitude for the black sable fur I shall lead back to you your people who have left you. I shall be as unseparable from you as the breast is from the neck and the seat from the loins." Were these not my words? (26) Now I return to those words of mine: In gratitude for the sable fur I shall restore to you your Borte ujin, even if I have to destroy all the Merkit. In gratitude for the sable fur we shall bring back to you your wife Borte, even if we have to crush all the Merkit! Send a message to my younger brother[9] Jamukha. He is likely to be near the little river Khorkhonakh.[10] I shall set out from here for the field with twenty thousand men as

---

[6] A part-Chinese, part-Mongol princely title.
[7] A tribe on the middle and lower reaches of the Selenga river.
[8] The title 'father' in this context signifies that Chinggiz Khan approaches him as a petitioner and recognizes him, as it were, as his 'superior'.
[9] He means: 'brother by choice'.   [10] On the Onon river.

the right wing. My younger brother Jamukha is to ride with twenty thousand men as the left wing. He shall choose the time for the enterprise.' These were his words. When Temujin with his two companions . . . had returned home from To'oril Khan, he sent the two forth. He sent them forth with the order: 'Tell this to my friend Jamukha: I have been attacked by the three Merkit, and my bed has been plundered. Are we not of the same people? How shall we go about our revenge? Half my breast has been torn away. Are we not relations of the same liver? How shall we inflict punishment?' This message for his friend Jamukha was brought by them to Jamukha, and similarly the words that To'oril Khan had spoken about the Kereit: 'Remembering the assistance and goodwill extended to me by father Yesugai, I shall be your comrade and go to the field with twice ten thousand men as the right wing. Tell this to my younger brother Jamukha. My brother Jamukha shall go to the field with twice ten thousand men and he shall choose the meeting place.'

Borte is freed; Temujin wins friends and allies.

2. Hunting

(31) . . . When Temujin, To'oril Khan and Jamukha together had overturned the Tatar yurts of the Merkit and had carried away the noblewomen, they made their way back. . . . Temujin and Jamukha returned together towards Khorkhonakh. To'oril Khan, however, went . . . to . . . where he hunted for the game of that area intending to return afterwards to . . . the Black Forest by the Tula river.

Further campaigns and friendships.

3. Allies

(35) . . . Altan, Khuchar and Sacha beki held council together and afterward said to Temujin: 'We want to make you Khan.[11] If you become . . . Khan, we shall ride at the head against the enemy, and without delay we shall bring back for you their most beautiful and highborn girls and women and their palace yurt, and from their

[11] Prince, ruler.

state and people, the soft-cheeked women and girls and the slim-limbed geldings. When you hunt the cunning wild animals, we shall be the first to drive them toward you from the circle. We shall drive the bodies of the wild animals of the steppe, all together, close toward you. We shall drive the hind legs of the mountain game, all together, close toward you. If on the day of the fight we do not follow your command, tear us away from our possessions and wives and women and throw our black heads on to the ground! If in days of peace we should fail in our alliance to you, cut us off from the men and from our women and children and banish us to some ungoverned land!' With such vows and oaths they raised Temujin to be Khan with the title Chinggiz Khan.

Distribution of offices.

4. Rewards

(36) ... Then Chinggiz Khan, now being the ruler, said to Bo'orchu and Jelme: 'At the time, when apart from my shadow, I had no companion, you two were my shadow and you brought peace to my mind. You shall remain in my mind! When, apart from the tail, I had no whip, you two were the tail and you brought peace to my heart. You shall remain in my bosom! Since you two stood by me in the beginning, should you not be the superiors of all these others here?' (37) Chinggiz Khan went on: 'If heaven and earth strengthen and protect me in my power, then you who wished to leave friend Jamukha and longed for me and who came to join me, you shall surely remain my companions, as of old, bringing me good fortune. I invest you with a fief, each in his place.'

Soon Chinggiz Khan found himself at war with Jamukha. He suffered an early defeat, but managed, together with Ong Khan, to beat his enemy in spite of the numerous allies the latter had found. Together Chinggiz Khan and Ong Khan went on to subjugate several more tribes.

5. Frustrated Marriage Intentions

(59) Chinggiz Khan wished to add to this bond of friendship yet a second bond of friendship. He intended to ask on Jochi's[12] behalf

[12] His eldest son.

for Sanggum's younger sister . . . and to give to Sanggum's son . . . our . . . in exchange. When he made his request, however, Sanggum, who considered himself very superior, said: 'Whenever one of our women goes to them she stands in the corner by the door looking all the time at the place (60) of honor on the opposite side. But when one of their women comes to us she sits at the place of honor looking toward the corner by the door.' Thus he spoke, feeling highly superior and despising us and he refused to give . . . but took the request as an offense. As a result of these words, the love in Chinggiz Khan's heart for Ong Kahn and . . . for Sanggum diminished a little.

Soon afterward, Chinggiz Khan was secretly informed that Ong Khan was plotting to attack him and as a result an open struggle developed between them which led eventually to Ong Khan's downfall.

6. *A People Is Enslaved*

(77) Now that he had defeated the Kereit people, he shared them out on all sides to be stripped of their possessions and to be enslaved. To . . . of the Suldut he gave one hundred . . . people as a token of his gratitude. In addition Chinggiz Khan ordered as follows: Jakhagambu, Ong Khan's younger brother, had two daughters. The elder . . . Chinggiz Khan took for himself. The younger one, Sorkhakhtani [Sorqaqtani = Seyurkhokhataitai] beki,[13] he gave to Toluy. Because of this he pardoned Jakhagambu and did not enslave him, but decided that he, together with his servants and other people subject to him, should remain as a united group, and should form the other shaft. In addition Chinggiz Khan ordered as follows: 'To these two . . . in recognition of their merits I shall give Ong Khan's golden palace tent, just as it stands, and also the golden wine vessels, bowls and beakers and the people who have been looking after these things. And the Ongkhojit and Kereit shall be their bodyguards. I shall also invest you with the right to carry the quiver and to drink from the beaker, and you shall enjoy the privileges of the Darkhan[14] down to your

[13] Mother of the later Great Khans, Möngkä (1251–9) and Qubilai (1259–94), and of Hülägü, the conqueror of Persia (d. 1265). She was a Nestorian Christian.
[14] Privileged nobles.

children and your children's children! When you attack the enemy you shall take as booty whatever you may find! When you kill the animals of the steppe you shall take as many as you kill!' These were his orders. In addition Chinggiz Khan ordered as follows: 'Since these two . . . saved my life, I was able, with the help of eternal heaven, to subjugate the Kereit people and thus to attain the highest position. When later on my most distant descendants occupy the throne they shall remember, generation after generation, those who have done such service!' When (78) they enslaved the people of the Kereit, they continued sharing them out until nobody wanted any more of them. When the ten thousand [of the tribe] of the Tube'en, were shared out they all continued taking them until they had enough. They enslaved the Dungkhait without as much as a day's delay. Only the heroic Jirgin, capturers of the bloodstained enemy clothes, could not be torn apart in this way and shared out. After he had dissolved the people of the Kereit in this way he spent the winter in the mountains. . . .

The great tribe of the Naiman was defeated, and further tribes came under Chinggiz Khan's rule. Finally the ruler of the Naiman, Küchlüg (Guchuluk), was defeated in a decisive battle and compelled to flee westward into the area of the Qara-Khitai in Central Asia.

7. Elevation To Be Great Khan

(95) . . . After Chinggiz Khan had brought the people with the felt tents under his sway, they assembled in the Year of the Tiger[15] (1206) at the source of the Onon river and planted there the white standard with jagged edge of nine points (tuq). They, there and then, gave to Chinggiz Khan the title Khan or Emperor [cf. below, p. 26]. He then gave to Mukhali[16] the title Go-ong or Imperial Prince. He then sent out Jebe on a campaign in pursuance of King Küchlüg of the Naiman. After that the people of the Mangkholjin were organized, and after he had done that Chinggiz Khan gave the following order: 'I shall organize the army in units of a thousand,[17] and those who have come with me

[15] A year in the Mongol Cycle of Twelve Animals (also widespread among other peoples).
[16] One of the most important generals.
[17] The Mongol army is organized on the decimal system.

to help found the empire shall be made leaders of a thousand and in addition I shall reward them with words of gratitude.' The following were appointed as leaders of a thousand. . . .

Further appointments, including a chief Shaman;[18] distribution of pastures.

8. One of the Most Important Generals

(99) Chinggiz Khan turned to Khorchi: 'You once made a prophesy, and then through the many years, from the days of my youth to now, you endured wetness and cold with me, and bore yourself like a saint. You, Khorchi, said at the time: "If the prophesy comes true and heaven grants what you desire, make me the owner of thirty women!" Since it has now come true, I grant them to you: Look at the most beautiful women and the most beautiful girls from the conquered peoples and choose thirty women for yourself!' This was his order. In addition he ordered: 'Khorchi shall add to the three thousand Ba'arin [soldiers from tribes enumerated individually in the text] and thus swell their numbers to ten thousand. These shall be commanded by Khorchi. I set him in command over the ten thousand so that he may be my frontier guard against the forest peoples, and consequently he may freely choose his own pastures right up to the forest peoples along the Irtysh river. Without Khorchi's permission the forest peoples may do neither this nor that. If they act without his permission short shrift will be made of them.' This was his order. Further, Chinggiz Khan said to Jurcheday: 'This was your chief merit: When in the sandy deserts of (100) Khalakhaljit we fought with the Kereit people, and when we were filled with anxiety, . . . swore an oath of allegiance. You carried out what he swore to do, when in the attack . . . you defeated the thousand guards, the most valuable of the troops, letting none escape. And when you reached the center of the enemy, you shot an . . . arrow into the red cheek of . . . . In this way, eternal heaven opened the door for me, and gave me free rein. If you had not wounded him, what, indeed, might have become of us? This was Jurcheday's greatest merit! When, afterward, we had disengaged from the enemy, and moved

[18] Priest.

down the Kalka, I kept thinking of him as of the shelter afforded
by a high mountain. Then we went down to the edge of the lake
... to collect water. Then, however, we went once more ... to
the battlefield to fight against the Kereit, with Jurcheday at our
head. Heaven and earth strengthened our power so that we overwhelmed the people of the Kereit and made them captive. After
the most important states had been dealt with, the prestige of the
Naiman and the Merkit was destroyed. They could no longer
resist us and were scattered. After the fight in which we scattered
the Merkit and the Naiman, ... of the Kereit had been allowed,
for the sake of his two daughters, to remain in a united group
with those people who belonged to him. But when he rose a
second time and broke away from us, Jurcheday lured him into a
trap. Through a ruse he seized him with his own hands, when he
had irrevocably turned away from us, and put an end to him.
And for the second time the people of this man, without exception,
fell to him. This was Jurcheday's second great merit!' Because he
had staked his life on the day when so many fought together, and
had staked his life on the day when so many died, Chinggiz Khan
gave Ibakha beki to Jurcheday. And he said to Ibakha: 'I have not
said of you that you were not of good disposition nor that your
appearance or your face was unpleasant. I give you to Jurcheday,
you who have come close to my breast and legs and who had
descended in the order of rank. (101) I give you to him in recognition of my deep indebtedness; in recognition of my indebtedness
to Jurcheday for his services, when on the day of the battle he acted
as a shield, as a protection against my enemies; when he brought
back to us the people who had deserted us, and brought together
again the people who had scattered. For ages to come, my descendants, when they occupy Our Throne, shall remember their
indebtedness to him for having given such services, and they shall
not act contrary to my word and shall maintain the status of
Ibakha and her descendants down to the most distant generation!'
This was his order. Chinggiz Khan continued speaking to Ibakha:
'Your father ... had given you two hundred servant girls as a
dowry, and he had also given you the two cooks. ... Now, as you
are going, give me before you go, so that I shall remember you,
one hundred of your servant girls and also your cook. ...' Having
been given these, Chinggiz Khan said to Jurcheday: 'I give to

you my Ibakha. And you shall keep four thousand men under your command!' Thus he proclaimed the conferring of his favors.

(Erich Haenisch, *Die Geheime Geschichte der Mongolen* [*The Secret History of the Mongols*], [Leipzig, 1941], pp. 10–101.)

9. *Chinggiz Khan: Ruler by the Grace of God*

(28) . . . At this time [after the victory over Ong Khan, cf. p. 22] there arose a man of whom I have heard from trustworthy Mongols that during the severe cold that prevails in those regions he used to walk naked through the desert and the mountains and then to return and say: 'God has spoken with me and has said: "I have given all the face of the earth to Temujin and his children and named him Chinggiz Khan. Bid him administer justice in such and such a fashion."' They called this person Teb-Tengri [Most Heavenly], and whatever he said (29) Chinggiz Khan used implicitly to follow. Thus he too [Teb-Tengri] grew strong; and many followers having gathered around him, there arose in him the desire for sovereignty. One day, in the course of a banquet, he engaged in altercation with one of the princes; and that prince, in the midst of the assembly, threw him so heavily upon the ground that he never rose again.

(Juvaini, *The History of the World-Conqueror*, trans. J. A. Boyle [Manchester, 1958], I, 39 [=Part I, 28–9].)

The Tatars [=Mongols] claim to be the true masters of the earth. God had created the earth merely for their sake so that they should exercise their rule and enjoy it. According to the Mongols even the birds of the air report that they are the masters of the world, and that the whole earth pays them tribute perforce. They maintain that even the birds of the air and the wild animals in the desert eat and drink only by the grace of their emperor.

Once, when a Frank [European] came to one of the great emperors [Great Khans] and was asked: 'What presents have you brought for me?' he replied: 'I have not brought a present since I did not know your power.' The prince replied to that: 'Did not the birds of the air tell you about it when you entered [my] country?'

To this he replied: 'It may well be that they said something, but I did not understand their language.' At this [the prince] was mollified and spared him.

(Ugo Monneret de Villard, *Il libro della peregrinazione nelle parti d'Oriente di Frate Ricoldo da Montecroce*, [Rome, 1948], pp. 114f.)

10. The Structure of the Army

(108) ... who had founded the empire with him and had borne with him all the toil he appointed leaders of a thousand. When he set up units of a thousand, he appointed leaders of the thousand, of each hundred and each ten. When he set up units of ten thousand, he appointed leaders of the ten thousand. To those leaders of ten thousand or of one thousand who had merited some reward he gave a reward, and to those who had merited favorable mention he gave such mention. The order given out by Chinggiz Khan went as follows: 'I used to have eighty men for the watch by night and seventy bodyguards as sentries by day. Now that I, fortified by the eternal powers and by heaven and earth, have brought the whole empire under my control, from each unit of a thousand you shall select for me and commission bodyguards for the day sentry duties. After their commissioning, that is the commissioning of night watchmen, quiver bearers and day sentries, you shall make up the number of the troops to ten thousand.' Further Chinggiz Khan gave an order to each unit of a thousand regarding the selection and commissioning of bodyguards: 'When the sons of the leaders of ten thousand, of a thousand and of a hundred and also the sons of the common people are chosen to be commissioned as our bodyguards, then only those shall be commissioned who are skilled and handsome and suitable for service with us. The sons of the leaders of a thousand shall on being commissioned bring one of their younger (109) brothers and ten of their men. The sons of the leaders of a hundred shall on being commissioned bring one of their younger brothers and five of their men. The sons of the leaders of units of ten and of the common people shall on being commissioned also bring one of their younger brothers and three of their men. They shall be provided with horses from their units.

These people who look after our service shall be made more powerful, and for this purpose the ten men from their units of a thousand
and a hundred shall pay their dues to the sons of the leaders of a
thousand. And apart from any share that their fathers may have
granted them in those men and horses which they have personally
acquired or bought, and apart from their salaries, they shall be
allotted and provided with as much as is to be allotted according
to the scale laid down by us. Similarly, in addition to their salaries,
the sons of the leaders of a hundred shall receive dues from their
five men; and the sons of the leaders of ten, as well as the sons of
the common people, shall receive dues from their three men!'
Then another order was given: 'When the leaders of a thousand,
of a hundred, and of ten, as well as the men, have received and
heard this our order, anybody who contravenes it shall be subject
to punishment! If the men who are to be commissioned as our
bodyguard should avoid and decline the service, or should not be
able to undertake the service any longer, we shall commission
others and punish that man and banish him behind Our Eyes to a
distant country! Those people who wish to come and serve Us in
order to be trained within Our service shall not be prevented!'
These were his words.

Further military orders.

11. Honoring the Old Bodyguard

(113) Chinggiz Khan said: 'You, my night guards, who have become gray in my service, who in cloudy nights lay around my yurt
with its lookout flaps and allowed me to sleep quietly and in peace
and thus brought me to this throne! You, my lucky night guards,
who in starry nights lay around my palace yurt, and saw to it that
I never started up from my bed, you have brought me to the high
throne! You, my faithful night guards, who stood quietly and
immovably around my yurt of plaited willow during blizzards
which threatened to sweep you away, in cold that makes you shud-
der and in rain that comes down like a torrent, and who have thus
calmed my heart; you brought me to the seat of joy! You, my
reliable night guards, who, without moving an eye, stood in defense
in the thick of the enemy around my yurt with its firmly trodden
(114) soil; you, my speedy night guards, who, without delay,

rushed back to your posts whenever the birchwood quivers made the slightest movement; you, my fast-footed night guards, who never rallied too late, whenever the willow-wood quivers made the slightest movement; you, my lucky night guards, shall all be called 'Old Night Guards'! You seventy day guards who have entered with . . . shall be called the 'Great Day Guards'! You elite troops of Arkhai, you shall be called the 'Old Elite Troops', and the quiver bearers with . . . and . . ., you shall be called the 'Great Quiver Bearers'!' This was the order.

Various campaigns were launched in different directions, ending in 1211–15 with the war against the north Chinese Kin Empire and the Khitai people.

12. The Persian Campaign

(129) . . . Then it happened [1218] that Chinggiz Khan's envoys, a hundred men led by Ukhuna, were held up and killed by the Muhammadan people.[19] Whereupon Chinggiz Khan said: 'How could I possibly allow the Muhammadan people to wrench away my golden guide rope!' And he decided to go to war[20] against the Muhammadan people to retaliate and to take revenge for the death of Ukhuna and his hundred-man embassy.

(Haenisch, *Geheime Geschichte der Mongolen*, pp. 108–29.)

13. The Mongol Invasion and the Muslims

(233) . . . For several years—writes the author Ibn al-Athīr—I put off reporting this event. I found it terrifying and felt revulsion at recounting it and therefore hesitated again and again. Who would find it easy to describe the ruin of Islam and the Muslims . . .? O would that my mother had never borne me, that I had died before and that I were forgotten! (234) Though so many friends urged me to chronicle these [events], I still waited. Eventually I came to see that it was no use not complying. The report

[19] By order of the Khwārizm-Shāh Muhammad II (1200–20), who at that time ruled the greater part of Persia.

[20] This campaign destroyed the empire of the Khwārizm-Shāhs (between 1218 and 1224) and brought Mongol troops as far as Caucasia and Russia.

comprises the story of a . . . tremendous disaster such as had never happened before, and which struck all the world, though the Muslims above all. If anyone were to say that at no time since the creation of man by the great God had the world experienced anything like it, he would only be telling the truth. In fact nothing comparable is reported in past chronicles. The worst they recall is the treatment and extinction of the Israelites and the destruction of Jerusalem by Nebuchadnezzar. But what is Jerusalem compared with the areas devastated by those monsters, where every city is twice the size of Jerusalem? What are the Israelites in comparison with [the number of] those they massacred, for a single city whose inhabitants were murdered numbered more than all the Israelites together. It may well be that the world from now until its end . . . will not experience the like of it again, apart perhaps from Gog and Magog. Dadjdjāl [the Muslim equivalent of Antichrist] will at least spare those who adhere to him, and will only destroy his adversaries. These [the Mongols], however, spared none. They killed women, men and children, ripped open the bodies of the pregnant and slaughtered the unborn. Truly: we belong to God and shall return to him; only with him is strength and power!

Now, then, to report how the sparks [from these events] flew in all directions, and the evil spread everywhere. It moved across the lands like a cloud before the wind. A people set out from China, overran those fair lands of Turkestan, Kashgar and Balāsāghūn, and advancing into Transoxiana toward Samarkand and Bukhara, took them and dealt with their inhabitants in a way which we will recount later. Then one detachment advanced to Khurasan and plundered, devastated, killed and ravaged [the inhabitants] in every way imaginable. After that they pushed toward Rayy [to the east of modern Tehran], Hamadan, into the [Zagros] mountains and on to the threshold of Iraq. Then they turned to Azerbaijan and Arrān, devastated these [areas] and killed the majority of the inhabitants. Only here and there could someone save himself and escape. In less than one year things happened the like of which [until then] had never been heard.

When they had finished with Azerbaijan and Arran they moved toward Derbent in Shirvan and conquered its cities; only the castle where their king was staying saved itself. On they moved into the country where the Alans [=Ossetians] and Lezghians lived, together with other tribes; they overran them, robbing, looting and laying waste. Eventually they invaded the country of the Qıpchaq, one of the most numerous Turkish peoples, crushing all who tried to stand in their way. Those remaining fled to the swamps and mountains, and abandoned their land which the Tatars occupied. All this they did in the shortest imaginable time: they did not stop any longer than was necessary for further advance.

Another detachment turned toward Ghazna [=Ghazni, in present-day eastern Afghanistan] and its surrounding area, and moved on into the neighboring areas of India, to Seistan [Sijistān] and Kerman (235). They behaved here in the same way as their fellows, perhaps even worse. Never had anything like it been heard of. Even Alexander [the Great] who all sources agree in saying was the ruler of the world, did not come to dominate it so rapidly, but needed ten years to do so: he did not kill anyone, but was content with the submission of the people. But in just one year they [the Mongols] seized the most populous, the most beautiful, and the best cultivated part of the earth whose inhabitants excelled in character and urbanity. In the countries that have not yet been overrun by them, everyone spends the night afraid that they may appear there, too. Incidentally, they do not need a baggage train or stores, since they have with them sheep, horses and other animals, and live exclusively off their meat. The animals on which they ride as they advance pound the earth with their hooves and eat the roots of plants; barley is unknown to them [as fodder]. This is the reason why [the Mongols] do not need any supplies when in camp.

Their religion consists in the adoration of the rising sun. They regard no [food] as forbidden and thus eat any animal, even dogs, pigs and the like. They do not know marriage, and several men will go with one woman; if a child is born, it does not know its father.

Thus Islam and the Muslims were struck, at that time, by a disaster such as no people had experienced before. Part of this was due to those accursed Tatars. They came from the East and committed actions that anybody upon hearing will consider horrifying. God willing, you will now learn about them in detail. Part of this [disaster] is also due to the intrusion into Syria of the cursed Franks [=crusaders] from the West, their attack on Egypt, and their conquest of the coastal strip of Damietta. They might even have seized Egypt and Syria had it not been for God's grace and his help against them [as mentioned earlier]!

... May God grant victory to Islam and the Muslims, for he is the most powerful help and support of Islam. If God wishes to inflict harm on a people, there is no way of averting it, and no one but he can intercede. The Tatars succeeded in their advance only because of the lack of any defense. This was due to the fact that the Khwārizm-Shāh Muhammad [II; from 1200] after having conquered the [Iranian] countries had killed and annihilated their rulers. Therefore he alone was left. When he had fled, there remained nobody in these countries who could have defended and protected them. God has only to lay his plans, and already the reality begins to take shape. Now we shall report everything as it happened.

(Ibn al-Athīr, *Chronicon, quod perfectissimum inscribitur*, ed. K. J. Tornberg [12 vols.; Leiden, 1851–76], XII, 233–5.)

14. The Capture of Bukhara

(75) ... In the Eastern countries Bukhara is the cupola of Islam and in those regions she is like unto the City of Peace [Baghdad]. Her environs are adorned with the brightness of the light of doctors and jurists and her surroundings embellished with the rarest of high attainments. (76) Since ancient times she has in every age been the place of assembly of the great savants of every religion. Now the derivation of Bukhara is from *bukhār* [Vihāra], which in the language of the Magians [correctly: the Buddhists] signifies center of learning. ...

Chinggiz Khan, having completed the organization and equipment of his armies, arrived in the countries of the Sultan [the Khwārizm-Shāh Muhammad II]; and dispatching his elder sons and the *noyan*s in every direction at the head of large forces, he himself advanced first upon Bukhara, being accompanied by Toluy alone of his elder sons and by a host of fearless Turks that knew not clean from unclean, and considered the bowl of war to be a basin of rich soup and held a mouthful of the sword to be a beaker of wine.

He proceeded along the road to Zarnūq [near Otrār], and in the morning when the king of the planets raised his banner on the eastern horizon, he arrived unexpectedly before the town. When the inhabitants thereof, who were unaware of the fraudulent designs of Destiny, beheld the surrounding countryside choked with horsemen and the air black as night with the dust of cavalry, fright and panic overcame them, and fear and dread prevailed. They betook themselves to the citadel and closed the gates, thinking, 'This is perhaps a single detachment of a great army and a single wave from a raging sea.' It was their intention to resist and to approach calamity on their own feet, but they were aided by divine grace so that they stood firm and breathed not opposition. At this juncture, the World-Emperor, in accordance with his constant practice, dispatched Dānishmend Ḥājib upon an embassy to them, to announce the arrival of his forces and to advise them to stand out of the way of a dreadful deluge. Some of the inhabitants, who were in the category of 'Satan hath gotten mastery over them' [Koran 58:20], were minded to do him harm and mischief; whereupon he raised a shout, saying: 'I am such-and-such a person, a Muslim and the son of a Muslim. Seeking God's pleasure I am come on an embassy to you, at the inflexible command of Chinggiz Khan, to draw you out of the whirlpool of destruction and the trough of blood. (77) It is Chinggiz Khan himself who has come with many thousands of warriors. The battle has reached thus far. If you are incited to resist in any way, in an hour's time your citadel will be level ground and the plain a sea of blood. But if you will listen to advice and exhortation with the ear of intelligence and consideration and become submissive and obedient to his command, your lives and property will remain in the stronghold of security.' When the people, both nobles and commoners, had heard his words, which bore the brand of veracity, they did not refuse to accept his advice, knowing for certain that the flood might not be stemmed by their obstructing his passage nor might the quaking of the mountains and the earth be quietened and allayed by the pressure of their feet. And so they held it proper to choose peace and advantageous to accept advice. But by way of caution and security they obtained from him a covenant that if, after the people had gone forth to meet the Khan and obeyed his command, any harm should befall any one of them, the retribution thereof should be on his head. Thus were the people's minds set at ease, and they withdrew their feet from the thought of transgression and turned their faces toward the path of advantage. The chief men of Zarnūq sent forward a delegation bearing presents. When these came to the place where the Emperor's cavalry had halted, he asked about their leaders and notables and was wroth with them for their dilatoriness in remaining behind. He dispatched a messenger to summon them to his presence. Because of the great awe in which the Emperor was held a tremor of horror appeared on the limbs of these people like the quaking of the members of a mountain. They at once proceeded to his presence; and when they arrived he treated them with mercy and clemency and spared their lives, so that they were once more of good heart. An order was then issued that everyone in Zarnūq—be he who he might—both such as donned *kulah* and turban and such as wore kerchief and veil, should go out of the town on to the plain. The citadel was turned into level ground; and after a counting of heads they made a levy of the youths and young men for the attack on Bukhara, while the rest of the people were suffered to return home. They gave the place the name of Qutlugh Balıgh [roughly 'Fortunate Town']. A guide, one of the Turcomans of that region, (78) who had a perfect knowledge of the roads and highways, led them on by a little frequented road; which road has ever since been called the *Khan's Road*. . . .

Dayir Bahādur was proceeding in advance of the main forces. When he and his men drew near to the town of Nur [Nūrata] they passed through some gardens. During the night they felled the trees and fashioned ladders out of them. Then holding the ladders in front of their horses they advanced very slowly: and the watcher on the walls thought that they were a caravan of merchants, until in this manner they arrived at the gates of the citadel of Nur; when the day of that people was darkened and their eyes dimmed. . . .

To be brief, the people of Nur closed their gates; and Dayir Bahādur sent an envoy to announce the arrival of the World-Conquering Emperor and to induce them to submit and cease resistance. The feelings of the inhabitants were conflicting, because they did not believe that the World-Conquering Emperor Chinggiz Khan had arrived in person, and on the other hand they were apprehensive about the Sultan [Khwārizm-Shāh]. They

were therefore uncertain what course to take, some being in favor
of submission and surrender while others were for resistance or
were afraid [to take any action]. Finally, after much coming and
going of ambassadors, it was agreed that the people of Nur should
prepare an offering of food and send it to the Lord of the Age
together with an envoy, and so declare their submission and seek
refuge in servitude and obedience.

(79) Dayir Bahādur gave his consent and was satisfied with only
a small offering. He then went his own way; and the people of Nur
dispatched an envoy in the manner that had been agreed upon.
After the envoys [sic] had been honored with the Emperor's
acceptance of their offering, he commanded that they should
surrender the town to [the general] Sübödäi, who was approaching
Nur with the vanguard. When Sübödäi arrived they complied
with this command and delivered up the town. Hereupon an
agreement was reached that the people of Nur should be content
with the deliverance of the community from danger and the
retention of what was absolutely necessary for their livelihood and
the pursuit of husbandry and agriculture, such as sheep and cows;
and that they should go out on to the plain leaving their houses
exactly as they were so that they might be looted by the army.
They executed this order, and the army entered the town and
bore off whatever they found there. The Mongols abided by this
agreement and did no harm to any of them. The people of Nur
then selected sixty men and dispatched them, together with
Il-Khoja, the son of the Emir of Nur, to Dabus to render assistance
to the Mongols. When Chinggiz Khan arrived, they went forth to
meet him bearing suitable [presents] in the way of *tuzghu* and
offerings of food. Chinggiz Khan distinguished them with royal
favor and asked them what fixed taxes the Sultan drew from Nur.
They replied that these amounted to 1500 dinars; and he commanded them to pay this sum in cash and they should suffer no
further inconvenience. Half of this amount was produced from
the women's ear-rings, and they gave security for the rest and
[finally] paid it to the Mongols. And so were the people of Nur
delivered from the humiliation of Tatar bondage and slavery, and
Nur regained its splendor and prosperity.

And from thence Chinggiz Khan proceded to Bukhara, and in
the beginning of Muharram, 617 [March 1220], he encamped

before the gates of the citadel. .... (80) And his troops were more numerous than ants or locusts, being in their multitude beyond estimation or computation. Detachment after detachment arrived, each like a billowing sea, and encamped round about the town. At sunrise twenty thousand men from the Sultan's auxiliary army (*bīrūnī*) issued forth from the citadel together with most of the inhabitants; being commanded by Gök Khan and other officers. .... Gök Khan was said to be a Mongol and to have fled from Chinggiz Khan and joined the Sultan ...; as a consequence of which his affairs had greatly prospered. When these forces reached the banks of the Oxus [now Amu Darya], the patrols and advance parties of the Mongol army fell upon them and left no trace of them. ....

On the following day when from the reflection of the sun the plain seemed to be a tray filled with blood, the people of Bukhara opened their gates and closed the door of strife and battle. The *imām*s [priests] and notables came on a deputation to Chinggiz Khan, who entered to inspect the town and the citadel. He rode into the Friday mosque and pulled up before the *maqṣūra* [place of the priest in prayer], whereupon his son Toluy dismounted and ascended the pulpit. Chinggiz Khan asked those present whether this was the palace of the Sultan; they replied that it was the house of God. Then he too got down from his horse, and mounting two or three steps of the pulpit he exclaimed: 'The countryside is empty of fodder; fill our horses' bellies.' Whereupon they opened all the magazines in the town and began carrying off the grain. And they [the Mongols] brought the cases in which the Korans were kept out into the courtyard of the mosque, where they cast the Korans right and left and turned the cases into mangers for their horses. After which they circulated cups of wine and sent for the singing-girls of the town to sing and dance for them; while the Mongols raised their voices to the tunes of their own songs. (81) Meanwhile, the *imām*s, *shaikh*s, *sayyid*s, doctors and scholars of the age kept watch over their horses in the stable under the supervision of the equerries, and executed their commands. After an hour or two Chinggiz Khan arose to return to his camp, and as the multitude that had been gathered there moved away the leaves of the Koran were trampled in the dirt beneath their own feet and their horses' hoofs. In that moment, the Emir Imām

Jalāl ad-Dīn 'Ali b. al-Ḥasan Zaidī, who was the chief and leader of the *sayyid*s of Transoxiana and was famous for his piety and asceticism, turned to the learned *imām* Rukn-ad-Dīn Imāmzāda, who was one of the most excellent savants in the world . . ., and said: '*Maulānā*, what state is this? *That which I see do I see it in wakefulness or in sleep, O Lord?*' *Maulānā* Imāmzāda answered: 'Be silent: it is the wind of God's omnipotence that bloweth, and we have no power to speak.'

When Chinggiz Khan left the town he went to the festival *muṣallà* and mounted the pulpit; and, the people having been assembled, he asked which were the wealthy amongst them. Two hundred and eighty persons were designated (a hundred and ninety of them being natives of the town and the rest strangers, viz. ninety merchants from various places) and were led before him. He then began a speech, in which, after describing the resistance and treachery of the Sultan . . ., he addressed them as follows: 'O people, know that you have committed great sins, and that the great ones among you have committed these sins. If you ask me what proof I have for these words, I say it is because I am the punishment of God. If you had not committed great sins, God would not have sent a punishment like me upon you.' When he had finished speaking in this strain, he continued his discourse with words of admonition, saying, 'There is no need to declare your property that is on the face of the earth; (82) tell me of that which is in the belly of the earth.' Then he asked them who were their men of authority; and each man indicated his own people. To each of them he assigned a Mongol or Turk as *basqaq* [tax collector] in order that the soldiers might not molest them, and, although not subjecting them to disgrace or humiliation, they began to exact money from these men; and when they delivered it up they did not torment them by excessive punishment or demanding what was beyond their power to pay. And every day, at the rising of the greater luminary, the guards would bring a party of notables to the audience-hall of the World-Emperor.

Chinggiz Khan had given orders for the Sultan's troops to be driven out of the interior of the town and the citadel. As it was impossible to accomplish this purpose by employing the townspeople and as these troops, being in fear of their lives, were fighting, and doing battle, and making night attacks as much as was possible, he now gave orders for all the quarters of the town to be set on fire; and since the houses were built entirely of wood, within several days the greater part of the town had been consumed, with the exception of the Friday mosque and some of the palaces, which were built with baked bricks. Then the people of Bukhara were driven against the citadel. And on either side the furnace of battle was heated. On the outside, mangonels were erected, bows bent and stones and arrows discharged; and on the inside, ballistas and pots of naphtha were set in motion. It was like a red-hot furnace fed from without by hard sticks thrust into the recesses, while from the belly of the furnace sparks shot into the air. For days they fought in this manner; the garrison made sallies against the besiegers, and Gök Khan in particular, who in bravery would have borne the palm from male lions, engaged in many battles; in each attack he overthrew several persons and alone repelled a great army. But finally they were reduced to the last extremity; resistance was no longer in their power; and they stood excused before God and man. The moat had been filled with animate and inanimate and raised up with levies and Bukharians; the outworks had been captured (83) and fire hurled into the citadel; and their khans, leaders and notables, who were the chief men of the age and the favorites of the Sultan and who in their glory would set their feet on the head of Heaven, now became the captives of abasement and were drowned in the sea of annihilation. . . . Of the Qangli no male was spared who stood higher than the butt of a whip and more than thirty thousand were counted amongst the slain; whilst their small children, the children of their nobles and their womenfolk, slender as the cypress, were reduced to slavery.

When the town and the citadel had been purged of rebels and the walls and outworks levelled with the dust, all the inhabitants of the town, men and women, ugly and beautiful, were driven out on to the field of the *muṣallā* (summer mosque). Chinggiz Khan spared their lives; but the youths and full-grown men that were fit for such service were pressed into a levy (*ḥashar*) for the attack on Samarkand and Dābūsīya. Chinggiz Khan then proceeded against Samarkand and the people of Bukhara, because of the desolation, were scattered like the constellation of the Bear and departed into the villages, while the site of the town became like '*a level plain*'.

Now one man had escaped from Bukhara after its capture and had come to Khurasan. He was questioned about the fate of that city and replied: 'They came, they sapped, they burnt, they slew, they plundered and they departed.' Men of understanding who heard this description were all agreed that in the Persian language there could be nothing more concise than this speech. And indeed all that has been written in this chapter is summed up and epitomized in these two or three words.

(84) . . . Finally, when, by the order of the World-Emperor [Ögädäi, 1229–41] . . ., the keys of government were placed in the solicitous hands of the Minister Yalavach, those scattered and dispersed in nooks and crannies were by the magnet of his justice and clemency attracted back to their former homes, and from all parts of the world people turned their faces thitherward; for because of his solicitude the prosperity of the town was on the increase, nay it reached its highest pitch and its territory became the home of the great and noble and the place of assembly of patrician and plebeian.

Suddenly in the year 636/1238–39 a sieve-maker of Tārāb in the district of Bukhara rose up in rebellion in the dress of the people of rags [mystics], and the common people rallied to his standard; and finally things came to such a pass that [after the rebellion had been stamped out] orders were given for the execution of all the inhabitants of Bukhara. But the Minister Yalavach, like a good prayer, averted their evil fate and by his mercy and solicitude repelled from them this sudden calamity. . . . And day by day the bounty of God's favor, by dint of which mercy and compassion everywhere form the carpet of justice and munificence, shines forth like the sun in the mercy of Maḥmūd (= Yalavach) and the pearl of that sea, namely Mas'ūd [his son and successor]. . . .

(Juvaini, *History of the World-Conqueror*, trans. Boyle, I, 97–108 [= Part I, 75–84].)

15. Chinggiz Khan's Legislation (Yasa)

Since the Mongols had no script of their own, Chinggiz Khan had the Tatar children instructed in the Uighur[21] script. Therefore

[21] The Uighurs, a Turkish tribe in Central Asia, had obtained their script via the Christian and Manichaean missions from the Syrians. It is written downward and is still used by the Mongols.

Mongolian is written in Uighur letters just as the Egyptians [by which are meant the Copts] write with Greek and the Persians with Arabic letters. He also had recorded the following laws which he had proclaimed:

1. If it is necessary to write to rebels or send messengers to them they shall not be intimidated by an excessive display of confidence on our part or by the size of our army, but they shall merely be told: if you submit you will find peace and benevolence. But if you continue to resist—what then do we know [about your future]? Only God knows what then will become of you. In this the Mongols show confidence based on the Lord; through this they have been and will be victorious.

2. The pure, the innocent, the just, the learned and the wise of every people shall be respected and honored; the bad and the unjust shall be despised. Since the Mongols noted among the Christians sincerity and charity they held the Christians in the early stages of their rule in high esteem. But, later their affection turned to hatred; they could no longer approve the behavior of the Christians when many of them changed over to the Muslim faith.[22]

3. The rulers and the members of the class of leaders shall not be given any grandiose names as is the custom with other people, especially the Muslims. The occupant of the throne deserves only one title: Khan or Qā'ān.[23] His brother and his other relatives shall simply be called by their proper names.

4. When there is no war raging against the enemy, there shall be hunting; the young shall be taught how to kill wild animals, so that they become accustomed to fighting, and acquire strength and endurance, and will subsequently fight, without sparing themselves, against the enemy as though against wild animals.

[22] For many decades (after the death of Bar Hebraeus, 1286) the Mongols were fierce enemies of the Muslims. Only later in the Near East did they themselves adopt Islam (and the Turkish way of life). In Mongolia the Mongols are today Buddhists.

[23] In fact Chinggiz Khan's successor Ögädäi (1229–41) is called simply Qā'ān in the sources.

5. Soldiers shall not be less than twenty years old. They shall be organized in groups of ten, a hundred, a thousand and ten thousand men.

6. Each Mongol tribe shall contribute to the upkeep of the Khan from their annual surpluses and they shall provide him with horses, rams, milk and woolens.

7. Nobody shall leave the unit of a thousand, a hundred or ten to which he is assigned. Otherwise he himself, and the leader of the unit that has accepted him, shall be executed.

8. Every two miles there shall be staging posts with horses for envoys in transit.

9. The Khan shall not take anything from the estate of a man who dies without heirs; such a man's property shall pass to the person who has looked after him.

To remain concise, other laws of the Mongols will not be mentioned at this stage.[24]

(Gregorius Bar Hebraeus, *Chronicon Syriacum*, ed. Paul Bedjan [Paris, 1890], pp. 411–12.)

16. The Investiture of the Third Son Ögädäi as Administrator of the Empire

(132) ... And then Chinggiz Khan said: 'Why do you speak of Jochi in this way? Is not Jochi the eldest of my sons? In future you shall not speak about him like this!' To these words Chaghatai, Jochi's brother, replied, smiling: 'It goes without saying that Jochi is strong, and his abilities are universally recognized. One cannot take away on carts those he has killed with his mouth, and one

---

[24] These laws, in an extended and more elaborate form, but in the same order, appear also in the Persian language in *Jowaynī: Ta'rīkh-i Jahān gushā (The History of the World-Conqueror)*, ed. Mīrzā Mohammäd Qazwīnī, Vol. I (Leiden and London, 1912), pp. 16–25 (Gibb Memorial Series, vol. XVI/1). They also contain two short paragraphs on religious tolerance under Chinggiz Khan and his immediate successors and about the selection of captive girls for the ruler and the officers.

cannot plunder those he has killed with his speech. Among the sons, the two of us, Jochi and I, are the eldest. Let us together dedicate our strength to the Imperial Father. The one of us who has evaded his duty shall be cut in two by the other. The one of us who has lagged behind shall have his heels hacked through by the other! Ögädäi, however, is a prudent man. Let us elect Ögädäi! Ögädäi shall remain with you, the Imperial Father, and you shall instruct him in the ceremonial forms and in the skills of the Big Hat. That would be the right thing to do.' Whereupon Chinggiz Khan said: 'What does Jochi say? Speak!' Jochi said: 'Chaghatai has already said it. Together, Chaghatai and I, we will make our strength available and we will elect Ögädäi!' Chinggiz Khan replied: 'What will happen, when you act together? The Mother Earth is vast. Many are the rivers and lakes. I shall share out in such a way as to increase for you the distributable grazing areas and give you governorships of the states.' He continued: 'You two, Jochi and Chaghatai, shall keep to what you have said, and shall not give the people cause for derision, nor give the men any reason to roar with laughter! What happened earlier to the two . . . as a consequence of making just such an agreement, and then not keeping their words? What became of them? The descendants of those two, I am now about to share with you. Bearing them in mind, how could you be negligent in your duties!' Then he said: 'What does Ögädäi say? (133) Speak!' Ögädäi said: 'When, through the kindness of the Imperial Father, I am asked to make a statement, what shall I say for myself? How could I say, "I cannot"? I say, therefore, that I shall strive to the utmost to do the best within my power. I am only afraid that, later, it may come about, that among my descendants, there are those that, if they were wrapped in fresh grass this would not be eaten by the cattle, if they were wrapped in fat this would not be eaten by the dogs; that incompetents will be born who may miss a . . . -stag with a side-on shot, or a rat, shooting end-on. These are the concerns that I have to express. What else shall I say?' At this Chinggiz Khan said: 'If Ögädäi utters such words, there is something in it.' And he went on: 'What does Toluy[25] say? Speak!' Toluy said: 'I shall support my elder brother appointed by the Imperial Father, remind him when he forgets something, wake him when he has fallen asleep. I shall

[25] The younger son.

be his sworn companion and a whip for his red horse. I shall not go back on what I have promised, and I shall never be missing in the ranks. I shall accompany him on a long campaign just as I shall fight for him in a short war.' Then Chinggiz Khan praised him for having spoken in this way.

A short description of the campaign in Central Asia and Persia.

17. Muslim Governors

(137) When Chinggiz Khan had completed his conquest of the lands of the Muslims he appointed by a decree bailiffs for the various cities. There came from the city of Urgench two Muslims from the family of Khurumshi, father and son, named Yalavach and Mas'ūd. They explained to Chinggiz Khan the meaning and importance of the cities. When he had been advised so as to have some idea of their importance, he appointed his [Yalavach's] son Mas'ūd Khurumshi to administer together with our bailiffs the cities of . . . [in the country of Transoxiana[26]] and others. He went and fetched his father Yalavach and took him with him and gave him the city of Jung-du[27] of the Kitat[28] to administer. Since among the . . ., the Muslims, these two, Yalavach and Mas'ūd, were best versed in city affairs, he entrusted them together with the bailiffs, with the administration of the Kitat people.

(Haenisch, *Geheime Geschichte der Mongolen*), pp. 132–7.)

18. Chinggiz Khan's Death and Funeral

After several futile rebellions against the Mongols, the ruler of the Tanguts—on the southeastern fringe of Tibet—offered his submission to Chinggiz Khan.

He sent messengers to ask for peace, a treaty and a solemn oath, and said: 'I am afraid that he may not accept me as one of his "sons".' Chinggiz Khan granted his request. [The Tangut ruler]

---

[26] The Central Asian region north of the Oxus river, roughly present-day Turkestan.
[27] Present-day Peking.   [28] = Khitai.

then asked for a month's grace in order to prepare the handing over, and to lead away the people of the city. The respite he had asked for was granted. [The ruler] wanted to appear submissive [to Chinggiz Khan], and to express his admiration and submission, but Chinggiz Khan sent word to him: 'I am ill. He shall wait until I am better.' To . . . he said: 'Be his adjutant and . . . head of receptions when envoys and other visitors call on him.' The man acted accordingly and was permanently with him. But Chinggiz Khan's illness got worse day by day.

The ruler thought that as a result of this illness his end was inevitable. He gave an order to his beys: 'Do not let my death be known, do not weep or lament in any way, so that the enemy shall not know anything about it. But, when the ruler of the Tanguts and the population leave the city at the appointed time, annihilate them all.' On the fifteenth day of the middle month of the autumn, in the Year of the Pig, which corresponds to Ramadan 624 H. [= 15 August to 13 September 1227], he left the transient world and left throne, property and rule to his famous family. As he had ordered, the beys kept his death secret until [the Tanguts] had left their city. Then they slew them all. Then they took his coffin and started on their way back. On the way they killed every living being they met until they had reached the [home] horde with the coffin. All the princes, women and beys who were in the area came together and wept for the deceased.

In Mongolia, there is a big mountain called Burkan Kaldun. On one side of this mountain, many rivers run down. Alongside them, there are vast areas of trees and large forests. These are inhabited by the Taijut people. Chinggiz Khan, himself, had chosen this place for his funeral, and had ordered: 'This shall be the place for my grave and those of my family.' Chinggiz Khan's summer and winter camps were in this area; he had, himself, been born in Buluk-Buldaq on the lower Onon [river]. It is a six-day journey from there to Burkan Kaldun, where a unit of a thousand Oirats lived . . . and guarded this country.

. . . It had come about in this way: One day Chinggiz Khan had been hunting; at a certain place, a unique tree was growing. He rested under it, and was there refreshed. So he said: 'This place is suitable for my burial. This shall be noted!' When they [now] wept for him, the people who at the time had heard him say these words, repeated them. Thus princes and beys selected this spot [for his grave], according to his orders. It is said that in the very same year that he was buried there, trees and grass grew in the steppe to an unimaginable extent. Now, this forest is so dense, that it is impossible to make one's way through it. The original forest and place of his burial are no longer known. Not even the old field-guards who guard this place any longer can find a way to it.

(Rashīd ad-Dīn, *Jamiʿ at-tawārīk* = *Sbornik Letopisej*, Vol. I/2, ed. and trans. Olga I. Smirnova [Moscow and Leningrad, 1952], pp. 233–5.)

19. Ögädäi Is Elected Great Khan

(141) . . . In the Year of the Rat[29] [1228], the princes of the right hand,[30] under the leadership of Chaghatai and Batu,[31] and the princes of the left hand, under the leadership of Otchigin Noyan (Temügä, youngest brother of Chinggiz Khan), Yegu and Yesung-ge, the princes of the center under the leadership of Toluy, the princesses, the sons-in-law, the leaders of ten thousand and of a thousand, all came together for a general meeting near Kode'u aral, on the Keluren,[32] and made Ögädäi Khan their emperor, in strict accord with the order by which Chinggiz Khan had appointed him. And it was Chaghatai, the eldest, who installed his younger brother, Ögädäi Khan, as emperor. In doing this, Chaghatai, the eldest, and Toluy, these two, allotted to Ögädäi Khan the night guards, quiver bearers, and eight thousand day guards who had protected the golden life of their father, Chinggiz Khan, as well as the servants and ten thousand bodyguards who had served close to their Imperial Father. In the same way, they allotted to him the Middle Kingdom. When Ögädäi Khan had had himself made emperor, and the ten thousand bodyguards serving in the palace and the Middle Kingdom made over to him, he sent, after previous

[29] See p. 23, n. 15.
[30] Of the right wing of the army in the permanent army order.
[31] The second son of Jochi (d. 1227) and future conqueror of Russia (1237–40), died 1255 after becoming the first Khan of the Golden Horde.
[32] The place where the 'Secret History' was written.

consultation with the eldest[33] brother Chaghatai, the two . . . to war.

Campaigns in China, the Near East and Russia; consolidation of the internal institutions.

(Haenisch, *Geheime Geschichte der Mongolen*, p. 141.)

20. The Accession of the Ruler of the World (*Ögädäi*) *Qā'ān to the Throne and the Power of the World Empire*

(141) After God Almighty . . . had tried His servants upon the touchstone of calamity and melted them in the crucible of tribulation . . ., [according to the words of the Koran 55:106], and when in proportion to the wickedness of their deeds they had each of them borne the rope of punishment, and in accordance with the evilness of their actions and the uncleanness of their ways had drunk the brimful cup of 'the recompense of evil with its like'; it being ordained that every event hath its limit and every beginning its end [as the Prophet Muhammad has said] . . .; it became necessary in accordance with both reason and tradition that the treasures of the mercy of God . . . should again be opened up and the ease and comfort of His servants again provided for. . . . And the prefacing of these remarks and the laying of these foundations announces the tale of the transfer of empire to the Lords of the World Ögädäi Qā'ān and Möngkä Qā'ān. I shall begin by describing in due order the accession of Qā'ān (Ögädäi), expressing myself with conciseness and brevity so that those that honor this book with their perusal may not reproach the author of these lines with garrulity (142) but may understand the purpose of this narration and learn in what manner Qā'ān administered affairs and protected the commonweal; how he reduced the other climes, which were hesitating between hope and despair, to obedience and submission, some by threats and some by fair words, and brought them under his control and command; and how after his death Möngkä Qā'ān shored up the building of justice after its collapse and raised and strengthened the foundations thereof. May God Almighty grant the success of truth and righteousness!

[33] Jochi having died in the meantime.

Before he alighted at the quarter of kingship Qā'ān bore the name of Ögädäi. And Chinggiz Khan from the deeds he performed and the words he uttered was wont to deduce his fitness for the throne and [to rule over] kings and armies, and in his shutting and opening and loosing and binding used daily to find the signs of valor and prowess in dealing with the affairs of the State and the defense thereof against the hand of foes. And by suggestion and allusion he used to paint the picture of this idea in the hearts of his other sons 'like the picture on the stone', and gradually sowed the seed of this advice in their innermost minds.

When Chinggiz Khan returned from the lands of the West to his old encampment in the East, he carried out his intention to proceed against the Tangut [cf. pp. 43f]. And after the whole region had been purged of the evilness of his enemies and they had all been conquered and subjugated, he was overcome by an incurable disease arising from the insalubrity of the climate. He called to him his sons Chaghatai, Ögädäi, Ulugh-Noyan (= Great Noyan, a title] Kölgen, Jurcheday and Orkhon [?] and addressed them as follows: 'The severity of my illness (143) is greater than can be cured by treatment, and, of a truth, one of you must defend the throne and the power of the State and raise up that pedestal which has received so strong a foundation. . . . For if all my sons wish each of them to become Khan, and be the ruler, and not be subservient to one another, will it not be like the fable of the snake with one head and the snake with many heads?'

When he had finished speaking these words and admonitions, which are the pivot of their deeds and their *yasa* [=their laws], the aforesaid sons knelt down and said: 'Our father is the king and we are his thralls; we bow our heads to thy command and counsel' [from *Shāhnāmā* by Firdausi].

Chinggiz Khan then spoke as follows: 'If it is your wish to pass your lives in ease and luxury . . ., my advice, as I have lately given you to understand, is that Ögädäi should ascend the throne of the Khanate in my place because he stands out amongst you for the excellency of his firm counsel and the superiority of his perspicacious understanding; and that the government of the army and the people and the defense of the frontiers of the Empire should be executed by his auspicious advice and good counsel. I therefore make him my heir and place the keys of the Empire in the hand of his valor and ability. What is your advice, my sons, concerning this thought and what is your thought concerning this advice?'

They again laid the knee of courtesy [*adab*] upon the ground of fealty and submission and answered with the tongue of obedience, saying: 'Who hath the power to oppose the word of Chinggiz Khan and who the ability to reject it?' . . . (144) 'Our welfare and that of our followers is dependent upon that wherewith the counsel of Chinggiz Khan is bound up, and the success of our affairs is entrusted to his direction.'

'If then,' said Chinggiz Khan, 'your will be in agreement with your words and your tongues in accordance with your hearts, you must make a confirmatory statement in writing that after my death you will recognize Ögädäi as Khan, and regard his command as the soul in the body, and suffer no change or alteration of what has been decided today in my presence, nor deviate from my decree.'

All Ögädäi's brothers obeyed his commandment and made a statement in writing. Chinggiz Khan's illness grew worse, and it being impossible to remove him from where he was he passed away on the 4th of Ramadan, 624 [18 August, 1227].

The princes then all set out for their places of residence, intending in the new year to hold the assembly which in the Mongol tongue is called *quriltai*. They all returned to their *ordu*s and made preparations for this *quriltai*.

As soon as the chillness of the air and the violence of the cold had abated and the earth was cheered and gladdened by the blowing of the gentle zephyr . . ., the aforementioned sons and their kinsmen sent a relay of messengers to spread the tidings of the death of Chinggiz Khan throughout the world and to proclaim that in order that no harm might come to the Kingdom, it was necessary to hold an assembly and decide the question of the Khanate. Upon this each man left his *ordu* and set out for the *quriltai*. From the lands of the Qïpchaq [the frontier areas of the Cumans adjacent to Russia—at that time still unconquered] came the sons of Jochi (Tushi), Orda, Batu, Berke and others . . . (145); from Qanās [Qayas?], Chaghatai; from the Emil and the Qobaq, Ögädäi; from the East, their uncle Otchigin and others . . . , and from the other parts, the emirs and *noyan*s that were stationed on every side. As for Ulugh-Noyan and his younger brothers, they were already in the *ordu* of Chinggiz Khan.

All the above-mentioned persons gathered together in the region of the Keluren [Kerulen river, a tributary of the Arghūn which flows through the Dalai Nor, now Hulum Nor, and joins it on the right bank]; and when the world had begun to smile because of the alighting of the Sun at the house of Aries . . . when, moreover, the herbs and flowers had blossomed in the meadows and for wonder thereat the ringdoves . . . had sung a hundred songs in a thousand ways in unison with the nightingales . . . (146) . . . all the princes, *noyan*s and emirs together with so large an army that the plain was filled therewith and the desert straitened with their multitude . . . , first of all feasted and revelled for three days and nights in succession filled with joy and delight, the impurities of deceit and envy remote from their secret thought . . . and after some days they spoke of the affairs of the realm and the testament of Chinggiz Khan and read over again and again the written statements made by his sons that the Khanate should be settled on Ögädäi. This counsel they adopted, and all the princes with a unanimity unmingled with evil or strife said to Ögädäi: 'In accordance with the command of Chinggiz Khan it behoves thee with divine assistance to set thy foot upon the hand of kingship in order that all the mighty ones may with one accord gird the loins of their lives with the girdle of submission and servitude and incline their eyes and ears to obeying thy command.'

Ögädäi replied as follows: 'Although Chinggiz Khan's command was to this effect, yet there are my elder brothers and uncles, who are more worthy than I to accomplish this task, and moreover, in accordance with the Mongol custom, it is the youngest son from the eldest house that is the heir of his father, and Ulugh-Noyan is the youngest son of the eldest *ordu* and was ever in attendance on Chinggiz Khan day and night, morning and evening, and has seen, and heard, and learnt all his *yasa*s and customs. Seeing that all these are alive and here present, how may I succeed to the Khanate?'

(147) All that day till nightfall they debated together with gaiety and friendly emulation. And in like manner for full forty days they donned each day new clothes of different color and quaffed cups of wine, at the same time discussing the affairs of the kingdom. And every day Ögädäi in a different way and in a style at once subtle and correct expressed these same sentiments. When the forty days

had come to an end, on the morning of the forty-first . . . the knots
of all the princes and every class of freeman and slave having been
resolved, all the princes of one accord went up to Ögädäi and said:
'This task Chinggiz Khan has confided to thee of all his sons and
brethren and has entrusted to thy counsel the binding and loosing,
the tying and untying thereof. How then may we suffer any
change or alteration of his words or allow any transformation or
violation thereof? Today, which according to the astrologers and
*qam*s [shamans] is a fortunate day and a favorable and auspicious
time, thou must with the aid of God . . . be established upon the
throne of universal sovereignty and adorn the world with justice
and beneficence.'

Finally, after much importunity on their part and much re-
fusing on the part of Ögädäi, he obeyed the command of his father
and followed the advice of his brothers and uncles. In accordance
with their ancient custom they removed their hats and slung their
belts across their backs; and it being the year 626/1228-9 Chaghatai
took his right hand and Otchigin his left and by the resolution
of aged counsel and the support of youthful fortune established
him upon the throne. Ulugh-Noyan took a cup, and all present
in and outside the Court thrice knelt down and uttered prayers,
saying, 'May the kingdom prosper by his being Khan!'

(148) . . . And they named him [gave him the title of] Qā'ān,
and in accordance with the usual custom all the princes, in service
and obeisance to Qā'ān, knelt three times to the sun outside the
ordu; then reentering they held an assembly of mirth and sport
and cleared the plains of merriment of the thorns of sorrow.

The world-ruling Emperor seated himself upon the ladder of
vigilant fortune, Heaven-assisted and powerful, and the princes,
Orion-like, girded the zone of service about the loins of affection
before the sun of the heavens of greatness and power; while on the
left were the ladies, each of them richly endowed with fairness
and beauty, in their exquisite freshness and brightness resembling
flowers and in their sweetness and purity like unto the verdure of
spring. . . . The eyes of Time were brightened by the presence of
Qā'ān and the world by his influence became without hatred or
anger. . . . The days from rest and quiet acquired the pleasantness
of nights, and the nights from the geniality and brilliance of the
fire of wine became like broad day.

(149) Qā'ān then ordered that they should open the deposits of the treasuries collected during so many years from the countries of the East and the West for the behoof of Chinggiz Khan, the sum total of which could not be contained within the bellies of ledgers. He closed the mouths of the censorious with rejection of their advice and allotted his portion to each of his relatives and soldiers, his troops and kinsfolk, noble and base, lord and liege, master and slave, to each in accordance with his pretensions; and left in his treasuries for the morrow neither much nor little, neither great nor small. . . .

And when he had done with feasting and bestowing gifts and presents, in accordance with the custom [. . . quotation from Koran 43:22] he commanded that for three days in succession they should prepare victuals for the spirit of Chinggiz Khan; also that from moonlike virgins, delightful of aspect and fair of character, sweet in their beauty and beautiful in their glances, graceful in motion and elegant in repose, such that 'God hath promised to them that fear Him', they should select forty maidens of the race of the emirs and *noyans* to be decked out with jewels, ornaments and fine robes, clad in precious garments and dispatched together with choice horses to join his spirit.

And when he had finished with these matters he began to concern himself with the administration of the kingdom and the management of affairs.

First of all he made a *yasa* [an order] that such ordinances and commands as had previously been issued by Chinggiz Khan should be maintained, and secured, and protected against the evils of change, and alteration, and confusion. Now, from all sides there had come talebearers and informers to report and make known the doings of each of the emirs and governors. But Qā'ān said: 'Every hasty speech which until the day of our accession hath issued from the mouth of any man, we shall pardon and cancel it; but if from henceforth any man shall set foot to an action that contravenes the old and new ordinances and *yasa*s, the prosecution and punishment of that man shall be proportionate to his crime.'

And after decreeing these *yasa*s he dispatched armies to all the climes of the world.

In Khurasan and Iraq the fire of strife and unrest had not yet died down and Sultan Jalāl ad-Dīn [cf. p. 3] was still active there. Thither he dispatched Chormaghun with a number of emirs and thirty thousand warriors. (150) To the lands of the Qıpchaq and Saqsīn and [Volga-] Bulghar he sent Kögödäi and Sübödäi Bahādur with a like army. Likewise to Tibet and Solangai [northern Korea] he dispatched greater or lesser forces; to Khitai [northern China] he decided to proceed in person accompanied by his brothers. . . .

(Juvaini, *History of the World-Conqueror*, trans. Boyle, I, 178–90 [=Part I, 141–50].)

21. The Western Campaign 1236–42

(145) Chormakhun Khorchi subjected the people [sic; reporter mistook Baghdad to be a population group instead of a geographical location] Baghdad. When Ögädäi learned that that country was reputed to be beautiful and its products renowned for their excellence, he gave him the order: 'Chormakhun Khorchi shall reside right there as governor, and you shall send here, year after year, yellow gold, embroideries interlaced with yellowish gold, brocades, damasks, fine pearls and mother-of-pearl, long-necked and high-legged . . . horses, . . . camels, . . . and to carry the burden . . . mules!' The various princes sent to war in support of Sübödäi, like Batu, Börü, Göyük and Möngkä, subjugated the people of . . . and massacred the Orus [Russians], or carried them off, down to the last man. Of the inhabitants of the cities . . . some were enslaved, others were merely made subject. After setting up governors and bailiffs they returned home. As a reinforcement . . . the emperor sent . . . there. He ordered him to take up residence there as governor.

From the Qıpchaq campaign, Batu sent by messenger a report to Ögädäi Khan: 'Through the power of eternal heaven and the grace of the Imperial Uncles, we have destroyed the city of Mtskheti [in Georgia] and made the Russian people slaves. We have subjected eleven states and peoples to our rule, and have tightened the golden rein. Afterward, we arranged to meet for a farewell feast, and set up the large tent. When we eventually sat down to the feast, I, who after all was a little older than the princes here present, drank once or twice [from the beaker] before they did. This was resented by Börü and Göyük, and, without taking part in the feast, they rode away. Such treatment (146) was I given. On riding away, Börü said: 'Batu, surely, is our equal. How, then, could he drink first! He is like the old wives with beards. He should be hacked with the heel, he should be trampled down with the sole!' Göyük said: 'Those quiver-bearing women, we shall hit them on the breast with a heavy stick!' And . . . said: 'I shall tie a wooden tail to them!' These were their words.— 'Surely, when we are sent to war against enemy people of foreign race, we should remind ourselves that our position is unsafe, but instead, I have been insulted in this way by the two, Börü and Göyük, and they have left without my consent. Now, they shall know the decision of the Imperial Uncle!' This was the report he sent. These words of Batu made the ruler very angry, and he refused to grant an audience to Göyük, but said: 'The scoundrel! On whose authority does he make bold to revile an elder brother? A single egg may stink! He, himself, has rebelled against the breast of the elder brother! I shall put him in the vanguard, and make him climb mountain-like city walls until the nails of his ten fingers are ground away! I shall give him the post of commander and make him climb strong and well-trampled city walls, until the nails of his five fingers are worn away!—And you, dirty, evil, mean . . . , who taught you to be so loudmouthed and to talk big against a member of Our family? I shall send the two, Göyük and . . . , together [for punishment]! . . . ought to be beheaded. But you would say this was being partial. As to Börü, tell Batu to send him to Chaghatai, the elder brother, and inform him about it. Brother Chaghatai shall decide about him!' . . . from the ranks of the imperial princes, and the princes . . . from the ranks of the other princes, made the following suggestion: 'There was an order given by your father, Chinggiz Khan, according to which matters of the battlefield should be decided in the field, and domestic matters at home. If the ruler would allow us to say so: The ruler is enraged about Göyük. This is a battlefield matter (147). Therefore it might well be right to pass it to Batu for settlement.' The ruler approved these words and, moderating his anger, received Göyük in audience. He rebuked him with the reproachful words: 'It is said of you, that when you go to war, while you are on the way, of those men who had buttocks, not even the buttocks are left. It is said of you, that the men in your army appeared broken down and worn out. Do you, perhaps, imagine that the Russian people there allowed themselves to be conquered from fear of your impetuosity and fury? Thinking that you conquered the Russian people single-handed, you have become arrogant and you have come to behave with enmity toward an elder brother. A phrase of our father, Chinggiz Khan, says: 'Numbers bring fear; depth brings death.' Although it appears as though you did it single-handed, in fact, you marched protected by the other two; ... only in a common action, in conjunction with all the other parts, did you conquer the Russians and the Qıpchaq. You have captured one or two Russians or Qıpchaq people, but as far as gaining the hoof of a buck and displaying it as booty, this you have not yet achieved. Once, pretending to be a hero, you left the yurt, and then returned, talking provocatively, as though you had done it all by yourself. As comrades at my side, ... have restrained my enraged mind and, like a broad ladle, prevented the kettle from boiling over. They called the case a battlefield matter and one to be decided by Batu. And so, Batu shall decide about the two, Göyük and ... !' With these words, he sent them off to him. 'Börü's case shall be decided by brother Chaghatai,' he said. ...

(151) Ögädäi Khan went on: 'The empire founded by my father, Chinggiz Khan, in the midst of troubles, I wish to free from its troubles. I want to give it happiness by letting it set its foot on the ground and its hand to the soil. Wherever I sit on the throne of my Imperial Father, I command, that, in order that the people shall not suffer from want, the population shall, each year, provide from the flock a two-year-old sheep for the soup. From every hundred sheep, one sheep shall be taken and handed to the poor and needy within that tribe. Further, when the brothers (princes), the whole of the army and bodyguards come together, how can drink be provided for all these from among the people? For this purpose, mares shall be selected from the various units of a thousand in the different regions, be milked, and then entrusted to the care of milkers. Then, by a system of rota, the camp stewards shall look after the mares. Further, when the brothers assemble, I would like to give them presents and tokens of favor. I shall put silk and bars of silver, quivers, bows, armor and weapons in store, and have the stores guarded. Storekeepers and rice-keepers shall

be selected from the various regions, and shall be entrusted with guarding them. Further, I shall assign grazing grounds and water to the people of the empire. Regarding the assignment of grazing grounds, it might be right to select and provide grazing managers from the individual units of a thousand. Further, in the Chol country, there is nothing but game. (152) In order to create a little more space [for grazing] for the people, the two, ... and ..., shall supervise the camp elders there, and shall dig out and line with stone, the wells in Chol. Further, when the couriers ride, we make them travel where there are people. This means that, on the one hand, the couriers are delayed, and on the other, the people are inconvenienced. Now, We shall introduce everywhere the following rule: the individual units of a thousand, in the various regions, shall provide postmasters and stableboys, and, at each stage, a post station shall be established, so that couriers need no longer be directed where there are people, without cogent reasons, but shall ride via the mail stages. That would be best. Those affairs which the two ... have considered and laid before Us, and which We consider right, shall be decided by brother Chaghatai. If these proposals which are to be laid before him are found right, and he accepts, brother Chaghatai's decision shall be acted upon.' The elder brother, Chaghatai, agreed without exception to these measures that had been proposed to him, and the reply came: It shall be done! Further, brother Chaghatai sent word: 'From here I shall provide a connection to link up with your mail stages. Then, I shall send a messenger from here to Batu, so that Batu shall provide also a connection to link up with my mail stages.' These were his words. Further, he added this to his message: 'Of all the points you raised, the idea of providing mail stages was the best suggestion of all!' Upon hearing this Ögädäi Khan said: 'The princes and brothers of the right hand, all together, with the elder brother, Chaghatai, and with Batu at their head, and the brothers and all the princes of the left hand with Otchigin and ... at their head, the sons-in-law and the princesses of the original empire, and the leaders of ten thousand, a thousand, a hundred, and of ten, have all agreed to the proposals. Its contents are as follows: "For the soup of the ruler of the world, a two-year-old ram should be provided every year from the flock, and, for the poor and needy, a one-year-old lamb should be provided from every hundred sheep.

If, on the setting up (153) of mail routes, postmasters and stable-boys were provided, this would be a relief for the whole people and would make the couriers' service easier." Everybody has agreed to this proposal.' Thereupon the ruler's order was presented to the elder brother, Chaghatai, for his opinion, and approved by him. Then, consequently, according to the command of the ruler, from the individual units of a thousand in the various regions all over the empire, every year, a two-year-old ram was to be provided from each flock for the soup, and from every hundred sheep a one-year-old lamb. Mares were provided, and herdsmen were engaged. Herdsmen, storekeepers and rice-keepers were selected. Postmasters and stableboys were appointed, and after calculating the distances between the individual stations, mail stages were set up. He charged the two . . . with the administration, and arranged for each mail stage twenty stableboys; for all the stages twenty stableboys each. And he ruled: 'If with regard to the horses for the relays, to the sheep for the rations, to the mares for the milk, to the cattle to draw the carts, and to the carts, the measures laid down here by us are found to be short by even a short rope, then a fine shall be imposed like that for chopping through the neck! If a spoon, or the spoke of a wheel, is found missing, a fine shall be imposed like that for cutting off the nose!' This was his order.

Ögädäi Khan said: 'One of the good things I have achieved since I succeeded my Imperial Father whose high throne I occupy, is that I made war against the Jakhut [= Kin, according to Haenisch] people, and destroyed their empire. My second achievement is the fact that I have established mail stages between which our couriers carry on the express service, and to facilitate the conveyance of my important state papers. Yet another achievement is that, in places where there was so far no water, I saw to it that wells were found and dug out, and so I helped the population to get water and grass. Moreover, for those peoples with cities, I set up a garrison and appointed bailiffs, and thus made life secure (154) for the people of the empire, so that they can set their feet on the ground and their hands to the soil. Thus, since I succeeded my Imperial Father I have achieved four new things. But on the other hand, after I had been put on the high throne by my Imperial Father, and had had the burden of his numerous states put by him on my shoulders, I did wrong in allowing myself to fall victim to the wine of grapes. This is one thing of which I am guilty. The second thing of which I am guilty is that, foolishly yielding to the word of a woman, I committed a wrong by having girls brought to me from the state of my uncle Otchigin. Yet another thing of which I am guilty, is that, as ruler and master of the empire, I wrongly relied on unjust actions. Furthermore, I am guilty of having killed Dokholkhu. If I am asked, why this should be a crime, [I would say]: That I had a man like him killed in secret who had repeatedly risked his life for my Imperial Father, his true master, is a crime and an injustice. Who will now stake his life for me as he had done? I charge myself with guilt, because I had a man killed without trial and in secret, who, more than anyone, had proved his loyalty to my Imperial Father. Further, through building stockades and earth mounds, I used to enclose the game created by heaven and earth for the benefit [of everybody], from greed, so that it should not wander into the lands of my brothers, and consequently I had to hear words of hatred from my brothers. This, too, was wrong. Therefore, as the successor of my Imperial Father, I have achieved four good things and am guilty of four wrongs.' These were his words.

(Haenisch, *Geheime Geschichte der Mongolen*, pp. 145–54.)

22. Ögädäi's Building Activities

During the seven years [between 1234/35 and 1240/41] . . . [Ögädäi] enjoyed life and amused himself. He moved from summer to winter camp and vice versa, serene and happy, and took permanent delight in beautiful women and moonfaced enchantresses.

At every opportunity, he allowed his sublime thoughts to overflow lavishly into the most just and charitable of good deeds, into the eradication of injustice and enmity, into the development of cities and districts, as well as into the construction of various buildings. He never neglected any measure designed to strengthen the framework of peace, and to lay the foundations of prosperity. In earlier years, he had already brought with him from China various craftsmen and masters skilled in the arts. Therefore in his main camp ('yurt') in Karakorum, where he contentedly resided most of the time, he now had erected his palace with a very high base and columns as befits the lofty thoughts of such a ruler. Each side of the palace was an arrow-shot long. In the centre, a sumptuous high pavilion ('kiosk') was built; the building was handsomely decorated with paintings and representations, and it was called *qarshi* [Mongolian = Palace]. The Khan designated it his sublime residence. [Thereafter] the order was put out, that each of his brothers, sons and the other princes residing close to him should build a handsome house near the palace. Everybody obeyed the order. When these buildings were completed and snuggled one against the other they formed a whole settlement. [Furthermore the Great Khan] ordered that experienced goldsmiths should make for the drinking house a centerpiece of gold and silver in the shape of animals such as elephants, tigers, horses, and the like. They were set up, together with large drinking vessels which were filled with wine and fermented mare's milk (*qumys*). In front of each figure a silver basin was set up: from the orifices of these figures wine and mare's milk poured into the basins.

[Once, the ruler] asked: 'Which is the best city on earth?' The reply was: 'Baghdad.' He therefore had a great city built on the banks of the river Orkhon, and he called it Karakorum. A mail route was established connecting it with the Chinese lands. . . . Every five parasangs [a parasang is roughly an hour's journey] there was a staging post. At each stage, a unit of a thousand was stationed to protect the posthouse. He ordered that, daily, five hundred vehicles with food and drink should arrive there from the provinces. The supplies were to be stored in sheds and distributed from there. [Exceptionally] large vehicles were built for grain and wine, each of them to be drawn by eight oxen. [Furthermore] a day's journey away from Karakorum, he had a pavilion built by Muslim masters in a place were once Afrasiyāb [the mythical King of Tūrān]'s falcon houses had stood. . . . In spring he stayed there for falconry. . . . A tent was erected there which could hold a thousand persons, and which was never dismantled. Its poles were of gold, its interior was covered in fabrics; it was called the 'Golden Horde' (*Sira Ordu*). In the autumn, [the ruler] stayed . . . four days in Karakorum and kept a forty-day fast. In winter, he . . . hunted in the . . . mountains. . . . Returning to Karakorum, he [used to stop] two traveling hours away from the city, where he had had a towering pavilion built . . . . He took a meal there . . . and stayed one day. The next day everybody put on clothes of the same colour, and they entered the palace (*qarshi*). At the head of them all appeared young entertainers. In the palace, he recuperated for a month and distributed alms from his treasures to the notables and to the simple people. Every evening, he organized a competition in archery and crossbow shooting, as well as in wrestling, and he honored the winners. Moreover, he ordered that a fence should be erected in . . . from poles and clay. Its length was to be two days' journey, with one opening in it. . . . At hunting time . . . all army units stationed in the vicinity were ordered to form a circle, after which [the hunters] moved into the enclosure and held a battue. According to an order previously given, the animals were driven through the opening. The troops formed a ring and stood shoulder to shoulder. At first, the Great Khan, with a group of his courtiers, rode into the enclosure, amused himself for a while, and shot at the animals. When he got tired of it, he rode on to a hill in the center of the enclosure. Now, one after the other, the princes and beys rode in, and, finally, the common soldiers, and shot at the animals. Eventually, some [of the animals] were let out again for breeding. The beaters [?] distributed the game impartially to all units of the princes, the beys, and the warriors; nobody was cheated. The whole company went through the ceremony of kissing the dust and offering gifts. After a feast lasting ten days, each clan returned to its tents and homes.

(Rashīd ad-Dīn, *Jāmi at-tawārīch* = *Sbornik Letopisej*, vol. II, trans. Ju. P. Verkhovsky [Moscow and Leningrad, 1960], pp. 40–2.)

23. Anecdotes from the Life of Ögädäi

(161) . . . The above is but a brief account of his actions. It may be that those who hear and read this history will regard these statements as belonging to the category of 'The fairest poetry is the falsest'. In order to prove their truth we shall in a succinct manner free from the contingencies of detraction or hyperbole recount some few anecdotes wherefrom these statements may be fully confirmed. . . .

(i) It is laid down in the *yasa* (law) and custom of the Mongols that in the season of spring and summer no one may sit in water by day, nor wash his hands in a stream, nor draw water in gold or silver vessels, nor lay out washed garments upon the plain; it being their belief that such actions increase the thunder and lightning. For in the country where they live it rains most of the time from the beginning of spring until the end of summer, and the clashing of the thunder is such (162) that when it roars 'they thrust their fingers into their ears because of the thunder-clap, for fear of death', and the flashing of the lightning is such that 'the lightning almost snatches away their eyes' (Koran 2:18, 19). And it has been observed that when it lightnings and thunders they become 'as mute as fishes'. Every year that one of them is struck by lightning they drive his tribe and household out from amongst the tribes for a period of three years, during which time they may not enter the *ordu* of the princes. Similarly if an animal in their herds and flocks is so struck, they proceed in the same manner for several months. And when such a happening occurs they eat [almost?] no food for the remainder of the month, and as in the case of their periods of mourning, they hold a celebration (*süyürmishī*) at the end of that month.

One day Qā'ān was returning from his hunting ground together with [his brother] Chaghatai when at noon they beheld a Muslim sitting in midstream washing himself. Now Chaghatai was extremely zealous in enforcing the *yasa* and spared no one who had deviated even slightly from it. When he caught sight of this man in the water, from the flame of the fire of his anger he wished to commit the earth of his being to the wind of annihilation and to cut off the source of his life. But Qā'ān said: 'Today it is late and we are tired. This man shall be held in custody until tomorrow, when we can inquire into his case and ascertain the reason for his violating our *yasa*.' And he ordered Dānishmend Ḥājib to take charge of the man till the morning, when his innocence or guilt might be discovered; he also told Dānishmend, in secret, to have a *balish* of silver thrown in the water where the man had been sitting and to instruct the man, when he was examined, to say that he was a poor man with many obligations, that this *balish* was his whole capital, and that it was for this reason that he had acted so rashly.

On the next day the guilty man was examined in Qā'ān's presence. Qā'ān listened to the excuse with the ear of acceptance, but by way of precaution someone went to the spot and the *balish* was taken out of the water. Then Qā'ān said: 'To whom could it occur to meditate breaking our *yasa* and commandment (163) or swerving a single hairsbreadth therefrom? But it seems to be that this man is a person of poor estate and little property and so has sacrificed himself for a single *balish*.' He commanded that the man should be given ten more *balish* in addition to the one; and a written statement was taken from him that he would not commit a similar action again. And so he not only escaped with his life but acquired property. . . .

(ii) When they first rose to power they made a *yasa* that no one should slaughter animals by cutting their throats but should slit open their breasts after the Mongols' own fashion.

A Muslim bought a sheep in the market, took it home, closed the gates securely and slaughtered the animal after the Muslim fashion in [the lane between] two or three houses, not knowing that he was being watched by a Qıpchaq [Cuman?], who, awaiting his opportunity, had followed him from the market. When he drew the knife across the sheep's throat, the Qıpchaq leapt down from the roof, bound him tight, and bore him off to the Court of the World-Emperor. Qā'ān examined the case and sent out scribes to investigate. When the circumstances were made known to his clear intellect, he spoke as follows: 'This poor man has observed the commandment of our *yasa* and this Turk has infringed it.' The Muslim's life was spared and he was treated with favor (*soyurghamishī*), while the ill-natured Qıpchaq was handed over to the executioners of Fate.

(iii) A troupe of players had come from Khitai (northern China) and acted wondrous Khitaian plays such as (164) no one had ever seen before. One of these plays consisted of tableaux of every people, in the midst of which an old man with a long white beard and a turban wound round his head was dragged forth upon his face bound to the tail of a horse. Qā'ān asked who this was meant to portray. They replied that it represented a rebellious Muslim, for that the armies were dragging them out of the lands in this manner. Qā'ān ordered the show to be stopped and commanded his attendants to fetch from the treasury all sorts of jewels from the lands of the Khurasan and the two Iraqs, such as pearls, rubies, turquoises, etc., and also gold-embroidered webs and garments, and Arab horses, and arms from Bukhara and Tabriz; and likewise what was imported from Khitai, being garments inferior to the others, small horses and other Khitaian products; and all these things he commanded to be laid side by side so that it might be seen how great was the difference. And he said: 'The poorest Muslim has many Khitaian slaves, while the great emirs of Khitai have not one Muslim captive. And the reason for this can only be the beneficence of the Creator, who knoweth the station and rank of every nation; it is also in conformity with the ancient *yasa* of Chinggiz Khan, according to which the blood-money for a Muslim is forty *balish* and for a Khitaian a donkey. In view of such proofs and testimonies how can you make a laughing stock of the people of Islam? This crime you have committed ought to be punished, but I will spare your lives. Count that as a total gain; depart from my presence forthwith and be seen no more in this neighborhood.'

N.B. By 'Khitai' might be meant members of the people who from 916 until 1125 ruled northern China (known there as K'itan), and some of whom later on conquered Central Asia (the so-called Qara-Khitai) and ruled there until they were overthrown by the Mongols.

(iv) A certain ruler ... sent a messenger to him and expressed a desire to yield him homage and obedience, sending among other gifts a polished ruby which had come down to him from the victories of his ancestors. (165) The name of Muhammad the Prophet of God was written on top of the stone, while beneath it in due order were impressed the names of his forefathers. Qā'ān commanded the jewelers to leave the name of Muhammad for luck's sake but to erase the names of the sultans and to set his own name after the name of the Prophet ... and that of the divine sender.

(v) A poor man, who was unable to earn a living and had learnt no trade, sharpened pieces of iron into the shape of awls [?] and mounted them on pieces of wood. He then sat down where the retinue of Qā'ān would pass and waited. Qā'ān caught sight of him from afar and sent one of his attendants to him. The poor man told him of the weakness of his condition, the smallness of his property and the largeness of his family and gave him the awls.

But when the messenger saw his clumsy awls, whereof even a hundred would hardly have been worth a barleycorn, he thought them unworthy of being presented to Qā'ān and so left them with him and [returning] told what he had seen. Qā'ān ordered him [to go back and] bring all the awls that the man had with him. And taking them in his hand he said: 'Even this kind will serve for herdsmen to mend the seams of their *qumiz* skins with.' And for each awl he gave the man a *balish*.

(xliii) (182) When the crops were growing so much hail fell as to destroy them all. And at the time of this disaster there was such scarcity of corn in [the capital] Karakorum that a single maund could not be obtained for a dinar. Qā'ān ordered the heralds to proclaim that whoever had sown corn should not give way to anxiety, for his crop had suffered no harm. If they watered their fields again, and tilled them, and there was no harvest, they would receive the full equivalent from his treasury and granaries. It so happened that so much corn was reaped that year that there had never been such a crop and harvest since they had first begun to till the ground.

(xliv) (183) Three persons were brought to him for a crime they had committed. He ordered them to be put to death. When he left his audience-hall he came upon a woman scattering dust [on her head] and crying out aloud. 'Why art thou doing this?' he asked. 'Because,' she replied, 'of those men whom thou hast ordered to be put to death, for one of them is my husband, another my son and the third my brother.' 'Choose one of them,' said Qā'ān, 'and for thy sake he shall be spared.' 'I can find a substitute for my husband,' replied the woman, 'and children too I can hope for; but for a brother there can be no substitute.' He spared the lives of all three.

(Juvaini, *History of the World-Conqueror*, I, 204–8, 226–7 (=Part I, 161–5, 182–3].)

24. The Summer Residence

(194) . . . And when the life of spring had reached its maturity . . . , he [the Qā'ān] would return to his summer residence. And since the garden and palace in the town lay upon his way, he would

reside there for several days in his wonted manner carrying out the commandments of God (*amr-i-ma'rūf*) and would thence move on toward his destination. And when he left there he would go to a small palace ('kiosk') which he had built on a hilltop three miles from the town, through which he also passed in returning from his winter residence. On both occasions he would amuse himself for four or five weeks in this spot, and offerings of food would be brought out to him from the town. And from thence in the summer he would go into the mountains, where there would be erected for him a Khitaian pavilion, whose walls were made of latticed wood, while its ceiling was of gold-embroidered cloth, and it was covered all over with white felt: this place is called *Sira Ordu*. In these parts there are cool waters and much grass. Here he would remain until the sun entered Virgo [end of August] and there was a fall of snow. And here (195) his bounty would flow more freely than in his other pleasances. And departing from hence he would arrive at his winter residence by the end of autumn, which is the beginning of their winter. There he would make merry for three months, and during these months his generosity and munificence were under some restraint and did not flow so freely. . . .

(Juvaini, *History of the World-Conqueror*, I, 238–9 [=Part I, 194–5].)

25. The Accession of Göyük to the Throne

(203) . . . In the year in which Qā'ān was to bid farewell to the comforts of this life and to foreswear the pleasures of this vile world (1241), he had sent for Göyük, bidding him turn the reins of homecoming and direct his will and desire toward hurrying to his presence. In compliance with this command Göyük pressed the spurs of haste and loosened the bridle of speed; but when the time was at hand when the touch of plague that arises from length of distance was to have been expelled by closeness of propinquity and the veil of absence and exile removed, Fate's inevitable decree was carried out, and no respite was given for those thirsting in the desert of separation to quench their thirst with a drop of the limpid water of reunion or for father and son to anoint their eyes with the collyrium of each other's beauty. When Göyük received tidings of that irremediable calamity he saw fit to make still greater haste,

and grief for what had happened did not suffer him to halt until he reached the [river] Emil. Neither did he tarry here, for there was a report of the coming of Otchigin, but proceeded to his father's *ordu*: and the hopes of the ambitious were dashed by his arrival. And in that neighborhood he took up his abode. State business was still entrusted to the counsel of his mother Törägänä Khatun, and the binding and loosening of affairs was in her hands, and Göyük did not intervene therein to enforce *yasa* or (204) custom nor did he dispute with her about these matters.

And when messengers were dispatched to far and near to bid princes and *noyan*s and summon sultans and kings and scribes, everyone left his home and country in obedience to the command. And when the world, because of the coming of spring, had set the foot of beauty upon the head of the stars and drawn the pen of oblivion through the Garden of Iram;[34] and the earth . . . had donned a covering of every manner of flower; and the springtime . . . had with blossoms made its whole body a mouth and with lilies converted all its limbs into tongues; . . . then it was that the princes arrived, each with his horsemen and servants, his army and retinue. The eyes of mankind were dazzled by their accoutrement, and the fountain of their enemies' delight was troubled by the harmony that reigned among them all. Seyurkhokhataitai (Sorkhakhtani) beki and her sons arrived first with such gear and equipage as '*eye hath not seen nor ear heard*'. And from the East there came . . . Otchigin and his children . . . and the other uncles and nephews that reside in that region. From the *ordu* of Chaghatai came . . . (205) and the other grandsons and great-grandsons. From the country of Saqsīn and Bulghar [east of the river Volga], since Batu did not come in person, he sent his elder brother Orda [Hordu] and his [four] younger brothers. . . . And distinguished *noyan*s and leading emirs (=beys), who had connections with one or other party, came in attendance on the princes. From Khitai there came emirs and officials; and from Transoxiana and Turkestan the Emir Mas'ūd (cf. p. 43) accompanied by the grandees of that region. With the Emir Arghūn there came the celebrities and notables of Khurasan, Iraq, Lur(istan), Azerbaijan, and Shirvan. From Rum

[34] A mythical imitation of paradise. Mentioned several times in the Koran, e.g. 89:7.

[Asia Minor] came Sultan Rükn ad-Dīn [of the Seljuq] and the ruler of Little Armenia [Cilicia]; from Georgia, the two [kings named] David; from Aleppo, the brother of the Lord of Aleppo; from Mosul, the envoy of Sultan . . . ; and from the City of Peace, Baghdad, the chief qadi Fakhr ad-Dīn. There also came . . . envoys from the Franks [the West Europeans: John de Plano Carpini], and from Kerman and Fars also; and from [the Imām of the Ismailis] . . . of Alamut [northwest of modern Tehran] and from two of his deputies.

And all this great assembly came with such baggage as befitted such a court; and there came also from other directions so many envoys and messengers that two (206) thousand felt tents had been made ready for them; there came also merchants with the rare and precious things that are produced in the East and the West.

When this assembly, which was such as no man had ever seen nor has the like thereof been read of in the annals of history, was gathered together, the broad plain was straitened and in the neighborhood of the *ordu* there remained no place to alight in, and nowhere was it possible to dismount. . . . There was also a great dearth of food and drink, and no fodder was left for the mounts and beasts of burden.

The leading princes were all agreed as to committing the affairs of the Khanate and entrusting the keys of the Empire to one of the sons of Qā'ān. Köten aspired to this honor because his grandfather had once made a reference to him. Others were of the opinion that Sirämön [probably = Solomon], when he came of age, might be a suitable person to charge with the affairs of the Kingdom. But of all the sons of Qā'ān Göyük was most renowned for his might, and ruthlessness, and intrepidity, and dominion; he was the eldest of the brothers and had had most practice in the handling of difficult matters and most experience of weal and woe. Köten, on the other hand, was somewhat sickly, and Sirämön was but a child. Moreover Törägänä Khatun favored Göyük, and Beki and her sons were at one with her in this, and most of the *noyan*s were in accord with them in this matter. It was therefore agreed that the Khanate should be settled upon Göyük and that he should ascend the throne of the Kingdom. Göyük, as is the custom, for some time rejected the honor and recommended instead now this person, now that.

Finally on a day chosen by the practitioners of the science of the *qam* all (207) the princes gathered together and took off their hats and loosened their belts. And [Yesü?] taking one hand and Orda the other they set him on the throne of Dominion and the cushion of Kingship and seized their goblets; and the people that were present inside and outside the audience-hall knelt down three times and called him 'Göyük Khan' [1246]. And in accordance with their custom they gave declarations in writing that they would not change his word or command, and uttered prayers for his welfare; after which they went out of the hall and knelt three times to the sun. And when he reposed again upon the throne of greatness, the princes sat on chairs on his right and the princesses on his left, each in exceeding grace like a precious pearl. And in the place of cupbearers was every youth of graceful mien, and violet cheeks, and rosy complexion, and sable locks, and cypress form, and blossom-like mouth, and pearly teeth, and happy aspect. . . . And the minstrels . . . opened their lips in song before the Chosroes of the World, and all others were tongue-tied for awe and dread. And in this manner till midnight (208) of that day the wine cups were filled to the brim. . . . When they had grown drunk, after uniting in praising and belauding the Monarch of the Face of the Earth, they departed to their sleeping quarters; and on the next day . . . the princes, *noyan*s and common people '*came strutting to the King's court* . . .'. [Göyük] sat down in his audience-hall upon the throne . . . ; and noble and commoner were granted permission to enter, and everyone sat in his own place and began [to praise the ruler] [several verses from Firdausī's *Shāhnāmā*]. The princesses and concubines [?] strutted in with the beauty of youth, like envoys of the materials of gaiety, and held cups of wine before them. . . . And they seated themselves upon the left like the northern zephyr. And all the men and women (209) and youths and maidens had donned garments of fine pearls, whose sparkle and luster was such that the stars of the night out of jealousy wished to be scattered before the time of scattering. And in the drinking-bout of enjoyment they stretched out for cups of pleasure and set the foot of merriment in the arena of amusement, gratifying their eyes by gazing on the songstresses and their ears by hearkening to the songs; and their hearts were exalted by the succession of joys and delights. . . .

And on this wise for seven days . . . they were employed. . . . The distribution of these valuables he entrusted to the counsel and discretion of Seyurkhokhataitai, who had the greatest authority in that *quriltai*. The first to receive their share were the princes and princesses that were present of the race and lineage of Chinggiz Khan; as also all their servants and attendants, noble and base, graybeard and suckling; and then in due order the *noyan*s, the commanders of *tümen* (ten thousand men), thousands, hundreds, and tens, according to the census, the sultans, *malik*s, scribes, officials, and their dependents. And everyone else who was present, whoever he was, did not go portionless, nay everyone received his full share and appointed lot. . . .

(Juvaini, *History of the World-Conqueror*, I, 247–55 [=Part I, 203–9].)

26. Reply of the Great Khan Göyük to Pope Innocent IV
(In Persian)

Through the power of eternal heaven [God], of the Ocean-like Khan of the great and mighty people; our order (*yarlıgh*) [*this in Turkish*].

This is a directive sent to the great Pope; may he take note of it and comprehend it. We . . . written in the language [?] of the lands of the King [=Emperor Frederick II?] . . . [very obscure and not easily readable part of a sentence]. This [letter] was conferred about, and the request for [your] submission was heard by your envoys. If you act according to your word, then come: you, the great Pope, and the Kings, all in person, to pay homage to us. Then, we shall make known the orders (*yasa*) which exist.

Further, you have said there would be an advantage for me in [accepting] baptism. You have imparted this to me, and sent a request [to this effect]. This your appeal, I have not understood.

Furthermore, you have sent [the following] message: 'You have conquered all the lands of the Hungarians and [other] Christians. This seems strange to me. What was their crime? Tell me [about it].' This your message I have not understood either. [Well then:] Chinggiz Khan and the Great Khan [Ögädäi] have both transmitted God's order [that all the world should be subordinated to the Mongols] to be taken note of. [But] they disregarded God's order to such an extent that those mentioned by you even held a great [Council?], and they behaved arrogantly [in refusing], and killed our messengers and envoys. Thus the eternal God himself has killed and exterminated the people [in] these countries. How could anybody, without God's order, [merely] from his own strength, kill and rob? And when you go on to say, 'I am a Christian, I honor God', I despise [?]. . . . How [do you think] you know whom God will absolve and in whose favor he will exercise his mercy? How do you think you know, that [you dare to] express such an opinion?

Through the power of God, all empires from sunrise to sunset have been given to us, and we own them. How could anybody achieve anything except on God's order? Now, however, you must say from a sincere heart: We shall be obedient, we, [too], make [our] strength available. You personally, at the head of the Kings, you shall come, one and all, to pay homage to me, and to serve me. Then, we shall take note of your submission. If, however, you do not accept God's order and act against our order, we shall know that you are our enemies.

This is what we make known to you. If you act against it, how then can we know [what will happen]? Only God knows.

Written at the end of Jumādā II 644 of Hijra (= early November, 1246).

(After Paul Pelliot, 'Les Mongols et la Papauté', Part I, in *Revue de l'Orient chrétien*, XXIII [1922–3], 3–30, at pp. 13–23, with facsimile; repeated in Albert Maria Ammann, *Kirchenpolitische Wandlungen im Ostbaltikum*, Orientalia Christiana Analecta CV [Rome, 1936], p. 284f.)

The following is a contemporary translation of this letter:

Epistola domini Tattarorum ad papam Innocentium IV.

Dei fortitudo, omnium hominum imperator, magno pape litteras certissimas atque veras. Habito consilio pro pace habenda nobiscum, tu papa et omnes Christiani, nuntium tuum nobis transmisisti, sicut ab ipso audivimus, et in tuis litteris habebatur. Igitur si pacem nobiscum habere desideratis, tu papa et omnes reges

et potentes, pro pace diffinienda ad me venire nullo modo post-
ponatis, et tunc nostram audietis responsionem pariter atque
voluntatem. Tuarum continebat series litterarum quod debemus
bapticari et effici Christiani. Ad hoc tibi breviter respondemus,
quod hoc non intelligimus, qualiter hoc facere debeamus. Ad
aliud, quod etiam in tuis litteris habebatur, scilicet quod miraris
de tanta occisione hominum et maxime Christianorum et potissime
Pollonorum, Moravorum et Ungarorum, tibi taliter respondemus,
quod etiam hoc non intelligimus. Verumtamen ne hoc sub
silentio omnimodo transire videamur, taliter tibi dicimus re-
spondendum: Quia littere Dei et precepto Cyngis-Chan et Chan[35]
non obedierunt et magnum consilium habentes nuntios occiderunt,
propterea Deus eos delere precepit et in manibus nostris tradidit.
Alioquin, quod si Deus non fecisset, homo homini quid facere
potuisset? Sed vos homines occidentis solos vos Christianos esse
creditis, et alios despicitis. Sed quomodo scire potestis cui Deus
suam gratiam conferre dignetur? Nos autem Deum adorando in
fortitudine Dei ab oriente usque in occidentem delevimus omnem
terram; et si haec Dei fortitudo non esset, homines quid facere
potuissent? Vos autem si pacem suscipitis et vestras nobis vultis
tradere fortitudines, tu papa cum potentibus Christianis ad me
venire pro pace facienda nullo modo differatis; et tunc sciemus,
quod vultis pacem habere nobiscum. Si vero Dei et nostris litteris
non credideritis et consilium non audieritis, ut ad nos veniatis,
tunc pro certo sciemus, quod guerram habere vultis nobiscum.
Post haec quid futurum sit, nos nescimus, solus Deus novit.[36]
(Cyngis-Chan primus Imperator. Secundus Ochoday-Chan.
Tertius Cuiuch-Chan. Non plus continebatur in litteris Domini
Tattarorum missis ad Papam.)

(From Pelliot, 'Les Mongols et la Papauté', pp. 13–14.)

[35] The second 'Khan' refers to the Qā'ān Ögädäi.
[36] Here, in fact, the letter ends. In the next sentence Pelliot conveys general
information.

II

THE MONGOLS IN THE EYES
OF THE EUROPEANS
(REPORTS OF ENVOYS)

1. The Tatars: Marriage

(56) Everybody can take as many wives as he can support. Some have a hundred, some fifty, some ten, some more, some fewer. As a general rule they are allowed to marry all their (57) relatives except their own mother, their own daughter, and their sisters by the same mother; they may, however, marry their sisters on their father's side, and even their father's other wives (with the exception of their own mother) after his death.[1] On the death of a brother, another younger brother or some other younger member of the family has the obligation of marrying the wife of the deceased. They are free to marry all other women without discrimination, and they actually buy them at a high price from their parents. After the death of her husband it is not easy for a widow to conclude a second marriage, unless somebody should want to marry his stepmother.

There follow details about clothing and dwellings.

2. Religious Customs: The Worship of God

(61) (I) They believe in one god, the creator of all the visible and invisible world; they also believe that all the good and all (62) the chastisements in this world originate from him, but they worship him neither with prayers, nor with hymns of praise, nor with any other religious ceremonies. Nevertheless, they still have certain

[1] With the Muslims it was frequently customary to pass on the father's harem as inheritance.

idols made out of felt in the shape of human figures, which they set up on both sides of the entrance to the yurt.[2] Beneath these idols, they put some felt figures which look like an udder, and which, they believe, protect their herds (63) and provide them with an abundance of milk and young animals. Other idols are made from silken material, and they are highly honored.

Some Mongols put these idols on a beautiful covered cart in front of the door of the yurt, and anybody who steals anything from this cart is put to death without pardon. These idols are manufactured in the following way: all (64) the older distinguished ladies from the particular army camp come together, and produce them with suitable reverence. When this is done, they kill a sheep and eat it, while they burn the bones in a fire. They do the same if a child falls ill, making an idol in the described manner and suspending it above its bed. The dukes,[3] the commanders over a thousand and over a hundred men, always have a [stuffed] (65) he-goat [as an idol] in the middle of their camp.

They sacrifice to these idols the first milk from all cattle and all mares, and, before they start eating and drinking, they sacrifice the first bits of food and drink. In the same way, when they kill an animal, they offer to the idol on the cart the heart of the animal on a dish, and leave (66) it there until the following morning; then they take it out of his gaze, and cook and eat it.

(II) They also make an idol in honor of their first Emperor [Chinggiz Khan], which they set up in a reverent fashion on a cart outside the camp, as we have seen ourselves outside the *ordu*[4] of the present Emperor [Göyük], and they offer to it many presents. They also offer it horses which nobody then dares to ride for the rest of their lives. (67) Similarly, they offer it other animals, and if they kill one of them for food, they do not break its bones, but burn them. They also bow toward the south, as if to a god, and force other distinguished people who subject themselves to them to bow in the same way.

The following is an example of this: When, recently,[5] Michael, one of the Grand Dukes (68) of Russia,[6] had come to subject himself to Batu, they first of all made him pass between two fires. Then, they ordered him to bow toward the south in front of

[2] The tent.   [3] Beys.   [4] Horde, camp.
[5] 1246.   [6] From Chernigov.

Chinggiz Khan. But he replied he would be pleased to bow before Batu and even his servants, but never before the image of a dead man, since this was not allowed to a Christian. When, in spite of frequent repetitions of the order, he still did not want to bow, (69) the Khan [Batu], mentioned above, sent him word through the son of Yaroslav, that he would be killed if he continued in his refusal. The other man replied that he would rather die than do something that is forbidden to Christians. At this Batu sent a man from his bodyguard who drove his heel into [the Russian's] heart and stomach until he fainted. One of his knights standing nearby (70) [Feodor] encouraged him with the words: 'Be steadfast! For this pain will not last long for you, and eternal joy will follow immediately.' Then his head was cut off with a small sword, and in the same way the head of that knight was cut off with the same weapon.

(III) Furthermore, they worship the sun, the moon [other reading: the heavenly lights], and the fire, and honor them, just as [they do] the water and the earth, by offering them the first of any food and (71) drink, particularly in the morning before they eat and drink. Since, with regard to their worship of god, they have no binding religious rules, they have up to now, as far as we know, not forced anybody to deny his faith or religion, if one disregards what has just been told about Michael. But what they will do in future, we do not know. Some people think, however, that if they had sole power, which God forbid, they would compel everybody to bow in front of that idol.

This can be deduced from the following incident which occurred during our recent stay in their country. Andrew, Grand Duke of Chernigov[7] [which is also situated in Russia], had been denounced to Batu for exporting Tatar horses from the country and selling them abroad. Although this accusation was not proved, he was executed.

(72) When his younger brother heard about this, he came with the wife of the dead man to the said Khan Batu, to beg him on his knees, not to wrest their land from them as well. Upon this, Batu told the young man to marry the wife of his own brother, and equally he ordered the woman to take the other man (her brother-in-law) for a husband according to the Tatar custom. The man

[7] Obviously a mistake.

replied he would rather die than act against his religion. Nevertheless, the woman was handed to him, although both of them resisted with all their power, but the Tatars led them both to a [common] bed, laid the young man on the woman, notwithstanding her wailing and crying, and with brutal force compelled the two of them similarly and without further argument to perform the marriage act.

3. Enumeration of What They Regard as Sin

(73) Although they possess no book of religious law which obliges them to do right and avoid doing wrong, they nevertheless have certain traditions that either they or their forefathers have devised, and, according to these, certain actions are considered sinful. It is, for instance, a sin to poke one's dagger into the fire, or to touch the fire in any way with it, or to take meat from the kettle with the dagger, or even to hack [meat] with the hatchet near the fire. For they think that this would take the head [i.e., the force] from the fire. It is sinful to lean on the whip with which they beat their horses—they do not use spurs—furthermore, to touch arrows with the whip, to catch or to kill young birds, to strike a horse with the rein, or again to break one bone with the help of another, to pour milk or other drinks on the ground, or to urinate inside a tent. Anybody (74) who does so intentionally pays for it with his life, but if he does so unintentionally, he has to pay a large sum of money for the exorcist to purify the people, and also to see that the yurt with all its contents passes between two fires. Until the yurt has been cleansed in this way, nobody is allowed to enter it, or to take anything away from it. Furthermore, if anybody is given a morsel of meat, and cannot swallow it, but has to spit it out again from his mouth, they dig a hole underneath the yurt, drag the person in question through this opening, and then kill him without pardon. Furthermore, (75), anybody stepping on the threshold of the yurt of a duke is equally punished with death.[8] They have many other similar superstitious customs, but it would be impossible to list them all.

On the other hand, killing people, invading other countries, seizing other people's property against all the rules of law, whoring,

[8] See below p. 105 (Rockhill's *The Journey of William of Rubruck*).

committing wrongs against other people, disregarding God's commandments and prohibitions, all this is not considered sinful. They know nothing of an eternal life, or of damnation without end. But they do believe that, after their death, they will live on in another world, that there they will breed cattle, eat, drink, and do everything else, in the same way as people do things during their lifetime in this world.

4. Prophesy and Cleansing from Sin

(76) (I) They set great store by prophesy, interpreting signs, looking at the entrails of sacrificial animals, witchcraft, and conjurings. If they receive a reply from the demons themselves, (77) they believe that God is speaking to them. They call this god Itoga, but the Cumans[9] call him Kam. They fear and adore him to an extraordinary extent; they devote to him many sacrifices as well as the first part of food and drink. They adjust all their actions according to the replies he gives.

When they plan a new enterprise, they do not start (78) on its execution until the moon begins to change or until full moon. They, therefore, call the moon the Great Emperor, bend their knees before him, and beg him to avert evil. Moreover, they regard the sun as the mother of the moon, since the moon receives its light from it.

(II) In short, they think that everything is purified by fire. When, therefore, envoys come to them, or princes, (79) or any other persons whoever they may be, they and the gifts they bring must pass between two fires to be purified, so as to prevent them practising witchcraft, or bringing poison or some other evil.

Furthermore, if cattle or men are killed by lightning, which happens frequently in their areas, or when any other such adversity occurs which, according to their superstition, makes them unclean or lays them open to adversity, the exorcist must similarly (80) perform a purification rite. In fact, one might say, they set all their hopes on such things.

[9] In their own language Qıpchaq, called by the Russians Polovtsy; a Turkish people who at that time migrated to Hungary and there merged into the Magyar culture.

5. Death and Burial

(III) If somebody among them falls mortally ill, they plant a lance wrapped in black felt on his dwelling. Then no stranger dares to cross the boundary of the home of such a sick person. When the sick person is about to breathe his last, almost all of them leave him, because nobody present at his death is allowed to enter the camp of a Khan or the Great Khan until the ninth month. If the sick person was of high rank, however, when he dies, they bury him secretly in the steppe at a place of which he (81) had been particularly fond. He is buried together with his yurt, sitting in the middle of it, and he has a table in front of him with a bowl full of meat and a jug full of mare's milk (*qumys*), and, at the same time, a mare and her foal are buried, as well as a horse with saddle and bridle. Another horse, however, is eaten at the burial feast, its (82) skin is stuffed with straw, and it is then [impaled on a long pole and] suspended on two or four poles, slightly raised, above the grave. In this way, when the dead person arrives in the other world, he has a yurt to live in, a mare to give him milk and to serve as the basis for a future herd of horses, and finally he also has horses there to ride on. The bones of the horse they eat are burnt for the benefit of the soul [of the dead man].

(83) Women frequently meet to burn bones for the benefit of the soul of their husbands, as we have seen with our own eyes, and have been told by other people in that country. Ögädäi Khan, the father of the present Great Khan [Göyük], grew some shrubbery for the benefit of his soul, as we have seen ourselves, and therefore ordered that nobody be allowed to cut anything from it; if, in spite of this, anyone cuts a branch from it, he is beaten, robbed, and miserably maltreated, as we have witnessed ourselves. Therefore, when one day we were in great need of a rod with which to whip our horse, we nevertheless took good care not to cut a branch from it.

The dead person also has gold and silver put in his grave, the cart on which he used to drive is broken up, his yurt is pulled down, and for three generations nobody is allowed to mention his name.

(84) Some of their dignitaries are buried in a different way: They go secretly into the steppe, and at some place there, after

having removed the grass together with the roots [i.e., the turf], they dig a big pit, and in the side of the pit they dig yet another hollow [a passage] below the surface. After this, they place the favorite slave of the dead man underneath the corpse, and leave him there until he is close to giving up the ghost. Then they pull him out and allow him to breathe a little. They repeat this three times; if, eventually, he has managed to survive, he is from then on free, can do as he likes, and enjoys great respect in the yurt and among the relatives of the dead man. The corpse, however, is placed with all the objects mentioned above, in the hollow that has been dug in the side of the pit. Finally, they fill with soil the pit in front of the hollow, where the dead man rests, and put the turf back as it (85) had been before, so that later nobody can find the place any more. At the same time, they conduct the other ceremonies, as told above, but they leave his yurt standing outside [the grave] in the steppe.

There are two burial places in their country. In one of them they bury their Khans, beys, and all other people of noble descent. Wherever they may be at the time of their death (86), they are brought there, if at all possible, and much gold and silver is placed in the grave with them. In the other burial place are buried those who had been killed in Hungary, and there were many of them.

Entry to these places is forbidden to everyone but the guards who are placed there to watch over them. If anybody should make bold to enter, he is seized, robbed, beaten, and grievously mal-treated. We ourselves, ignorant as we were, inadvertently crossed the fence of the burial place of those killed in Hungary; the guards approached us and were about to shoot their arrows at us. Since we were envoys and did not know the custom of the land, however, they released us and allowed us to go away.

6. Purification in the Event of Death and Being Struck by Lightning

The relatives, however, and everybody else living in the yurts of those who have died, must undergo purification by fire in the following way: They light two fires, and (87) near these fires they plant two lances in the ground, and stretch a rope between the points of the two lances. On this cord they fasten a few rags, and then make people, cattle, and the [movable] yurts, pass under this cord and the rags tied to it [representing idols], and between the two fires. On each side, right and left, stand two women sprinkling water while they repeat certain charms. If in the process some carts break or if anything should fall to the ground, the exorcists take it. If anybody is killed by lightning, all the people living in the yurts concerned must pass between the fires in the way just described. The yurt itself, the bed, the carts, the felt blankets, the clothes and whatever else belonged to the person killed, are indignantly rejected as unclean by everybody, and nobody dares even to touch these objects.

7. *The Good Characteristics of the Tatars*

(88) In the whole world there are to be found no more obedient subjects than the Tatars, neither among lay people nor among the monks; they pay their lords more respect than any other people, and would hardly dare lie to them. Rarely if ever do they revile each other (89), but if they should, the dispute never leads to blows. Wars, quarrels, the infliction of bodily harm, and manslaughter do not occur among them, and there are no large-scale thieves or robbers among them. Consequently their ordas and the carts in which they keep their treasures are not secured by either locks or bolts. If any animal goes astray, the finder either leaves it to its fate or takes it to those persons who are expressly appointed for this purpose. The owner of the lost animal (90) makes his inquiries to them and has it returned to him without further difficulty.

They treat one another with due respect; they regard each other almost as members of one family, and, although they do not have a lot of food, they like to share it with one another. Moreover, they are accustomed to deprivation; if, therefore, they have fasted for a day or two, and have not eaten anything (91) at all, they do not easily lose their tempers, but sing and enjoy themselves as though they had eaten a superb meal. While riding they can endure extreme cold and at times also fierce heat; they are neither soft, nor sensitive [to the weather]. They do not seem to feel in any way envious of one another, and (92) no public trials occur among them. No one holds his fellow in contempt, but each helps and supports the other to the limit of his abilities.

Their women are chaste, and nothing is ever heard of any im-
modesty among them. Nevertheless jokingly they will use rather
shameful and immodest words. It is said, mutiny rarely if ever
takes place. And although they get drunk frequently (93), they do
not either quarrel or fight in their drunkenness.

8. Their Bad Characteristics

They are extremely arrogant toward other people and look down
on all others with disdain. In fact, they regard them, both noble
and humble people alike, as little better than nothing. We observed
at the Court of their Great Khan, that they showed a lack of proper
respect to such as the Grand Duke of Russia, Yaroslav, who surely
is a noble man, and also to the son of the King and Queen of
Georgia (94) as well as to many mighty sultans. On the contrary,
those Tatars who were instructed to attend upon them, even if
they were of extremely low station, would always precede them
and take the first and foremost position; frequently the visitors
would have to sit behind their backs. Toward other people the
Tatars tend to anger and are easily roused. They are the greatest
liars in the world in dealing with other people [than Tatars], and
hardly a true word escapes from their mouths. Initially they flatter,
but in the end they sting like scorpions. They are crafty and sly,
and wherever possible they try to get the better of everybody else
by false pretenses. If they intend some mischief against others
they have an admirable ability to keep their intentions secret, so
that (95) others cannot take any precautions or countermeasures
against their clever plans.

They are messy in their eating and drinking and in their whole
way of life. Drunkenness is honorable among them; when anyone
among them has drunk too much he will be sick on the spot, but
even so will carry on drinking again. At the same time they are
mean and greedy, and if they want something, they will not stop
begging and asking for it, until they have got it. They cling fiercely
to what they have, and in making gifts they are extremely miserly.
(96) They have no conscience about killing other people. In short,
if one tried to enumerate all their bad characteristics there would
be too many to be put on paper.

There follows a paragraph on food.

9. *Their Customs and Laws*

(102) They have a law or custom by which they kill any man and woman whom they have found committing adultery, and if a virgin has committed fornication they also kill them, man and woman. If anybody is caught in robbery or theft within the countries under their jurisdiction, he is cut down without mercy. If, furthermore, anyone (103) betrays their plans, especially those with regard to an intended war, he is dealt a hundred strokes on his back, laid on as hard as can be by a peasant with a big stick. If humbler people make a mistake in anything, they cannot expect any pardon from their superiors, but receive a thorough thrashing.

They do not make any distinction between the son of a concubine and the son of the wife, but the father gives to each whatever he pleases, and if he belongs to the ranks of the dukes [beys], then the son of the concubine is as much a duke as the son of the wedded wife. When a Tatar has many (104) wives, each of them has her own yurt and her own household; the man eats, drinks, and sleeps one day with one woman, and the other with the other women in turn. But one of them has a higher rank than the others, and with her the man stays more often than with the others. Although so many women live together in one marriage, they do not readily quarrel among themselves.

(105) The men do nothing but occupy themselves with their arrows and to a small extent look after their herds; for the rest they go hunting and practice archery. For they are all, men and boys, good shots. As soon as their children are two or three years old they start riding; they are able both to drive their horses and to gallop on them. They are also given small bows, suitable to their age, and taught how to shoot. For they are very agile and also courageous.

The girls and women gallop on their (106) horses just as skillfully as the men. We also saw them carrying bows and quivers. Both men and women can stay in the saddle for a long time. They have very short stirrups and look after their horses very well, just as they generally endeavor to take care of everything [belonging to them]. All work rests on the shoulders of the women; they make fur coats, clothes, shoes, bootlegs, and everything else made from leather. They also drive the carts and mend them, load the camels, and are very quick and efficient in all their work. All women wear trousers, and some of them shoot with the bow as accurately as the men.

There follows a synopsis of the rise of the Mongol Empire.

10. Chinggiz Khan's Legislation and Death

(135) Then Chinggiz Khan returned to his own country. Here he enacted his laws and promulgated orders to which the Tatars strictly adhere. Only two of them shall be mentioned here. The first order says: Anybody who puffed by pride and on his own authority without election by the princes aspires to Imperial dignity, shall be executed without grace or pardon. Consequently, before the present Emperor Göyük Khan was elected, one of the princes, an actual grandson of Chinggiz Khan, was executed (136) for this crime, since he wanted to make himself Emperor without election by the princes.

The other order says they must subjugate the whole world, and must not live in peace with any people who has not first surrendered to them; and this will apply until the time when they themselves are annihilated. For they had already made war for forty-two years and have still to rule for another eighteen [before their destruction]; then, so they say, according to some prophesy made to them, they are to be conquered by another nation; but they do not know themselves which nation that will be. And those who are able to escape will, so they say, have to observe that law which their future conquerors will also observe. (That means: Both the victors and the defeated will have to observe the commandments of Chinggiz Khan.)

Further he ordered that there should be commanders for every thousand men, for every hundred, for every ten men, and for the darknesses, that is, for ten thousand men,[10] and on this pattern he built the whole army organization. (137) He gave many other orders, but it would take us too far beyond the scope of our subject to list them all here; moreover, they are not known to us. After he

[10] *Tümen* = 10,000; here connected with Russian *t'ma* = darkness.

had completed giving his laws and orders, he was struck by lightning[11] and died.

There follows a section on Chinggiz Khan's descendants.

11. The Powers of the Emperor and His Dukes

(141) The Great Khan of the Tatars has extraordinary power over all his subjects; nobody dares to settle in any part of his empire without his express direction. (142) In fact he determines the places of residence for the dukes, the dukes in their turn those of the commanders of a thousand, they in turn those of the commanders of a hundred, and the last those of the commanders of ten. If, moreover, at any time or any place he gives them an order, be it for war [or for peace], be it for life or for death, they obey without question.

Even when he demands somebody's unmarried daughter or sister for a wife, she is given to him [instantly] without argument. Actually, every year, or at any rate every few years, he orders the maidens from everywhere throughout the Tatar lands (143) to be assembled, so that he may choose and keep those he likes; the others he gives to those around him as he sees fit.

If he sends any envoys, however great their number may be, to any place, his subjects must provide them with post horses without delay and supply them with the necessary provisions; and if there come to him from anywhere people bringing tribute or envoys, they have equally to be provided with horses, carts, and provisions. (144) If, on the other hand, envoys come to them from elsewhere, they have to suffer great deprivations and shortage of food and clothing, for their provisions are poor and scanty, especially if they come to see princes [rather than the Khan], and if their stay here is drawn out; in that case what is provided for ten people is hardly enough for two. Both at the courts of the princes and on the journey they are given food only once a day, and then very little. Even so, they have little opportunity to make even a modest complaint, if they are wronged; they just have to bear it patiently.

(II) And as if this were not enough, everyone, including princes and noblemen, and even people of a more lowly status, continually

---

[11] No other source refers to this.

demand presents from the envoys, and if they do not get what they want, they look down on them with disdain, and in fact treat them as though they were not there. If, in fact, the envoys should have been sent by a powerful lord, they are not satisfied with an ordinary gift, but say: 'You come from such a powerful lord, why then, do you offer such trifling gifts?' And they refuse to accept [such a meager gift]. If, therefore, the envoys hope to succeed with their business they are forced to give more. In this way we ourselves could not avoid using for presents a large portion of the donations given to us by the faithful to defray our expenses.

(145) Further, it is important one should know that all property is in the hands of the Great Khan so that nobody dares to say: 'This belongs to me and that belongs to the other.' But everything, household chattels, cattle and people, is the property of the Khan. Only recently he issued an express order to this effect.

The dukes, in their turn, enjoy the same absolute power over their [subordinate] people. In fact, men and women, Tatars as well as others, are distributed among the dukes [as their property]. If a duke sends his envoys anywhere, the people, the Khan's men just as all the other people, are equally obliged to provide without argument post horses, the necessary provisions and servants, both to look after the horses and to wait on the envoys personally. The dukes [beys], like everyone else, are under an obligation to provide the Great Khan with mares as dues, for one, two, or three years, as he may see fit, (146) so that he may have the benefit of their milk. The subjects of the dukes have to provide precisely the same for their lords; for nobody is free among them. In short, the Khans and the dukes take from the property of the subjects whatever and however much they like, and also have unlimited rights to dispose of their persons as they wish.

The author now reports about the election of Ögädäi as Great Khan in 1229 and concerning some campaigns.

12. The Conduct of War: The Organization of the Army

(160) Of this we can report as follows: Chinggiz Khan laid down that there should be one man in charge of every ten soldiers, called a commander of ten [corporal]; in charge of ten such units

there should be a commander of a hundred, in charge of ten of these a commander of a thousand, and finally in charge of ten of these a high commander. In their language, this latter number [ten thousand] is called darkness.[12] At the head of the whole army are then two or three dukes (*duces* or holders of a *tugh*, i.e., of a commander's standard), but again, one of them has the supreme command.

In the event of war, should one or two or three or more of these ten men flee, they [those who fled] are all punished by death. Moreover, should all of these ten flee, unless (161) all the other men belonging to their unit of a hundred flee, then they are all punished by death. In short, unless there is a general retreat, all those fleeing are punished by death. If, on the other hand, one or two or three throw themselves boldly into battle and the rest of the ten they belong to do not follow, the latter must pay for it with their lives, and if one or more of the ten soldiers are taken prisoner, then unless their other comrades free them, they equally must pay with their lives.

There follow details about arms, tactics, warfare, and so on.

13. The Tyranny of the Tatars over Their Vassals

(187) In those countries whose princes they allow to return home, they install their own *basqaq*s or governors, to whose beck and call the princes and the common people are all equally subject. If the inhabitants of a city or a country do not do what they require, these *basqaq*s brand them as disloyal toward the Tatars, and as a result the city or region in question is laid waste and the inhabitants killed. For, at the order of the prince to whom that country is subject, the Tatars arrive in strength and completely without warning, and pounce upon the unsuspecting people, as happened recently while we were still in the land of the Tatars, to a city that they themselves had founded in the land of the Cumans and had populated with Ruthenes.[13] And not only the Tatar prince who has possessed himself of the land, or his governor, but any Tatar passing through this town or region gives himself, as it were, the

[12] Cf. p. 81 n. 10.
[13] This refers here to Russians in general (not specifically to Ukrainians).

airs of a lord there, and above all those among them who have a somewhat higher rank. Furthermore, they demand and receive without more ado, gold and silver and anything they want, at any time and in any amount they like.

(188) If quarrels break out between the vassal princes they have to go to the Great Khan to present their case there, as happened recently with the two sons of the King of Georgia. One of them, called Melik,[14] was the son of a legal union; the other, called David, an illegitimate son.[15] Now the dying father had bequeathed part of his kingdom to the bastard. Upon this, the other one who was younger set out with his mother for the court of the Great Khan, since the previously mentioned David had also gone there. In the course of the journey Melik's mother died. She had been the real queen of Georgia, and her husband had ascended the throne only on marriage to her, since in that country succession along the female line is also valid.

When the two rivals arrived, they presented magnificent (189) gifts, particularly the legitimate son who laid claim to the land which his father had bequeathed to his son David, who as a bastard had no right to it. The other argued against this: Although I am the son of a concubine, I still demand to be given my right according to the traditional law of the Tatars who do not distinguish between the son of the legitimate wife and the son of the servant. As a consequence, judgment was given against the son of the legitimate marriage. David, as the elder brother, was set even above the legitimate son, and he was allowed to retain the land given to him by his father peacefully and without further challenge. In this way, the other son lost both the (190) gifts which he had made in vain, and his case against his brother David.

They also exact tribute from those nations who live at some distance from them, and who are in alliance with other nations whom they still somehow fear and who have not yet been conquered by them. They treat them gently, as it were, so as not to incur the wrath of the army [of the nation whom they fear], and also so that others should not be afraid of submitting to them.

That was the case with the Obesians[16] or (191) Georgians from

[14] Melik in Arabic (and Persian) means 'king'.
[15] This refers to the litigation between David IV and David V, 1245–6.
[16] Abkhasians.

whom, as was mentioned before, they receive a tribute of fifty thousand or forty thousand hyperpera.[17] Yet other nations are at present left in peace by them; but as we gathered from them, they do intend to make war against them.

There follows a list of the countries conquered by the Mongols.

14. The Fate of the Enslaved Prisoners of War

(199) In the lands of the Saracens and of other nations amidst whom they live, as it were, as lords, they take all the more skilled craftsmen and use them for their own work; and the other craftsmen have to pay tribute to them out of their work. They [the slaves] store all their crops in the barns of their lords who out of this allow them only just enough for sowing and for their own upkeep. Of the others, however, everyone receives each day merely a piece of bread rather small in weight, and they give them nothing else except a little meat three times a week; this privilege applies only to the craftsmen living in the towns. (200) If, furthermore, it pleases the lords and their wives and sons, they take all the young people and make them walk behind them as their retainers with all their other servants. These number henceforth among the Tatars; in reality, however, they number rather among the prisoners, for, although they are counted among the Tatars, they are not held in the same respect as the Tatars, but are treated as slaves and exposed to all dangers just like other prisoners. In war they are placed in the front ranks, and if a swamp or a dangerous river has to be crossed, they have to attempt the crossing first.

Moreover, they have to do all the work needed, and if they make a mistake over anything, or do not obey instantly, they are beaten just like animals. In short, they are given little to eat, little to drink, and the most miserable clothes, unless they (201) are able to improve their lot by earning a little money for themselves, like the goldsmiths and other skilled craftsmen. But some of them have such bad masters, that they will not grant them anything, and because of all the work they must do for their masters, they have no time to work for themselves, unless they steal the time from the necessary breaks granted to them or from their sleep, and even

---

[17] The Byzantine unit of currency.

that they are only allowed to do [i.e., to work for themselves], if they have permission to marry and own a home of their own. ·

But the others, who are kept as slaves in the yurts of their masters are in the sorriest position in the world. For (202) we very frequently saw them walking about in fur trousers in the hot blazing sun, while the rest of their bodies were completely naked. In winter, on the other hand, they suffer abominably from the cold. We saw some of them, for instance, who had lost their toes and the fingers of their hands because they had been frostbitten in the fierce cold. We heard of others who had either died or at least had suffered from the icy frost to such an extent that they could hardly use their limbs any longer.

There follows now a longish section with advice on how to repel the Mongols.[18] After that, there is a description of John's travels containing information mainly about the countries through which he had passed, and their inhabitants.

15. Ceremonies at the Coronation of the Emperor[19]

(242) In 1246 Göyük underwent the following ceremony. When all the nobles and barons were assembled in the appointed place, they set up a gilt throne in their midst, placed the ruler on it, put a sword before him and said: 'We wish, request and command, that you shall be lord and master over all of us.' To this he replied: 'If you want me to be your master, are all of you prepared and determined to do whatever I command, to come when I call and request you, to go wherever I send you, and to kill anybody I name?' They all replied: 'Yes.' Upon this he said to them: 'From now on my own word shall serve as a sword.' They all expressed their agreement.

After that they spread a felt blanket on the ground, placed him on it and said to him: 'Look upward and recognize God; look at the ground and see the felt blanket on which you are sitting! If you rule your empire well, if you are generous and do good deeds, if you make justice your guiding star and honor your princes and

---

[18] A comparable copious literature resulted later from the Turkish threat.
[19] From the report on the election and ascent to the throne of Göyük at which John was present.

barons, each according to his rank and dignity, you will rule in splendor and glory; the whole world will bow before your rule, and God will give you whatever your heart desires. If, however, you act to the contrary, you will become miserable, worthless, despised and so poor, that not even the felt on which you are now sitting will be left to you as your own.'

After these words, the beys made the wife of the Great Khan sit down on the felt blanket beside him, and when they were both seated on it, they lifted both of them high off the ground, and with loud voices and much shouting proclaimed them Emperor and Empress of all Tatars. Then they brought to the new Emperor an infinite quantity of gold, silver, precious stones and other valuables, which Chaghatai Khan[20] had left on his (243) death, and gave him complete authority and unlimited powers over them. But he immediately used these treasures to give such presents as he saw fit to all the princes and nobles who were there, and he ordered the rest to be kept back for his own use.

(244) Then general revelries began which, according to their custom, went on well into the night. Then boiled, unsalted meat was brought along on a cart, and a piece was given to every four or five persons. The people inside the tent were given meat and, instead of sauce (*salsa*), salted meat broth. This was the procedure followed whenever they held a banquet.

Finally, John describes some events at the court of the Great Khan, the handing over of Göyük's reply[21] (still in existence in the Vatican archives) and his return journey.

(Johann de Plano Carpini, *Geschichte der Mongolen und Reiseberichte 1245–1247*, trans. into German by Friedrich Risch [Leipzig, 1930], pp. 54–96, 102–6, 135–7, 141–6, 160–1, 187–202, 242–4.)

16. Their Way of Life and Their Dwellings

(8) After having left Soldaia[22] we came on the third day across the Tatars, and when I found myself among them it seemed to me of a

---

[20] It may be that it is not Chaghatai, the part-Khan of Central Asia, but Göyük's predecessor Ögädäi, who had died in 1241, who is meant here.

[21] Reproduced in Albert Maria Ammann, *Kirchenpolitische Wandlungen im Ostbaltikum bis zum Tode Alexander Newskis: Studien zum Werden der russischen Orthodoxien* (Rome, 1936), facing p. 284 (Orientalia Christiana Analecta CV).

[22] Sudaq on the Crimea.

truth that I had been transported into another century. I will describe to you as well as I can their mode of living and manners. Nowhere have they fixed dwelling places, nor do they know where their next will be. They have divided among themselves Scythia, which extends from the Danube to the rising of the sun; and every captain, according as he has more or less men under him, knows the limits of his pasture lands and where to graze in winter and summer, spring and autumn. For in winter they go (9) down to warmer regions in the south; in summer they go up to cooler regions to the north. The pasture lands without water they graze over in winter when there is snow there, for the snow serves them as water. They set up the dwelling in which they sleep on a circular frame of interlaced sticks converging into a little round hoop on the top, from which projects above a collar as a chimney, and this [framework] they cover over with white felt. Frequently they coat the felt with chalk, or white clay, or powdered bone, to make it appear whiter, and sometimes also [they make the felt] black. The felt around this collar on top they decorate with various pretty designs. Before the entry they also suspend felt ornamented with various embroidered designs in color. For they embroider the felt, colored or otherwise, making vines and trees, birds and beasts. And they make these houses so large that they are sometime thirty feet in width. I myself once measured the width between the wheel tracks of a cart twenty feet, and when the house was on the cart it projected beyond the wheels on either side five feet at least. I have myself counted to one cart twenty-two oxen drawing one house, eleven abreast across the width of the cart, and the other eleven before them. The axle of the cart was as large as the mast of a ship, and one man stood in the entry of the house on the cart driving the oxen. Furthermore they weave light twigs into squares of the size of a large chest, and over it from one end to the other they put a turtleback also of twigs, and in the front end they make a little doorway; and then they cover this coffer or little house with black felt coated with tallow or ewe's milk so that (10) the rain cannot penetrate it, and they decorate it likewise with embroidery work. And in such coffers they put all their bedding and valuables, and they tie them tightly on high carts drawn by camels, so that they can cross rivers [without getting wet]. Such coffers they never take off the cart.

When they set down their dwelling houses, they always turn the door to the south, and after that they place the carts with the coffers on either side near the house at a half stone's throw, so that the dwelling stands between two rows of carts as between two walls. The matrons make for themselves most beautiful [luggage] carts, which I would not know how to describe to you unless by a drawing, and I would depict them all to you if I knew how to paint. A single rich Mongol or Tatar has quite a hundred or two hundred such carts with coffers. Batu[23] has twenty-six wives, each of whom has a large dwelling, exclusive of the other little ones which they set up after the big one, and which are like closets, in which the sewing girls live, and to each of these [large] dwellings are attached two hundred carts. And when they set up their houses, the first wife places her dwelling on the extreme west side, and after her the others according to their rank, so that the last wife will be in the extreme east; and there will be the distance of a stone's throw between the yurt of one wife and that of another. The *ordu* of a rich Mongol seems like a large town, though there will be very few men in it. One girl will lead twenty or thirty carts, for the country is flat, and they tie the ox or camel carts the one after the other, and a girl (11) will sit on the front one driving the ox, and all the others follow after with the same gait. Should it happen that they come to some bad piece of road, they untie them, and take them across one by one. So they go along slowly, as a sheep or an ox might walk.

When they have fixed their dwelling, the door turned to the south, they set up the couch of the master on the north side. The side for the women is always on the east side, that is to say, on the left of the couch of the master, he sitting on his couch with his face turned to the south. The side for the men is the west side, that is, on the right. Men coming into the house would never hang up their bows on the side of the women. And over the head of the master is always an image of felt, like a doll or statuette, which they call the brother of the master; another similar one is above the head of the mistress, which they call the brother of the mistress, and they are attached to the wall; and higher up between the two of them is a little lank one, who is, as it were, the guardian of the whole dwelling. The mistress places in her house on the

[23] The first Khan of the Golden Horde in Russia (d. 1255-6).

right side, in a conspicuous place at the foot of her couch, a goat-skin full of wool or other stuff, and beside it a very little statuette looking in the direction of the attendants and women. Beside the entry on the women's side is yet another image, with a cow's tit for the women, who milk the cows; for it is part of the duty of the women to milk the cows. On the other side of the entry, toward the men, is another statue with a mare's tit for the men who milk the mares.

17. Banqueting

And when they have come together to drink, they first sprinkle with liquor this image which is over the master's head, then the other images in order. Then an attendant goes out of the dwelling with a cup and liquor, and sprinkles three times to the south, (12) each time bending the knee, and that to do reverence to the fire; then to the east, and that to do reverence to the air; then to the west to do reverence to the water; to the north they sprinkle for the dead. When the master takes the cup in hand and is about to drink, he first pours a portion on the ground. If he were to drink seated on a horse, he first before he drinks pours a little on the neck or the mane of the horse. Then when the attendant has sprinkled toward the four quarters of the world he goes back into the house, where two attendants are ready with two cups and platters to carry drink to the master and the wife seated near him upon the couch. And when he has several wives, she with whom he has slept that night sits beside him in the day, and it becomes all the others to come to her dwelling that day to drink, and court is held there that day, and the gifts which are brought that day are placed in the treasury of that lady. A bench with a skin of milk or some other drink, and with cups, stands in the entry.

In winter they make a capital drink of rice, of millet, and of honey; it is clear as wine; and wine is carried to them from remote parts. In summer they care only for *qumys*. There is always *qumys* near the house, before the entry door, and beside it stands a guitar player with his guitar. Lutes and vielles such as we have I did not see there, but many other instruments which are unknown among us. And when the master begins to drink, then one of the attendants cries with a loud voice, 'Ha!' and the guitarist strikes his guitar, and when they have a great feast they all clap their hands, and also dance about to the sound of the guitar, the men before the master, the women before the mistress. And when the master has drunken, then the attendant cries as before, and the guitarist stops. Then they drink all around, and sometimes they do drink right shamefully (13) and gluttonously. And when they want to challenge anyone to drink, they take hold of him by the ears, and pull so as to distend his throat, and they clap and dance before him. Likewise, when they want to make a great feasting and jollity with someone, one takes a full cup, and two others are on his right and left, and thus these three come singing and dancing towards him who is to take the cup, and they sing and dance before him; and when he holds out his hand to take the cup, they quickly draw it back, and then again they come back as before, and so they elude him three or four times by drawing away the cup, till he has become well excited and is in good appetite, and then they give him the cup, and while he drinks they sing and clap their hands and strike with their feet.

18. Food

Of their food and victuals you must know that they eat all their dead animals without distinction, and with such flocks and herds it cannot be but that many animals die. Nevertheless, in summer, so long as lasts their *qumys*, that is to say mare's milk, they care not for any other food. So then if it happens that an ox or a horse dies, they dry its flesh by cutting it into narrow strips and hanging it in the sun and the wind, where at once and without salt it becomes dry without any evil smell. With the intestines of horses they make sausages better than pork ones, and they eat them fresh. The rest of the flesh they keep for winter. With the hides of oxen they make big jars which they dry in admirable fashion in the smoke. With the hind part of the hide of horses they make most beautiful shoes. With the flesh of a single sheep they give to eat to fifty men or a hundred; for they cut it up very fine in a platter with (14) salt and water, for they make no other sauce; and then with the point of a knife or a fork which they make for the purpose, like that which we use to eat coddled pears or apples, they give to each of the bystanders a mouthful or two according to the number of the guests. Prior to this, before the flesh of the sheep is served, the master takes what pleases him; and furthermore if he gives to anyone a special piece, it is the custom that he who receives it shall eat it himself, and he may not give it to another; but if he cannot eat it all he carries it off with him, or gives it to his servant if he be present, who keeps it; otherwise he puts it away in his *captargac*, which is a square bag which they carry to put such things in, in which they store away bones when they have not time to gnaw them well, so that they can gnaw them later and that nothing of the food is lost.

Description of the preparation of *qumys*.

19. Hunting

(16) The great lords have villages in the south, from which millet and flour are brought to them for the winter. The poor procure [these things] by trading sheep and pelts. The slaves fill their bellies with ordinary water, and with this they are content. They catch also rats, of which many kinds abound here. Rats with long tails they eat not, but give them to their birds. They eat mice and all kinds of rats which have short tails. There are also many marmots which are called *soghur*, and which congregate in one hole in winter, twenty or thirty together, and sleep for six months; these they catch in great numbers. There are also conies, with a long tail like a cat's, and on the end of the tail they have black and white hairs. They have also many other kinds of small animals good to eat, which they know very well how to distinguish. I saw no deer there. I saw few hares, many gazelles. Wild asses I saw in great numbers, and these are like mules. I saw also another kind of animal which is called *argali*, which has quite the body of a sheep, and horns bent like a ram's, but of such size that I could hardly lift the two horns with one hand, and they make of these horns big cups. They have hawks and peregrine falcons in great numbers, which they all carry on their right hand. And they always put a little thing around the hawk's neck, which hangs down to (17) the middle of its breast, by which, when they cast it at its prey, they pull down with the left hand the head and breast of the hawk, so that it be not struck by the wind and carried upward. So it is that they procure a large part of their food by the chase.

20. Clothing

Of their clothing and customs you must know, that from China and other regions of the east, and also from Persia and other regions of the south, are brought to them silken and golden stuffs and cloths of cotton, which they wear in summer. From Russia, Moxel,[24] and from greater Bulgaria[25] and Pascatur,[26] which is greater Hungary,[27] and Kerkis,[28] all of which are countries to the north and full of forests, and which obey them, are brought to them costly furs of many kinds, which I never saw in our parts, and which they wear in winter. And they always make in winter at least two fur gowns, one with the fur against the body, the other with the fur outside exposed to the wind and snow; these latter are usually of the skins of wolves or foxes or papions; and while they sit in the dwelling they have another lighter one. The poor make their outside [gowns] of dog and kid [skins].

21. Battue

When they want to chase wild animals, they gather together in a great multitude and surround the district in which they know the game to be, and gradually they come closer to each other till they have shut up the game in among them as in an enclosure, and then they shoot them with their arrows. They make also breeches with furs. The rich furthermore wad their clothing with silk stuffing, which is extraordinarily soft, light and warm. The poor line their clothes with cotton cloth, or with the fine wool which they are able to pick out of the coarser. With this coarser they make felt to cover their houses and (18) coffers, and also for bedding. With wool and a third of horsehair mixed with it they make their ropes. They also make with felt covers, saddlecloths and rain cloaks; so they use a great deal of wool. You have seen the costume of the men.

[24] The land of the Moksha Mordvins on the middle Volga.

[25] Volga Bulgaria, the region around the former trading town of Bulgar, south of modern Kazan. Some of the Volga Bulgars were later absorbed into the Tatars and converted to Islam; the remainder who were not affected are apparently the Chuvash of today (west of Kazan).

[26] The land of the Bashkir, southwest of the Ural mountains.

[27] Whether the Bashkir were really related to the Hungarians and were only later absorbed by the Turks is not clear.

[28] The Kirgiz.

22. Hairstyle

The men shave a square on the tops of their heads, and from the front corners [of this square] they continue the shaving to the temples, passing along both sides of the head. They shave also the temples and the back of the neck to the top of the cervical cavity, and the forehead as far as the crown of the head, on which they leave a tuft of hair which falls down to the eyebrows. They leave the hair on the sides of the head, and with it they make tresses which they plait together to the ears.

23. The Headgear of the Women

And the dress of the girls differs not from the costume of the men, except that it is somewhat longer. But on the day following her marriage [a woman] shaves the front half of her head, and puts on a tunic as wide as a nun's gown, but everywhere larger and longer, open before, and tied on the right side. For in this the Tatars differ from the Turks; the Turks tie their gowns on the left, the Tatars always on the right. Furthermore they have a headdress, which they call *boghtaq*, made of bark, or such other light material as they can find, and it is big and as much as two hands can span around, and is a cubit and more high, and square like the capital of a column. This *boghtaq* they cover with costly silk stuff, and it is hollow inside, and on top of the capital, or the square on it, they put a tuft of quills or (19) light canes also a cubit or more in length. And this tuft they ornament at the top with peacock feathers, and round the edge [of the top] with feathers from the mallard's tail, and also with precious stones. The wealthy ladies wear such an ornament on their heads, and fasten it down tightly with an amice, for which there is an opening in the top for that purpose, and inside they stuff their hair, gathering it together on the back of the tops of their heads in a kind of knot, and putting it in the *boghtaq*, which they afterwards tie down tightly under the chin. So it is that when several ladies are riding together, and one sees them from afar, they look like soldiers, helmets on head and lances erect. For this *boghtaq* looks like a helmet, and the tuft above it is like a lance. And all the women sit their horses astraddle like men. And they tie their gowns with a piece of blue silk stuff at the waist and they wrap another band at the breasts, and tie a piece of white stuff below the eyes which hangs down to the breast. And the women there are wonderfully fat, and she who has the least nose is held the most beautiful. They disfigure themselves horribly by painting their faces. They never lie down in bed when having their children.

24. The Duties of the Women

It is the duty of the women to drive the carts, get the dwelling on and off them, milk the cows, make butter and *gruit*, and to dress and sew skins, which they do with a thread made of tendons. They divide the tendons into fine shreds, and then twist them into one long thread. They also sew the boots, the socks, and the clothing. They never wash clothes, for they say that God would be angered thereat and that it would thunder if they hung them up to dry. They will even beat (20) those they find washing them [and take their washing away from them.[29]] Thunder they fear extraordinarily; and when it thunders they will turn out of their dwellings all strangers, wrap themselves in black felt, and thus hide themselves till it has passed away. Furthermore they never wash their bowls, but when the meat is cooked they rinse out the dish in which they are about to put it with some of the boiling broth from the kettle, which they pour back into it. They also make the felt and cover the houses.

25. The Duties of the Men

The men make bows and arrows, manufacture stirrups and bits, make saddles, do the carpentering on [the framework of] their dwellings and the carts; they take care of the horses, milk the mares, churn the *qumys* or mare's milk, make the skins in which it is put; they also look after the camels and load them. Both sexes look after the sheep and goats, sometimes the men, other times the women, milking them. They dress skins with a thick mixture of sour ewe's milk and salt. When they want to wash their hands or head, they fill their mouths with water, which they let trickle on to their hands, and in this way they also wet their hair and wash their heads.

[29] This phrase omitted in Rockhill text.

26. Marriage

As to their marriages, you must know that no one among them has a wife unless he buys her; so it sometimes happens that girls are well past marriageable age before they marry, for their parents always keep them until they sell them. They observe the first and second degrees of consanguinity, but no degree of affinity; thus [one person] will have at the same time or successively two sisters. Among them no widow marries, for the following reason: they believe that all who serve them in this life shall serve them in the next, so as regards a (21) widow they believe she will always return to her first husband after death. Hence this shameful custom prevails among them, that sometimes a son takes to wife his father's wives, except his own mother; for the *orda* of the father and mother always belongs to the youngest son, so it is he who must provide for all his father's wives who come to him with the paternal household, and if he wishes it he uses them as wives, for he esteems not himself injured if they return to his father after death. When then anyone has made a bargain with another to take his daughter, the father of the girl gives a feast, and the girl flees to her relatives and hides there. Then the father says: 'Here, my daughter is yours: take her wheresoever you find her.' Then he [the bridegroom] searches for her with his friends till he finds her, and he must take her by force and carry her off with a semblance of violence to his house.

27. Justice

As to their justice you must know that when two men fight together no one dares to interfere, even a father dare not aid a son but he who has the worse of it may appeal to the court of the lord, and if anyone touches him after the appeal, he is put to death. But action must be taken at once without delay, and the injured one must lead him [who has offended] as a captive. They inflict capital punishment on no one unless he be taken in the act or confesses. When one is accused by a number of persons, they torture him so that he confesses. They punish homicide with capital punishment, and also cohabiting with a woman not one's own. By not one's own I mean not his wife or bondwoman, for with one's slaves one may do as one pleases. They also punish with death grand larceny, but as for petty thefts, such as (22) that of a sheep, so long as one has not repeatedly been taken in the act, they beat him cruelly, and if they administer a hundred blows they must use a hundred sticks. I speak of the case of those beaten under order of authority. In like manner false envoys, that is to say persons who pass themselves off as ambassadors but who are not, are put to death. Likewise sorcerers, of whom I shall however tell you more, for such they consider to be witches.

28. Ritual at Death: Burial

When anyone dies, they lament with loud wailing, then they are free, for they pay not taxes for the year. And if anyone is present at the death of an adult, he may not enter the dwelling even of Möngkä Khan[30] for the year. If it be a child who dies, he may not enter it for a month. Beside the tomb of the dead they always leave a tent if he be one of the nobles, that is of the family of Chinggiz, who was their first father and lord. Of him who is dead the burying place is not known. And always around these places where they bury their nobles there is a camp with men watching the tombs. I did not understand that they bury treasures with their dead. The Cumans[31] raise a great tumulus over the dead, and set up a statue to him, its face to the east, and holding a cup in its hand at the height of the navel. They make also pyramids to the rich, that is to say, little pointed structures, and in some places I saw great tiled covered towers, and in others stone houses, though there were no stones thereabout. Over a person recently dead I saw hung on long poles the skins of sixteen horses, four facing each quarter of the world; and they had placed also *qumys* for him to drink, and meat for him to eat, and for all that they said of him that he had been baptised. Farther east I saw other tombs in shape like great yards covered with big flat stones, some round, some (25) square, and four high vertical stones at the corners facing the four quarters of the world.

[30] Möngkä, Great Khan of the whole empire from 1251/2–9.
[31] Russian: Polovtsy; Turkish: Qıpchaq, a Turkish nomadic people in the present day Ukraine (tenth/eleventh century) who later almost without exception migrated to Hungary.

29. Sickness

When anyone sickens he lies on his couch, and places a sign over his dwelling that there is a sick person therein, and that no one shall enter. So no one visits a sick person, save him who serves him. And when anyone from the great *ordu* is ill, they place guards all round the *ordu*, who permit no one to pass those bounds. For they fear lest an evil spirit or some wind should come with those who enter. They call, however, their priests, who are these same soothsayers.

William of Rubruck now describes his visit to a provincial governor and his attempts to set up a Christian mission at his court and among the local population. Subsequently he traveled eastward through the area inhabited by the Mordvin people to the river Volga, to visit Sartaq, a prince of the Golden Horde (1255–7). Then he went on to see Khan Batu (d. 1255) and subsequently traveled through Central Asia to the Great Khan Möngkä (1251–9). In this context William lists the peoples of Central Asia.

30. An Audience with the Great Khan

(81) On the Octave of the Innocents (4 January, 1254) we were taken to court; and there came certain Nestorian[32] priests, whom I did not know to be Christians, and they asked me in what direction I prayed, I said 'to the east.' And they asked that because we had shaved our beards, at the suggestion of our guide, so as to appear before the Khan according to the fashion of the country. 'Twas for this that they took us for Tuins, that is idolaters. They also made us explain the Bible. Then they asked us what kind of reverence we wanted to make (82) the Khan, according to our fashion, or according to theirs. I replied to them: 'We are priests given to the service of God. Noblemen in our country do not, for the glory of God, allow priests to bend the knee before them. Nevertheless, we

[32] The Nestorians belong to a branch of Christianity which came into existence in the fifth century and was named after the Patriarch Nestorius of Constantinople who had been deposed in 431. They originated in Mesopotamia (which at that time was politically part of Persia) and spread to China, to the Turks and Mongols of Central Asia, and to the southerly point of India. Since the fourteenth century they have gradually disappeared except for a few small remnants.

want to humble ourselves to every man for the love of God. We come from afar: so in the first place then, if it please you, we will sing praises to God who has brought us here in safety from so far, and after that we will do as it shall please your lord, this only excepted, that nothing be required of us contrary to the worship and glory of God.' Then they went into the house, and repeated what I had said. It pleased the lord, and so they placed us before the door of the dwelling, holding up the felt which hung before it; and, as it was the Nativity, we began to sing:

> 'A solis ortus cardine
> et usque terrae limitem
> Christum cantamus principem
> natum Maria virgine.'

When we had sung this hymn, they searched our legs and breasts and arms to see if we had knives upon us. They had the interpreter examined, and made him leave his belt and knife in the custody of a doorkeeper. Then we entered, and there was a bench in the entry with *qumys*, and near by it they made the interpreter stand. They made us, however, sit down on a bench near the ladies. The house was all covered inside with cloth of gold, and there was a fire of briars and wormwood roots—which grow here to (83) great size— and of cattle dung,[33] in a grate in the center of the dwelling. He [Möngkä] was seated on a couch, and was dressed in a skin spotted and glossy, like a seal's skin. He is a [flat-nosed] little man, of medium height, aged forty-five years, and a young wife sat beside him; and a very ugly, full-grown girl called Cirina, with other children, sat on a couch after them. This dwelling had belonged to a certain Christian lady, whom he had much loved, and of whom he had had this girl. Afterward he had taken this young wife, but the girl was the mistress of all this *ordu* which had been her mother's.

He had us asked what we wanted to drink, wine or *terracina* which is rice wine, or *qara qumys*, which is clarified mare's milk,[34] or *bal*, which is honey mead. For in winter they make use of these four kinds of drinks. I replied: 'My lord, we are not men who seek

---

[33] Important fuel in areas where wood is scarce.
[34] Actually 'black *qumys*'.

to satisfy our fancies about drinks; whatever pleases you will suit us.'

So he had us given of the rice drink, which was clear and flavored like white wine, and of which I tasted a little out of respect for him, but for our misfortune our interpreter was standing by the butlers, who gave him so much to drink, that he was drunk in a short time. After this the Khan had brought some falcons and other birds, which he took on his hand and looked at, and after a long while he bade us speak. Then we had to bend our knees. He had his interpreter, a certain Nestorian, who I did not know was a Christian, and we had our interpreter, such as he was, and already drunk. Then I said: 'In the first place we render thanks and praise to God who has brought us from so far to see (84) Möngkä Khan, to whom God has given so much power on earth. And we pray Christ, by whose will we all live and die, to grant him a happy and long life.' For it is their desire, that one shall pray for their lives. Then I told him: 'My lord, we have heard of Sartakh[35] that he was a Christian, and the Christians who heard it rejoiced greatly, and principally my lord the king of the French. So we came to him, and my lord the king sent him letters by us in which were words of peace, and among other things he bore witness to him as to the kind of men we were, and he begged him to allow us to remain in his country, for it is our office to teach men to live according to the law of God. He sent us, however, to his father Batu[36] and Batu sent us to you. You it is to whom God has given great power in the world. We pray then your mightiness to give us permission to remain in your dominion, to perform the service of God for you, for your wives and your children. We have neither gold, nor silver nor precious stones to present to you, but only ourselves to offer to you to serve God, and to pray God for you. At all events give us leave to remain here till this cold has passed away, for my companion is so feeble that he cannot with safety to his life stand any more the fatigue of traveling on horseback.' My companion had told me of his infirm condition, and had adjured me to ask for permission to stay, for we supposed that we would have to go back to Batu, unless by special grace he gave us permission to stay.

Then he began his reply: 'As the sun sends its rays everywhere,

[35] Sartaq, Khan of the Golden Horde, 1255–75.
[36] See note 31 on page 45.

likewise (85) my sway and that of Batu reach everywhere, so we do not want your gold and silver.' So far I understood my interpreter, but after that I could not understand the whole of any one sentence: 'twas by this that I found out he was drunk, and Möngkä himself appeared to me tipsy. His speech, it seemed to me, however, showed that he was not pleased that we had come to Sartakh in the first place rather than to him. Then I, seeing that I was without interpreter, said nothing, save to beg him not to be displeased with what I had said of gold and silver, for I had not said that he needed or wanted such things, but only that we would gladly honor him with things temporal as well as spiritual. Then he made us arise and sit down again, and after awhile we saluted him and went out, and with us his secretaries and his interpreter, who was bringing up one of his daughters. And they began to question us greatly about the kingdom of France, whether there were many sheep and cattle and horses there, and whether they had not better go there at once and take it all. And I had to use all my strength to conceal my indignation and anger; but I answered: 'There are many good things there, which you would see if it befell you to go there.'

Then they appointed someone to take care of us, and we went to the monk. And as we were coming out of there to go to our lodgings, the interpreter I have mentioned came to me and said: 'Möngkä Khan takes compassion on you and allows you to stay here for the space of two months: then the great cold will be over. And he informs you that ten days hence there is a goodly city called (86) Karakorum.[37] If you wish to go there, he will have you given all you may require; if, however, you wish to remain here, you may do so, and you shall have what you need. It will, however, be fatiguing for you to ride with the court.' I answered: 'May the Lord keep Möngkä Khan and give him a happy and long life. We have found this monk here, whom we believe to be a holy man and come here by the will of God. So we would willingly remain here with him, for we are monks, and we would say our prayers with him for the life of the Khan.' Then he left us without a word. And we went to a big house, which we found cold and without a supply of fuel, and we were still without food, and it was night. Then he to whom we had been entrusted gave us fuel and a little food.

[37] The actual capital of the Mongol Empire.

Our guide being about to return to Batu begged of us a carpet or rug which we had left by his order in Batu's *ordu*. We gave it him, and he left us in the most friendly manner, asking our hand and saying that it was his fault if he had let us suffer from hunger or thirst on the journey. We pardoned him, and in like manner we asked pardon of him and all his suite if we had shown them an evil example in anything.

The following report deals with Europeans at Möngkä's court and with the Christians.

31. The Place of Religion at Möngkä's Court

(90) When the feast of the Epiphany [6 January][38] was nigh that Armenian monk called Sergius told me that he would baptize Möngkä Khan on that feast. And I begged him to do all in his power (91) that I might be present and be an eyewitness to it. And this he promised me. The feast came, but the monk did not call me; however, at the sixth hour I was called to court, and I saw the monk with the priests coming back from the court bearing his cross, and the priests had a censer and the Gospels. Now on that same day Möngkä Khan had had a feast, and it is his custom on such days as his diviners tell him are holy, or the Nestorian priests say for some reason are sacred, for him to hold court, and on such days first come the Christian priests with their apparel, and they pray for him and bless his cup. When they have left, the Saracen[39] priests come and do likewise. After them come the priests of idols, doing the same thing. The monk told me that Möngkä believed only in the Christians, but he wanted all to pray for him. But he lied, for he believed in none, as you shall learn hereafter, and they all follow his court as flies do honey, and he gives to all, and they all believe that they are his favorites, and they all prophesy blessings to him.

32. The Life of the Envoys at the Court of the Great Khan

So we sat for a long time before the *ordu*, and they brought us meat to eat, but I told them that we would not eat there, but that

[38] Presumably the first Sunday after Epiphany (i.e., in that year 11 January).
[39] = Muslim.

if they wished to provide us with food, they should give it to us in our dwelling. Then they said: 'Go then to your dwelling, for you have only been called to eat.' So we went back by way of the monk's, who was ashamed of the lie he had told us, and to whom I would not therefore speak of that matter. Some of the Nestorians, however, wanted to assure me (92) that he [Möngkä] had been baptized: I told them that I would never believe it, nor say so to others for I had not seen it. We came to our cold and empty dwelling. They had supplied us with couches and bed covering, and brought us fuel, and given to the three of us the flesh of one poor thin sheep for food for six days. Daily they gave us a bowl full of millet and a quart of millet mead, and they borrowed for us a kettle and a tripod to cook our meat; and when it was cooked we boiled the millet in the pot liquor. This was our diet; and it would have been quite sufficient, if they had let us eat in peace. But there were so many suffering from want of food, who as soon as they saw us getting our meal ready, would push in on us,[40] and who had to be given to eat with us. Then I experienced what martyrdom it is to give in charity when in poverty.

At that time the cold began to grow intense, and Möngkä Khan sent us three gowns of papion skin, which they wear with the fur inside, and these we received with thankfulness. They inquired also whether we had all the food we required. I told them that a little food sufficed us, but that we had no house in which we could pray for Möngkä Khan; for our hut was so small that we could not stand up in it, nor open our books as soon as we lit the fire. So they reported these words to him, and he sent to the monk to know whether he would like our company, and he replied cheerfully that he would.

From then on we had a better dwelling, living with the monk before the *ordu* (93), where no one lodged except ourselves and their diviners; but these latter were nearer and in front of the *ordu* of the first lady, while we were on the extreme eastern end, before the *ordu* of the last lady.

There follows a description of a Nestorian service and information about Möngkä's attitude toward the Christians.

[40] Surely also from curiosity!

33. *The Use of Oracles*

(95) ... So on the Sunday of Septuagesima [8 February] (96), which is as it were the Easter of the Armenians, we went in procession to the dwelling of Möngkä, and the monk and we two, after having been searched for knives, entered into his presence with the priests. And as we were entering a servant came out carrying some sheep's shoulder blades, burnt to coals, and I wondered greatly what he could do with them. When later on I enquired about it, I learnt that he does nothing in the world without first consulting these bones; he does not even allow a person to enter his dwelling without first consulting them. This kind of divination[41] is done as follows: when he wishes to do anything, he has brought him three of these bones not previously charred, and holding one, he thinks of the thing about which he wishes to consult it, whether he shall do it or not; and then he hands it to a servant to burn. And there are two little buildings beside the dwelling in which he lives, in which they burn these bones, and these bones are looked for diligently every day throughout the whole camp. When they have been charred black, they are brought back to him, and then he examines whether the bones have been split by the heat throughout their length. In that case the way is open for him to act. If, however, the bones have been cracked crosswise, or round bits have been started out of them, then he may not act. For this bone always splits in the fire, or there appear some cracks spreading over it. And if out of the three he finds one satisfactory, he acts.

34. *Law Proceedings*

When we were going into his presence, we were cautioned not to touch the threshold[42] (97). The Nestorian priests carried incense to him, and he put it in the censer and they censed him. They then chanted, blessing his drink; and after them the monk said his benison, and finally we had to say ours. And seeing us carrying Bibles before our breasts, he had them handed him to look at, and he examined them very carefully. When he had drunk, and the highest of the priests had served him his cup, they gave the priests

[41] A general custom among the Mongols.
[42] Still considered offensive by the Russians. But cf. also I Samuel 5:5.

to drink. After this we went out, and my companion who had turned his face toward the Khan bowing to him and following us in this fashion hit the threshold of the dwelling; and as we were proceeding in all haste to the house of Baltu, his son, those who were guarding the threshold laid hands on my companion, stopped him and would not allow him to follow us; and calling someone, they told him to take him to Bulgai, who is the grand secretary[43] of the court, and who condemns persons to death. But I was in ignorance of all this. When I looked back and did not see him coming, I thought they had detained him to give him lighter clothing, for he was feeble, and so loaded down with furs that he could scarcely walk. Then they called our interpreter, and made him stay with him. We on our side went to the house of the eldest son of the Khan, who has already two wives, and who lodges on the right side of his father's *ordu*; and as soon as he saw us coming, he got up from the couch on which he was seated, and prostrated himself to the ground, striking the ground with his forehead, and worshipping the cross. Then getting up (98), he had it placed on high in the most honored place beside him. He had as a master a certain Nestorian priest, David by name, a great drunkard, who was teaching him. Then he made us sit down, and had given the priests to drink. And he also drank, after having been blessed by them.

35. *Treatment of the Sick*

Then we went to the *ordu* of the second lady, who is called Cota and who is an idol follower, and we found her lying ill in bed. The monk obliged her to get up from her bed, and made her worship the cross with bent knees and prostrations, the forehead on the ground, he standing with the cross on the west side of the dwelling, and she on the east side. When this was done, they changed places, and the monk went with the cross to the east side, and she to the west; and he commanded her boldly, though she was so feeble she could scarcely stand on her feet, to prostrate herself three times, worshipping the cross facing the east, in Christian fashion: and this she did.

[43] Roughly 'steward'.

36. Worshipping the Cross

And he showed her how to make the sign of the cross before her face. After that, when she had lain down again on her bed, prayers having been said for her, we went to a third house in which the Christian lady used to live. On her death she was succeeded by a young girl who together with the daughter of the lord, received us joyfully, and all they in this house worshipped the cross most devoutly; and she had it placed in a high place on a silk cloth, and had food brought, to wit, mutton, and it was placed before the mistress, who caused her to distribute it to the priests. I and the monk, however, took neither food nor drink. When the meat had been devoured and a great deal of liquor drunk, we had to go to the apartment of that damsel (99) Cirina, which was behind the big *ordu* which had been her mother's; and when the cross was brought in she prostrated herself to the ground and worshipped it right devoutly, for she had been well instructed in that, and she placed it in a high place on a piece of silk; and all these pieces of stuff on which the cross was put belonged to the monk.

A certain Armenian who had come with the monk had brought this said cross from Jerusalem, as he said, and it was of silver, weighing perhaps four marks, and had four gems in the angles and one in the center; and it did not have the image of the Savior, for the Armenians and Nestorians are ashamed to show the Christ fixed to the Cross. And they had presented it to Möngkä Khan, and Möngkä asked him what he wanted. Then he said he was the son of an Armenian priest, whose church had been destroyed by the Saracens, and he asked his help to restore this church. Then [Möngkä] asked him with how much it could be rebuilt, and he said two hundred *yastuq* (bars)—that is, two thousand marks. And he ordered that he should be given letters to him who receives the tribute in Persia and Greater Armenia to pay him this sum of silver. The monk carried this cross with him everywhere, and the priests seeing how he profited thereby began to envy him.

So we were in the dwelling of this damsel, and she gave the priests much to drink. Thence we went to a fourth house, which was the last as to its position and its importance. For he [i.e. Möngkä] did not frequent that lady, and her dwelling was old, and she herself little pleasing; but after Easter (100) the Khan made her a new house and new carts. She, like the second, knew little or nothing of Christianity, but followed the diviners and idolaters. However, when we went in she worshipped the Cross, just as the monk and priests had taught her. There again, the priests drank; and thence we went back to our oratory, which was nearby, the priests singing with great howling in their drunkenness, which in those parts is not reprehensible in man or in woman.

Then my companion was brought in and the monk chided him most harshly, because he had touched the threshold. The next day came Bulgai, who was the judge, and he closely inquired whether anyone had warned us to be careful about touching the threshold, and I answered: 'My lord, we had no interpreter with us; how could we have understood?' Then he pardoned him, but never thereafter was he allowed to enter any dwelling of the Khan.

Report of a miraculous healing. Description of the surroundings of Möngkä's camp. References to China. Quarrels between Christians; fasting habits of the oriental Christians.

37. The Palace in Karakorum

(111) Here is a great palace, where he has his drinkings twice a year: once about Easter, when he passes there, and once in summer, when he goes back [westward]. And the latter is the greater [feast], for then come to his court all the nobles, (112) even though distant two months' journey; and then he makes them largess of robes and presents,[44] and shows his great glory. There are there many buildings as long as barns, in which are stored his provisions and his treasures.

In the entry of this great palace, it being unseemly to bring in there skins of milk and other drinks, Master William the Parisian had made for him a great silver tree, and at its roots are four lions of silver, each with a conduit through it, and all belching forth white milk of mares. And four conduits are led inside the tree to its tops, which are bent downward, and on each of these is also a gilded serpent, whose tail twines round the tree. And from one of these pipes flows wine, from another *qara qumys*, or clarified

[44] Right up to the beginning of modern times this was, as also in other parts of the Orient, the equivalent of the distribution of decorations in Europe.

mare's milk, from another *bal*, a drink made with honey, and from another rice mead, which is called *terracina*; and for each liquor there is a special silver bowl at the foot of the tree to receive it. Between these four conduits in the top, he made an angel holding a trumpet, and underneath the tree he made a vault in which a man can be hid. And pipes go up through the heart of the tree to the angel. In the first place he made bellows, but they did not give enough wind. Outside the palace is a cellar in which the liquors are stored, and there are servants all ready to pour them out when they hear the angel trumpeting. And there are branches of silver on the tree, and leaves and fruit. (113) When then drink is wanted, the head butler cries to the angel to blow his trumpet. Then he who is concealed in the vault, hearing this blows with all his might in the pipe leading to the angel, and the angel places the trumpet to his mouth, and blows the trumpet right loudly. Then the servants who are in the cellar, hearing this, pour the different liquors into the proper conduits, and the conduits lead them down into the bowls prepared for that, and then the butlers draw it and carry it to the palace to the men and women.

And the palace is like a church, with a middle nave, and two sides beyond two rows of pillars, and with three doors to the south, and beyond the middle door on the inside stands the tree, and the Khan sits in a high place to the north, so that he can be seen by all; and two rows of steps go up to him: by one he who carries his cup goes up, and by the other he comes down. The space which is in the middle between the tree and these steps by which they go up to him is empty; for here stand his cupbearer, and also envoys bearing presents; and he himself sits up there like a divinity. On [his] right side, that is, to the west, are the men, to the left the women. The palace extends from the north [southward]. To the south, beside the pillars on the right side, are rows of seats raised like a platform, on which his son and brothers sit. On the left side it is arranged in like fashion, and there sit his wives and daughters. Only one woman sits up there beside him, though not so high as he.

38. The Charming of the Weather

When then he heard that the work was finished, he ordered the master to put it in place and fix it well, and then toward Passion

Sunday [29 March] he started out with his light tents, leaving the big ones behind him. And the monk and we followed him, and he sent us another skin of wine. And on the way we passed between mountains where there was excessive wind and cold and much snow fell. So toward the middle of the night he sent to the monk and us, asking us to pray to God to temper this cold and wind, for all the animals in the caravan were in danger, particularly as they were then heavy with young and bringing forth. Then the monk sent him incense, telling him that he himself should put it on coals and offer it to God. I know not whether he did this, but the tempest, which had already lasted two days, abated when the third day of it was already beginning.

Description of the city of Karakorum. The life of the Christians there. A 'religious disputation' between Christians, Muslims, and Shamans.

39. The Position of the Shamans

(141) Their diviners are, as [Möngkä Khan] confessed to me, their priests; and whatever they say must be done is executed without delay. I will tell you of their office, as well as I could learn about it from master William and others who used to speak truthfully to me. They are very numerous, and always have a captain, like a pontiff, who always places his dwelling before the principal house of Möngkä Khan, at about a stone's throw from it. Under his custody are, as I have previously said, the carts on which the idols are carried. The others come after the *ordu* in positions assigned to them; and there come to them from various parts of the world people who believe in their art.

Some among them know something of (142) astrology, particularly the chief, and they predict to them the eclipses of the sun and the moon; and when one is about to take place all the people lay in their food, for they must not go out of the door of their dwelling. And while the eclipse is taking place, they sound drums and instruments, and make a great noise and clamor. After the eclipse is over, they give themselves to drinking and feasting, and make great jollity. They predict lucky and unlucky days for the undertaking of all affairs; and so it is that they never assemble an army nor begin a war without their assent, and long since the Mongols would have gone back to Hungary, but the diviners will not allow it.

40. Purification after Death

All things which are sent to the court they take between fires, and for this they retain a certain portion of them. They also cleanse all the bedding of deceased persons by taking them between fires. For when anyone dies, they put aside all that belongs to him, and they are not allowed to the other people of the *ordu* until they have been purified by fires. This I saw in connection with the *ordu* of that lady who died while we were there. On account of this [custom] there was a double reason why Friar Andrew and his companion should have gone between fires; they bore presents, and they were destined for one who was already dead, Göyük Khan.[45] Nothing of the sort was required of me, because I brought nothing. If any animal or any other thing falls to the ground while passing between the fires, it is theirs.

41. The Spring Festival

(143) On the ninth day of the month of May, they get together all the white horses of the herds, and consecrate them. And the Christian priests are obliged to come to this with their censer. Then they sprinkle new *qumys* on the ground and hold a great feast on that day, for they consider that they then first drink new *qumys*, just as in some places among us is done with wine at the feast of Bartholomew or Sixtus, and with fruit at the feast of James and Christopher. They [i.e., the Kam] are also called in when a child is born, to tell its fortune; and when anyone sickens they are called, and they repeat their incantations, and tell whether it is a natural malady or one resulting from witchcraft. And in this connection that woman of Metz, of whom I have spoken, told me a most remarkable thing.

42. Witchcraft

Once some valuable furs were presented, which were to be deposited in the *ordu* of her mistress, who was a Christian, as I have

[45] Great Khan since 1246, died in April, 1248.

previously said; and the diviners carried them between fires, and took of them more than they should have done. A certain servant woman who had charge of the treasure of this lady, accused them of this to her mistress; so the lady reproved them. Now it happened after this that this lady fell ill, and had shooting pains through her limbs. The diviners were called, and they, while seated at a distance, ordered one of the maids to put her hand on the painful spot, and to pull out whatever she should find. So she arose and did this, and she found in her hand a piece of felt, or some other thing. Then they told her to put it on the ground; when it was put there it (144) began to wriggle like some live animal. Then it was put into water, and it became like a leech, and they said: 'Lady, some sorceress has done you this harm with her sorceries.' And they accused her who had accused them about the furs. And she was taken outside the camp into the fields, and for seven days she was beaten and tried with other torments, so that she should confess. And in the meanwhile the lady died. When she heard of this she said to them: 'I know that my mistress is dead; kill me, that I may go after her, for I never did her wrong.' And as she would confess nothing, Möngkä commanded that she be allowed to live; and then those diviners accused the nurse of the daughter of the lady of whom I have spoken; and she was a Christian, and her husband was most respected among all the Nestorian priests. And she was taken to the place of execution with one of her maids, to make her confess; and the maid confessed that her mistress had sent her to speak to a horse, to get answer from it. The woman [i.e., the nurse] also confessed that she had done something to make herself liked by her master, so that he should show her favor, but she had never done anything which could have injured him. She was asked whether her husband knew what she had done. She made excuse for him, having burnt characters and letters she had made herself. So she was put to death; and Möngkä sent her husband, this priest, to the bishop who was in Cathay[46] to try him, though he had not been found guilty.

Finally William reports concerning the letter of reply, their taking leave of Möngkä and the return journey. This took them back through Central Asia to the Volga, and then along the western bank of the Caspian Sea and the southern side of the Caucasus to Asia Minor. From

[46] China.

there they went by way of Cyprus to 'Akko (Acre) where William set down his report in writing.

(William Woodville Rockhill, *The Journey of William Rubruck* [London 1909], pp. 8–144, *passim.*)

43. Praise of a Ruler

Of the honorable deeds of the ruler of the world, Möngkä Qā'ān, after his accession to the throne

(83) . . . In the introduction to this book there was some brief mention of his noble character and actions, and in the chapter on his accession there were included some more detailed references thereto. In order to corroborate what has been said we have recorded a story, which is the meeting place of justice and generosity, in order that mankind may know of a certainty that this narration is unmarked with the brand of extravagance and innocent of the sin of aberration.

Merchants had hastened to the presence of Göyük Khan [above, pp. 64ff] from all parts of the world and having concluded very large deals had been paid by drafts on the lands of the East and the West. But since he did not tarry long in his kingdom [but soon died], the greater part of that money remained unpaid and did not reach those merchants. And after his death, his wives, sons, and (84) nephews concluded deals on a still greater scale than during his lifetime and wrote drafts in the same way. And crowds of other merchants came one after the other and carried out transactions with them. When the position of those people [Göyük's family and supporters] changed and their cause was lost, there were some merchants who from former transfers had not obtained even a tenth of their due; some had not yet reached the stage of a transfer; some had delivered their wares but a price had not yet been fixed, and others had not yet received a draft.

When the World-Emperor Möngkä Qā'ān took auspicious repose upon the throne of success and the necklace of justice and equity had been strung, certain of these dealers approached him by way of a test partly hoping [to enjoy the benefit of] his justice and partly despairing of [achieving anything by] their petition for the money involved in this transaction; and they brought their case to his auspicious attention. All the Functionaries of Court and

Pillars of State were of the opinion that there was no obligation to pay the amount due on this transaction out of the Emperor's treasury and that no mortal would have cause to object or cavil [if payment was refused].

But on the principle of the verses . . . he spread the wing of compassion over them all and gave orders for the whole sum (85) to be met from the finances of his Empire. It amounted to 500,000 silver *balish* (bars), and had he withheld it none would have had cause to object.

With such bounty he stole away the glory of Ḥātim-like kings [Ḥātim was an Arab renowned for his generosity] and with such justice he cast dust into the eyes of Nūshirvān-like emperors [Nūshirvān was a Sassanid king]. And from what book of history has it been read or heard from reciters that a king paid the debt of another king? And no mortal ever discharged the obligations of his enemies. This is an instance of habits and practices from which one can deduce his behavior in other matters. . . .

An emperor like this, by the effect of his commands and prohibitions, cannot but be powerful and long-lived [Möngkä died, however, after a reign of only eight years, in 1259] in accordance with the Divine Word: . . . God Almighty grant him in sovereignty an unending life!

(Juvaini, *History of the World-Conqueror*, II, 602–4 [=Part III, 83–85].)

III

THE ILKHAN DYNASTY IN PERSIA (1256–1335/54)

A. THE DEVELOPMENT UP TO THE CONVERSION OF THE DYNASTY TO ISLAM

1. The Mongol Conquest of Baghdad (1258)

Out of fear, the order was proclaimed to barricade the streets, and to station numerous troops on the walls. The two Dawādārs,[1] the cupbearer, Suleimān Shāh and other heads of the army and the Mamluks sent, to help them, a large crowd got together from among the ordinary people of Baghdad and armed with various weapons. The next day, when the golden-winged *anka* [a miraculous bird] stretched its wings in the green nest of heaven, and the surface of the earth, after having been dark as the dwelling of the wretched, was filled with light and sound, like the heart of those who see their wishes fulfilled, the eagle standard of the Ilkhan, the bird of good fortune, proudly raised its neck from the head of fury and the fire of the fight burst forth, and the wood on which it fed was the doom of Baghdad. [. . . Arab double verse.] Inside the city it looked as though the sea were about to be smothered, or the edge of the *Thahlān* mountains to be shattered by the strength of the arm, or the sun to be covered in clay; or as though one were to flee the earthquake with a kick of the foot or to draw off the flame of the lightning and extinguish it with one's sleeve. They armed themselves for the fight and prepared the mangonels, ballistas and battering rams. The bird of arrows rose and flew from the curved-edged fortress of the bow [Koranic verse . . .] and the eagle of pain began to open its claws of fury. With the setting up of the

[1] Roughly 'Chancellor'.

siege tent, the large and small mangonels were brought into action and correctly conjugated right at the beginning by the efforts of those operating them, and as according to the laws of inflection the determining case is followed by the operative case,[2] so the pointed words of the arrows were shot in answer to predetermined questions. That day, the fight and the smoke of the battle lasted as long as the golden reined and yellow horse of the sun was made to gambol along the riding track of the heavens by the ordainer of destiny. The arrows and bolts, the lances and spears, the stones from the slings and catapults of both sides shot up to heaven at top speed like messengers of the prayer of the just, and briskly fell down like the judgment of fate. The people were killed, both from inside and outside, or were carried away wounded ... [... Persian hemistich]. [Then], the Ilkhan ordered that the hand should be withdrawn from the fight. In this way was Baghdad besieged and terrorized for fifty days. But, since the city was still holding out, the order was given for the baked bricks which were lying outside the city to be collected, and from them high towers constructed in all quarters, quite close to the streets and alleys of Baghdad. On top of these they set up the catapults. The city was filled with thunder and lightning by the striking of stones and the flares from the naphtha pots; a dew of arrows rained from the cloud of bows, and the inhabitants were trampled under foot by the forces of weakness and humiliation; the cry went up: 'We have no strength today against Goliath and his army.'[3] The river Tigris which flows through the center of Baghdad, as the Milky Way pours through the center of heaven, was blocked on all sides and all possibility of flight was barred. On the other side the Pādishāh's fiery storming army, a heaving sea, stood guard at the post of revenge: 'Behind him hell will open and his thirst will be quenched with stinking water.'[4] In the meantime, ... [three Shi'ite dignitaries] ... had, by means of a messenger, sent a letter to His Majesty Hülägü Khan, reading: 'We submit ourselves, our families and our lands, for we have

[2] Allusion to rules of grammar that are expressed by words which can also be taken to refer to ballistas.

[3] Koran 2:249 Cairo (= 250 Flügel).

[4] Koran 14:16 Cairo (= 19 Flügel). R. Bell adjusted from Rudi Paret: 'Afterwards he must expect hell. And he is given [there] the water from wounds to drink.' (Retranslated from German into English.)

knowledge passed on to us from our forebears, the twelve Imāms, and we know equally from the mouth of ʿAlī, ʿAlī, the prince of the true believers, the bravest among the armies, the most courageous on the seas, the bold, he who is served by pious wishes, *the friend of his friends, the enemy of his enemies*, the strongly built fast-striking one, the eloquent and bright-eyed one who trails behind him a train of riches, he who is the owner of the whirling sword,[5] who speeds up the gifts and favors slow in coming, and with his ring unites the commandments in truth, who combines the extremes of braveness and mildness, and is the entrance gate to all knowledge, whose mercies are extensive, whose strides are long, whose wit is sharper than the . . .'s sight, who has said: *if the hidden were unveiled*, the lion of God, the mighty—from ʿAlī ibn Abī Tālib's mouth we have knowledge that you will one day be the owners of this land, that the grip of your power will defeat its governor, and that he will give way before the verdict of greatness. In these words, they were referring to the following sentences of ʿAlī the Pleasing (May God glorify his countenance!): "When the bond, the indissoluble comes, you will in truth be destroyed, O mother of cruelty and home of injustices, O mother of adversity. Woe to you, O Baghdad! Woe to your inhabited palaces which have wings as the wings of peacocks which will be dissolved as salt in water. There will come the sons of Kantūra,[6] and their leader of mighty voice; they have faces like leather-covered shields and noses like the trunks of elephants; they will not enter a land without conquering it, and approach no flag without overturning it."'

Hülägü who was highly pleased about this gave them presents and certificates, and sent to them Takla and ʿAlā ad-Dīn, the Persian, who had been entrusted with the governorship. In this way the inhabitants of Ḥilla [south of Baghdad; mostly Shiʿites] put on the kaftan of security and drank from the cup of peacock friendship.

The caliph, quite secure against the internal enemies of the dynasty, against acquaintances who were less close to him than friends, against hidden enemies and open friends, against those who have had experience of gain and loss, [. . . Arab double verse]

---

[5] The popularly imagined double-edged sword Dhū 'l-Fiqār.

[6] The Turks as the descendants of Abraham's second wife Ketūra (Gen. 25:1 f.).

asked for means of relief in this terrible adversity and for means of averting this fearful attack: where there was a remedy for this torment and where in this general time of misfortune there was help. He wept and moaned:

> 'Every morning my sigh rises to the roof of heaven,
> and tells the world of the smouldering heart:
> The tear, teetering on the brink of the eye,
> threatens, as the Tigris, to burst its banks[7] at any moment.'

The vizier reported: The army of the Mongols is infinitely large, and there is no one present in the city who might be able to offer resistance to this enemy with chess figures. The efforts of the Mamluks and of this hastily gathered rabble are as ineffective as the *twitchings of a slaughtered animal*. By now defense against this enemy has become impossible, and his power becomes more and more overwhelming, resources and means of help are exhausted, and the people find it increasingly difficult to hold on to their courage. For the benefit of everybody and in the interest of the general welfare, it is necessary that the prince of the true believers, on the strength of the passage in the traditional writings [in the Ḥadīth] . . . desist from the fight with the Turks, that he may achieve salvation here for everyone, because the Turks themselves will not give up the fight, for they are *wrathful beyond measure*. It is the action of the wise, to humble themselves and to humiliate themselves; and it is a totally reasonable action, to flatter and show courtesy for the sake of the name and honour of the empire and the splendor of power [. . . two verses].

It would be best for the prince of the true believers to submit willingly and voluntarily, without argument or reservation, to the service of Hülägü Khan. The reason for the Ilkhan movements may well be greed for goods and riches; if the Caliph makes good use of this, once we have reestablished the system of good relations, we shall help ourselves and gain strength the best by means of intermarriage, and we shall make sure to lay the foundations of the means to victory, in such a way that a daughter of the Khanate shall be married to the prince of the faithful, and a pearl of the shell of the Imāmate shall be threaded onto the nuptial

[7] In the text: 'as Euphrates' (because of the verse meter instead of the more obvious Tigris).

necklace so that, through these preparatory arrangements, empire and religion shall fuse, so that sovereignty and splendor, Caliphate and power become one, in order to save the blood and the possessions of so many thousand Muslims on earth, and so that the dignity and greatness of the Caliphate shall be magnified with the aid of the mighty Pādishāh. [Arab hemistich by the author.]

You wish this to happen,
However, Time says: no!

The flood of fear and horror in the Caliph's mind heaved so mightily, that truth and error remained hidden from him, and the difference between sincerity and mendacity remained obscured, since outwardly these words seemed to agree with the prophesy and the success seemed to warrant the means; and in this sentence the Caliph accepted the correctness of the second part without considering whether the first part included any error, and confirmed what the enemy had thought. Anybody who is slow-witted enough to be taken in by the deceit of the enemy deserves his evil fate, and anybody who neglects being cautious will in spite of himself lose control over affairs and sadly and dejectedly will rightly say to himself [. . . Arab verse].

In short, when it was the day of fate for al-Musta'ṣim [the Caliph since 1242], a day black as pitch, like the clothing of 'Abba's family, and his judgment followed the guide of misfortune [there follows a series of further symbolic comparisons mentioning numerous former Caliphs], he made his way on Sunday, 10 February, 1258 (4 Ṣafar 656 H.) [Koranic verse], on a day of desperation and of faces lined with anguish,[8] on a day unhappy for both the prominent and the common people, [Koranic verse:] 'on a day, whose evil was far spread,'[9] with his two sons Abū Bakr and 'Abd ar-Raḥmān, with a great following of 'Alids and learned men, of holy men of the land and trusted men of the court, with his troops and followers, with most of his pages and protected relatives, to the stirrup of the Ilkhan majesty, and amid cries of 'Look up!' he passed along the broad road of destruction, that is out from the streets of Baghdad. [. . . verse.]

When they had reached the vicinity of Rabz, . . . the crowd was prevented from entering, and only the Caliph and his sons with

[8] Koran 76: 10 Cairo/Flügel.   [9] Koran 76: 7 Cairo/Flügel.

two or three servants were allowed to go in. Having waited for some time in the anteroom, the Caliph said to himself: [. . . Arab double verse].

Suleimān Shāh, the Dawādār and the cupbearer, together with a number of the closest confidants of the Caliph were executed by order of the Pādishāh [Hülägü]. In the morning, when the orange of Zulaikhā' [the sun] was placed at the rim of the dish of the horizon and the light by sleight of hand had conjured away from the mercury blanket of the sky the imprinted seals of the stars, the Ilkhan ordered the army to carry the torch of plunder and robbery into Baghdad. [. . . Arab half verse.]

First of all they razed to the ground the walls which were mentioned in the verse of the Koran, *'Erect between yourselves and them a rampart,'*[10] and filled in the moat which was as deep as the contemplation of rational men. Then, they swept through the city like hungry falcons attacking a flight of doves, or like raging wolves attacking sheep, with loose rein and shameless faces, murdering and spreading fear; [Koranic verse:] *'God leads the way to the house of salvation, and leads whom he will on to the right path.'*[11] The massacre was so great that the blood of the slain flowed in a river like the Nile, red as the wood used in dyeing, and the verse of the Koran: *'Both seed and stem perished'*[12] was recited about the goods and riches of Baghdad. With the broom of looting, they swept out the treasures from the harems of Baghdad, and with the hammer of fury, they threw down the battlements head first as if disgraced. The palaces whose canopies, on account of their ornamentation, had made the seats of paradise hide in shame and cover their shortcomings, were demolished. The verse was quoted: *'How many gardens and fountains and sown fields and splendid edifices have they not left behind'*[13] [. . . Persian double verse]. And a lament reached the ears . . . from roofs and gates: [. . . Arab verse]. The moving quill of events wrote on the leaves of the walls, and on the roofs reaching to the sky, the inscription: [. . . two verses]. Beds and cushions made of gold and encrusted with jewels were cut to pieces with knives and torn to

---

[10] Koran 18:95 Cairo (=94 Flügel).
[11] Koran 10:25 Cairo (=26 Flügel).
[12] Koran 2:205 Cairo (=201 Flügel).
[13] Koran 44:26 f. Cairo (= 25 f. Flügel).

shreds; those hidden behind the veils of the great harem [. . . Persian verse] were dragged like the hair of the idols through the streets and alleys; each of them became a plaything in the hands of a Tatar monster; and the brightness of the day became darkened for these mothers of virtues.

([Waṣṣāf] *Geschichte Wassafs*, ed. in Persian and trans. into German by Josef von Hammer-Purgstall, Vol. I [Vienna, 1856], pp. 68–75 = trans. pp. 66–72.)

2. *The Chief Wife of the Ilkhan Hülägü (1255–65)*

(92) Hülägü Khan[14] had a great number of wives and concubines. Among them were those who according to the *yasa*[15] had come down to him from his father [Toluy, the youngest son of Chinggiz Khan], and those whom he had chosen himself. Their names will be listed below. His chief wife [the 'Great Khatun'] was Doquz Khatun, from the highly respected tribe of the Kereit,[16] the granddaughter of Wang Khan.[17] Since she had also been the wife of his father, she had a position above the other ladies, although Hülägü had married some of them earlier; he took her in marriage only after he had crossed the Oxus [on the campaign against Persia]. [His father] Toluy had not yet consummated the marriage with her [see above, p. 22]. She commanded great respect and possessed absolute authority. Since the tribe of the Kereit adhered to the Christian faith, she strongly supported (94) the Christians, so that under her protection this 'nation'[18] had great influence. In order to please her, Hülägü supported and promoted this community, so that it was able to build new churches everywhere. Near Doquz Khatun's tent, there was always set up a [portable] chapel, where bells were rung.[19] This lady died four months after

[14] The conqueror of Persia (1255–7) and of Baghdad (1258).
[15] The law of Chinggiz Khan, cf. above, pp. 39ff.
[16] Those Mongol tribes which in 1007 had gone over to Nestorian Christianity, cf. above, pp. 22ff.
[17] Cf. above, pp. 21ff.
[18] In the Islamic world the religious communities form socially, economically, and frequently also racially exclusive communities in their own right and are linked to the head of state merely by the fact that their head is answerable to him.
[19] In the Islamic world the religious laws prohibit the building of churches and the ringing of bells.

Hülägü, and eleven days before the accession to the throne of [his son] Abaqa [August, 1265]. . . . Abaqa gave this portable chapel to her niece . . . , who had been a concubine of Hülägü, and who had been in constant contact with the horde of her aunt. In her way of life she followed entirely the example of her aunt. . . .

3. The Storage of the Mongol State Treasures

(316) Hülägü Khan handed the rich treasures which had been brought from Baghdad [in 1258 from the Caliph's court] to the ruler of Rayy[20] . . . for safekeeping, and had them taken to Azerbaijan [in north west Persia]; as was also the booty from the fortresses of the Assassins,[21] from Asia Minor, Georgia, Armenia, Luristan[22] and the land of the Kurds.[23] Then he ordered . . . that a strong fortress should be built in a very high place, on a mountain, on the banks of Lake Urmia,[24] near Selmās. (318) All the gold coins were melted down and made into gold bars which were deposited there. Some of the valuables and riches [from the booty] were sent to the Great Khan,[25] together with the news of the victory. At the same time Hülägü reported on the conquest of Iran, and announced his intention of marching against Syria and Egypt.[26] . . . (320) The Great Khan expressed extreme joy about this. . . .

4. The Death of the Ilkhan Abaqa in Delirium

On . . . 13 February, 1282, Abaqa traveled from the capital, Baghdad, to Hamadan. He arrived there on Wednesday, . . . 18 March, and took up residence in the palace. . . . The whole time, he gave himself to drink and amusements. On Wednesday, . . . 1 April, 1282, . . . after immoderate drinking, he had to

[20] A town in the vicinity of modern Tehran.

[21] A sectarian secret society which since the end of the eleventh century had committed numerous political murders.

[22] A district in the Zagros mountains in western Persia.

[23] Iranian people in eastern Asia Minor (on the upper reaches of the Tigris and Euphrates).

[24] In northwest Persia (Azerbaijan).

[25] The Great Khan was at that time Hülägü's brother Möngkä (1251–9). He was on a campaign in China.

[26] In this campaign Hülägü's army, in his absence, suffered in 1260 a decisive defeat which rid Egypt forever of the Mongol threat.

relieve himself at midnight. At that moment he met that which changes everything, the predetermined hour of his death, in the shape of a black bird sitting on a branch of the trees which stand there. He cried: 'What kind of a black bird is this?' and ordered his bodyguard to kill it with an arrow. But, however much they looked around, they could not find the black bird. Suddenly, [Abaqa] closed his eyes, and, seated on his golden chair, he gave up his cherished soul.

(After Rashīd ad-Dīn, *Ta'rīḫ-i-mubārak-i-Ġāzānī*[27] des *Rašīd al-Dīn Faḍl Allāh Abī-l'Ḫair: Geschichte der Īlḫāne Abāġa bis Gaiḫātū (1265– 1295)*, ed. Karl Jahn [Prague, 1941], p. 41 = Fazlullah Rashid-ad-Dīn, *Dzami-at-tavarich* [*Sbornik Letopisej*], Vol. III, ed. and trans. into Russian by 'Abd ül-Kerīm 'Alī Oġly 'Alī-zāde and A. K. Arends [Baku, 1957], p. 164.)

5. The Arrival of Prince Arghūn after Aḥmad's Accession to the Throne (1282), and the Fate of Some Viziers

(45)[28] After the festivities on the occasion of his accession, Aḥmad gave orders for the [state] treasure which was being kept on [the island of] Shāhū Talā [in Lake Urmia] to be brought to him. He shared it out among his wives, the princes, the emirs, the courtiers and the needy, as well as among the members of the army. Each person received one hundred and twenty dinars.[29] Suddenly, Prince Arghūn[30] arrived with two or three thousand mounted men, and rebuked him for not having delayed his accession until he had arrived to conduct Aḥmad to the throne.[31] Aḥmad, [in order to assuage him], received him honorably, and personally handed him twenty *balish* [each worth ten thousand dinars], which he had intended for him. A number of other princes . . . were also given something. During these days, Arghūn and [the bey] Qongortai became close friends; they made a contract in the horde of the

---

[27] Named for Ghāzān (1295–1304), the Mongol ruler of Persia to whom the work is dedicated. The author was for many years chief minister under this ruler and his successors until, in 1318, he was executed.
[28] Pages of the Persian text in Jahn's edition.
[29] Probably in silver.
[30] Nephew and successor (1284–91) of the Khan.
[31] As required by the code of honor of the close relations of the ruler.

Tuqini Khatun who had been instrumental in bringing them together, and they remained permanently in touch by means of messengers. This was to be used to incriminate Qongortai, as will be reported later. With Aḥmad's permission, Prince Arghūn returned [to his own horde] . . . , and sent envoys to Hamadan [in western Persia], to bring him the imprisoned 'Alā ad-Dīn 'Aṭā Malik and Majd al-Mulk. Majd al-Mulk had someone to speak for him at the court of Khan Aḥmad . . . , and he now recommenced his intrigue against the Minister of Finance . . . , and almost managed to get himself entrusted again with the administration. The Finance Minister, however, could strengthen his position once again : . . with the help of the Queen. He persuaded a number of people to denigrate Majd al-Mulk, and to incriminate him by means of both true and false statements. (46) Majd al-Mulk, then sent a message to Prince Arghūn, in which he declared that he was his trusted friend, [and that he knew] that the Minister of Finance had poisoned his [the prince's] father.[32] Because he had come to hear of this, attempts were now made on his life by the Finance Minister. The prince [Arghūn] ought to know about this, just in case something should happen to him. Now, this had come to the ears of a nephew of Majd al-Mulk, called Sa'd ad-Dīn. Since his uncle had just dismissed him from the treasury, because of embezzlement, he had gone away and hidden himself. Some men in the Finance Minister's confidence ensnared him and brought him before the minister, who dangled before him the prospect of the tax tenure of Persian Iraq [Jibāl; the old Media]. Now Sa'd ad-Dīn became trustful, and reported about the friendship between Majd al-Mulk and the Prince Arghūn, and about the messengers sent to him. Eventually, a *yarlıgh*[33] was issued that the nobleman 'Alā ad-Dīn 'Aṭā Malik [?] should have all his landed and other property which had been seized restored to him, and that he should be given an absolute pardon. . . . 'Alā ad-Dīn pointed out, that all the property of himself and his brothers actually belonged to the ruler, and he distributed it to the people, and allowed them to help themselves to everything. Further the two beys . . . were given orders to question Majd al-Mulk. Among his belongings they

---

[32] Abaqa, Arghūn's father, and Khan (1265–82) before Aḥmad's accession to the throne.

[33] Actually Dsārlıkh, i.e., a personal order of the ruler.

found a lion's skin painted with indecipherable signs and yellow and red lines. Since the Mongols were extremely afraid of witchcraft, they were worried about these written signs. Therefore, they dragged him before a court, and started an investigation against him. The Buddhist bonzes and the Shamans pronounced the verdict, that the pattern should be dissolved in water, and he should be made to drink the infusion so that the magic should be transferred to him. They wanted to make Majd al-Mulk undergo this procedure; but he refused, because the liquor had been prepared by Sheikh 'Abd ar-Raḥmān and had been kept among his belongings, and Majd al-Mulk was well aware that the former was not without deceit and trickery.

After his guilt had been established, the [investigating] bey . . . still would not let him be executed, and, however much he was pressed, he did not give way. Suddenly, he developed a pain in his foot; now, the Sheikh 'Abd ar-Raḥmān came to visit him, and tried to persuade him to agree to the execution. The Khan Aḥmad gave orders that he should be handed over to his [personal] enemies who should treat him according to the *yasa*. When the news spread that he was to be handed over, a large crowd gathered. [But even now], the Finance Minister . . . did not agree to his execution, and demanded that he should be pardoned. Other important persons . . . , however, were for it and dragged him to the palace of 'Alā ad-Dīn. From midday until the evening, [a list of] his valuables, accounts, *paizas*[34] and *yarlıgh*s was compiled at the gate [of this palace]. ['Alā ad-Dīn] got what he wished, and took what had been found there for himself. In this way, apart from the landed property, three hundred tomans from the Baghdad [tax] revenue were transferred to him; the landed property had an even higher value. . . . (47) [At the instigation of his enemies], he [i.e., Majd al-Mulk] was executed during the night of 14 August, 1284, in the horde of Aḥmad . . . and his severed head was sent to Baghdad. . . .

(From Rashīd ad-Dīn, ed. Jahn, pp. 45–7 of the Persian text.)

[34] Rods made of gold or other precious metal inscribed with the ruler's cipher, bestowing on the bearer absolute authority.

6. The Administration of Iran by the Mongols after Its Conquest. The Emir Arghūn

(ii) (242) . . . He [the Emir Arghūn] belongs to the Oirat tribe and his father Taidju was the commander of a thousand. The Oirat are one of the best known of the Mongol tribes, and to that tribe belong most of the maternal uncles of the children and grand-children of Chinggiz Khan [that is to say, these were married to Oirat girls whose brothers, therefore, were the uncles of their children], the reason being that at the time of his first rise to power the Oirat came forward to support and assist him and vied with one another in their alacrity to tender allegiance, and in recognition of their services an edict was issued concerning that tribe to the effect that the daughters of their emirs should be married to the descendants of Chinggiz Khan; and he likewise bestowed upon the chief of that tribe a daughter of his own. . . . This is the reason why all the princes take their wives from the Oirat.

The Emir Arghūn, after mastering the Uighur script and having grown into young manhood, encountered every manner of luck and good fortune. Young though he was he went to the Court of Qā'ān [Ögädäi] and was enrolled amongst the *bitikchi*s [secretaries]. (243) Day by day Qā'ān looked upon him with greater favor, and he was still in the flower of youth when he sent him to Khitai [northern China] together with Qaban on an important mission. He remained there some time, and upon his return to Qā'ān was nominated, because of his complete reliability to investigate [some administrative matter]. Upon arriving in Khurasan he commenced the investigation and then, in accordance with a decree, he sent all the parties to Court and returned thither himself also. At Court he assisted and supported Körgöz [one of the ac-cused]; and when the countries of Khurasan and Iraq were en-trusted to Körgöz, the Emir Arghūn was appointed *basqaq* [tax commissioner] to him and his *nökör* [roughly, plenipotentiary] or associate in the administration of affairs, so that Körgöz might carry out all business in consultation with him and embark upon nothing without him.

When Körgöz returned to Khurasan he began to administer the affairs of those countries independently, and the Emir Arghūn turned back. [Körgöz was now dismissed and imprisoned by

Törägänä; cf. p. 65.] ... Törägänä Khatun placed the territories
he had held, from the Oxus to Fars, Georgia, Rum [Anatolia] and
Mosul, under the command and control of the Emir Arghūn and
appointed Sharaf ad-Dīn to accompany him as *ulugh bitikchi*
[chief secretary], the other officials being retained in their posts.

In the year (244) 641/1243–4 the Emir Arghūn arrived in
Khurasan, where he read the *yarlıgh*s [orders of the Great Khans]
and reduced the affairs of the country to order. Then he left
[several officials] to collect the arrears of taxes.... He himself
set out for Iraq and Azerbaijan. When they reached Dihistān
Sharaf ad-Dīn received news that there was a plot against him at
Batu's Court. He set out for that court, whilst the Emir Arghūn
proceeded toward Tabriz, appointing [a number of secretaries].
Upon arriving in Tabriz he restored to order the affairs of that
region which had been disturbed by the proximity of the [Mongol]
great emirs such as ..., who regarded that territory as their own
property. He protected the revenue and caused these people to
withdraw their hands therefrom: he recovered from the grasp of
their control all the inhabitants, noble and base, both such as had
resorted to the protection of these men and such as had fled from
their tyranny and oppression. He put the affairs of that region to
rights, and in response to his fair and handsome treatment both
small and great were minded to follow and attend him.... The
Sultans of Rum, Syria, and Aleppo sent ambassadors to him and
sought his protection and favor; and he dispatched *elchi*s [envoys]
to those parts to secure the payment of tribute.

When Sharaf ad-Dīn arrived in Tabriz from the *ordu* of Batu
he made great exactions on the people there and elsewhere because of arrears in taxes. The Emir Arghūn opposed this although
Sharaf ad-Dīn persisted; and love and affection for him (245) became even more firmly implanted in men's hearts.... He left my
father the *sāḥib dīvān* [director of finance] as his deputy in the
lands of Azerbaijan, Georgia, Rum, etc., and appointed Bogha as
basqaq. By the time he reached Ṭūs Sharaf ad-Dīn had passed
away. The Emir Arghūn abolished the illegal taxes which he
had imposed on everybody to be collected by confiscation and
swept away that innovation, but such taxes as were already collected he dispatched [to the treasury].

... After the death of Qā'ān the princes had each of them taken possession of a region or district, made assignments (*iṭlāq*) on the taxes by means of drafts and transfers and issued *yarlıgh*s and *paiza*s [inscribed metal rods as proof of authority] [in their own name], which was contrary to their ordinances and *yasa*s. Accordingly the Emir Arghūn commanded the collection of every *paiza* and *yarlıgh* issued by the princes after Qā'ān's death.

When he [Arghūn] came to Göyük Khan he gave him many presents and he likewise sought the favor of the princes by the offering of gifts proportionate to the rank and importance of each ... Having finished the distribution of gifts he turned to the presentation of affairs of state. First he laid before the assembly, at which all the princes were present, those *paiza*s and *yarlıgh*s which they had issued and which he had retrieved from the holders. This was the most important of his services and produced the greatest effect. Göyük Khan showed him favor and confirmed him in the administration of all the territories he held. He gave him a tiger-headed *paiza* and a *yarlıgh* and transferred the affairs of all the *malik*s [small princes] and ministers to him. To none of these latter did he give a *yarlıgh* or *paiza*, and none (246) of the governors, *malik*s and *mutasarrif*s [governors] were allowed admittance to his presence except the Ṣāḥib Yalavach and his son from Khitai [northern China] and Transoxiana and the Emir Arghūn from the lands of the West.

... When returning from Court the Emir Arghūn arranged the affairs of each of his attendants, whoever he was, in accordance with his desire and ambition, appointing them to important tasks and great enterprises in conformity with their rank and station and granting the wishes of each of them, so that the great officers were united in loving him and ... they went back in attendance upon him filled with joy and exultation.

During the journey the Emir Arghūn opened his sealike hand in the manner of April rain, and all the lands of Turkestan and Transoxiana were immersed in his beneficence, and through the fame of his bountifulness and generosity the hearts [even] of strangers inclined toward him. He sent on messengers in advance to Khurasan and the [adjacent] countries to announce his return, and [the peoples of] all these lands and places set out to welcome him back and gathered together in Merv [now Mary]. ... For several days (247) they feasted in the royal palace, and he caused the palace to be rebuilt and the park restored, and each of the ministers at his instructions began to lay out a park and erect a mansion. . . . From thence he set out for Ṭūs, where he gave orders for the rebuilding of the Manṣūrīya and the palaces, which had fallen into such complete ruin. . . . He himself took up his abode in the meadows of Rādkān, where for some days he took his pleasure in the company of his peers and coevals. He was joined by the nobles from every side; affairs of state developed in accordance with his wishes; sadrs [officials] and maliks [kings] kept on arriving every day and he promoted their interests as his auspicious counsel saw fit. . . . [Toward the end of autumn] the Emir Arghūn set out for Tabriz by way of Māzändärān. He adjusted the affairs of each region or district as he came to it and so proceeded very slowly. When he reached the Āmul country my father came to meet him with all kinds of valuables, jewel-studded objects, and precious stones. . . . To these he added rugs and carpets and all the paraphernalia of banqueting, and for a day or two he held a feast. . . .

(248) . . . When the Emir Arghūn learnt of [various machinations against him] he ordered his deputies to prepare for the journey and draw upon the funds destined for the expenses of the Court, and he sent . . . in advance to serve as his ambassador and to report on the confusion that had arisen with the spreading of that rumor.

A month later he too set out and . . . journeyed to Court. The . . . and my father accompanied him, and by his orders the writer of these lines was also in attendance on him. When constant journeying had brought them to Ṭarāz (Talas) there came news of Göyük Khan's death [probably April, 1248]. . . . [Urged by the governor of Caucasia] (249) Arghūn returned . . . to Khurasan [and] prepared for the provisioning of [the governor] Eljigidai. Meanwhile the princes everywhere dispatched messengers and sent drafts in every direction so that the revenue for several years ahead was exhausted by these assignments, the great number of which together with the constant relay of Mongol tax collectors and the levies and demands of Eljigidai reduced the people to indigence and the emirs, maliks, and secretaries to impotence. . . . In Jumada I, 647 [August-September, 1249] [Arghūn] held it prudent to take a firm decision and set out [for Court]. And since no order from [the governor] was obeyed in Tabriz, he too at the Emir Arghūn's command set out from thence. When the Emir Arghūn reached the *ordu, yarghu*s [court sessions] were several times held and his case investigated. The truth of his words was plainly distinguished from [the governor's] lies. . . . With God's aid the Emir Arghūn (250) was victorious, and after remaining there awhile he obtained leave to return having succeeded in all his objectives.

Because of their displeasure, of which there were obvious signs, he was unable to go in person to the Court of Beki [= Seyur-khokhataitai/Sorkhakhtani] and [her son] Möngkä Qā'ān. In order therefore to present his excuses for failing to wait upon them he dispatched . . . , who was one of the most distinguished *malik*s, with gifts and presents to the Court. . . . The Emir Arghūn then journeyed homeward; . . . in the region of Almalygh he halted for a month or two to celebrate his nuptials with the daughter of one of the emirs of [the] Court. . . . The writer of these lines remained behind with the Emir Arghūn. When the latter left that place it was winter, and plain and hill were level with each other from the snow. . . . (251) [Soon after, while he was in Merv, Arghūn received a request to go to the great election meeting, and so he had to get on his way.] . . .

7. *Arghūn's Journey to the Great Election Meeting*

In Jumada II, 649 [August–September, 1251], he determined to set out for the *quriltai* [Great Election Meeting] and, in accordance with the edict, *ilchi*s were sent to summon all the *malik*s, emirs, and secretaries [to accompany him]. When they had reached the neighborhood of Ṭarāz he heard the glad tidings of Möngkä Qā'ān's accession to the throne of the Khanate [on 1 July, 1251]. He traveled at a faster pace and though the great quantities of snow hampered movement and precluded haste he paid no attention thereto. When he came to the neighborhood of . . . , the snow had leveled hollows and hillocks blocking the roads and filling the thoroughfare to more than the height of a horse. That day they halted where they were, but the next day the Emir Arghūn ordered all the horsemen to proceed in his company in advance of their horses. He turned aside from the road, crossed the stream, and proceeded along the hilltops. (252) He would make the horse-men dismount ten at a time to dig a road. Wherever there was a hollow he would fill it in, and the horsemen would then follow. . . .

By the grace of God Almighty the sun was shining that day so that by dint of great labor a parasang [roughly one hour's journey] had been traversed by evening, and by the bounty of the Glorious and Exalted Creator the dread of that danger had been dispelled. In the same manner he continued to deny himself rest and repose until he reached Beshbalıq, where the Emir Masʿūd Beg had arrived on his return from the Court of Möngkä Qāʾān. They received each other with all manner of refined courtesies and gave feasts and banquets. Then he departed from thence and sent on a messenger in advance to Möngkä Qāʾān to inform him of the exhaustion of their beasts of burden. The messenger was met by another bringing instructions for him to hasten [to the Khan's presence]. With this the gusts of the breeze of divine grace began to blow and the bud of hope of superabundant royal favor to un-fold. In obedience to this command the Emir Arghūn increased his pace and . . . [early in May, 1252] he reached Court. On the next day his companions arrived likewise and presented their offerings: and he was enrolled amongst the great ones of the realm. Later came the (253) . . . other notables who had been held up by the snow and cold, and they had the honor of making presents. When they had finished presenting their offerings the Emperor ordered an inquiry to be made into the state of land and people, and . . . certain emirs summoned them all and questioned the maliks [kings] and sadrs [senior officials]. Thereupon the Emir Arghūn made an oral report on the chaotic condition of finances and the deficit in tax payment occasioned by the constant succes-sion of unlawful assignments and a stream of harsh ilchis [state messengers] and tax gatherers; and acknowledged and admitted the shortcomings arising from the disordered state of affairs, which in turn was produced by the conditions of the time. Since his confession of negligence in the administration of affairs and his excuses therefor were reinforced with plain and evident proofs, the World-Emperor expressed his approval, being not unmindful of the services the Emir Arghūn had rendered in the past, and he distinguished him with increase of favor, and, in excess of kindness and beneficence, singled him out from all his peers and equals.

Möngkä Qā'ān then ordered all the *sadr*s who were present to be gathered together and consulted as to how the people's lot might be alleviated and the country so administered that the poor might be relieved and the lands restored to prosperity. For that which exclusively occupies the Emperor's mind is that the scented breezes of justice and equity should perfume the four corners of the world, that the hands of oppressors and tyrants should be restrained from harming the subjects of his realm, that the prayers of the servants of God Almighty should comprehend his daily increasing fortune and that the blessings of that fortune should be united with an auspicious era. Moreover there is not a shadow of doubt that everybody is best acquainted with the interests of his own country, and knows most about the cause of its ills, and by reason of that knowledge sees best how those ills may be cured. The Emperor commanded therefore that after careful consideration (254) they should each write a statement explaining what was right or wrong with their country, and how it had been caused, and how it might be remedied, so that he might order the necessary reforms according as his lofty understanding dictated.

In this, the ruler acted like an experienced physician.

In accordance with his command they each wrote a statement setting forth the griefs of the world, and the next day they were all ordered to present themselves in the place of audience. They were brought in before the Emperor and began to discuss the welfare of land and people in the aforesaid manner; and the gist of their conclusions was that the various levies and miscellaneous exactments from the people were [too] numerous, that the latter's dispersion was due to this cause and that therefore taxation should be fixed in the way it had been established in Transoxiana by the Minister Yalavach, that is, what was called *qopchur* [cattle tax], in accordance with which the amount of a person's annual payment was determined according to his wealth and ability to pay, and having discharged this fixed amount he might not be approached again during the same year nor might another assignment be made on him. So was the decision reached, and the Emperor gave orders that a wealthy man should be assessed at ten dinars and so in proportion down to a poor man at one dinar, all the revenue from this source to be employed to meet the expenses of the forced levy, the [mail] and the maintenance of ambassadors. Beyond this the people were not to be interfered with and nothing was to be taken from them by unlawful requisitions, nor were bribes to be accepted. And for every circumstance and (255) contingency he made a *yasa*, some of which are mentioned in the chapter on the accession of Möngkä Qā'ān.

And when the decrees and *yasa*s had been promulgated and the affairs of these countries settled upon the Emir Arghūn and the administration thereof entrusted to his hand, the Emperor first of all gave him a *yarlıgh* and a tiger-headed *paiza* and appointed [two] . . . to be his *nökör*s (advisers), an emir being likewise nominated as *nökör* on behalf of each of the [four] brothers . . . [of the Khan]. [Accordingly individual decrees were issued and dispatched to the governors of the various regions.] To all these the Emperor gave tiger-headed *paiza*s, whilst each of the others received gold or silver *paiza*s and also *yarlıgh*s according to their importance; after which he bade them depart. And all who were in attendance on them were numbered, and he presented them with Khitaian [Chinese] robes, even the donkey-drivers and cameleers that accompanied (256) them; and after receiving great honors and favors they departed, at the royal command, in the train of the Emir Arghūn. The writer of this history and . . . remained behind for a few days. They received a *yarlıgh* and a *paiza* confirming the office of *sāḥib-dīvān* [finance secretary] on behalf of the writer's father. . . .

When the Emir Arghūn arrived in Khurasan, all the ministers and *sadr*s presented themselves and he caused the *yarlıgh*s to be read out and expounded the *yasa*s of Möngkä Qā'ān. . . . And from each he exacted a written statement that he would not violate the principles thereof nor neglect the matters referred to therein; and that whoever acted contrary thereto and committed an act of oppression against the people would thereby incriminate himself and lay himself open to punishment. And in accordance with the royal decree he appointed emirs and secretaries, who for a number of days deliberated together regarding the fixing of the *qopchur* that had been ordered. [Certain officials were appointed to the various regions, among them the writer's father (257) who, however, since he had reached the age of sixty, was tired of administrative service, and he composed a poem about his present condition and his former frivolities, with alternate verses in Arabic and Persian. (258) In spite of this he was forced to continue in his office, but died at Isfahan on the way to Iraq.]

... When the Emir Arghūn had completed his business [in various parts of the country and had ended his talks with the Khan Batu of the Golden Horde] he hastened to meet Prince Hülägü [Möngkä's brother, who later was to conquer Baghdad and become Ilkhan of Persia], whom he reached in Kish [today Shahr-i Sebz, 'Green City,' southwest of Tashkent]. With his encouragement and favor he continued his journey to the Court of Möngkä Qā'ān. ... After (259) his departure from Hülägü ... went to the latter and laid before him a detailed list of all the ministers, *malik*s, emirs, and chief men, saying: 'I have charges against each of them and must go to the Court of Möngkä Qā'ān.' Hülägü replied: 'This matter is the concern of the Emir Arghūn and must be dealt with as he sees fit. At the command of Möngkä Qā'ān and with our agreement we have placed the keys of the government of those countries in his hands.' Now in the list of names ... had included that of the writer of these lines. When he came to my name the Prince said: 'If there is a charge against him let it be stated in my presence so that the matter may be investigated here and now and a decision given.' [The informer] repented of what he had said and excused himself; and returning from thence he joined the Emir Arghūn at Merv.

The latter now contracted a friendship with the Khoja Fakhr ad-Dīn such as had not previously existed between them, and they set out for Court in Rabī' I, 654 (March–April, 1256), the Emir Arghūn having appointed his son..., the Emir Aḥmad and the present writer for the management of affairs under Prince Hülägü.
...

When the Emir Arghūn reached the *ordu* of the World-Emperor, a number of calumniators and informers were already there awaiting his arrival. ... They made statements, and the Khitaian scribes set about casting the accounts, whilst the emirs of the *yarghu* [court administration] began to investigate the Emir Arghūn's case. Since the favor of the Judge of the Eternal Judgment still attended his affairs, his opponents achieved nought but trials and tribulation and in the arena of conflict nothing but disgrace and repentance. Some of the ringleaders had already passed away whilst actually in the *ordu*, and [the Emperor] handed over [the main informer] to the Emir Arghūn; and some were put to death on the spot and some executed upon his arrival in Ṭūs. . . .

(260) In the meantime, the census of the provinces having been completed, the World-Emperor apportioned them all amongst his kinsmen and brothers, as shall be mentioned in the proper place. And since . . . Möngkä Qā'ān was now moving toward the uttermost lands of Khitai, the Emir Arghūn was again ordered to return to the countries under his control together with all the *malik*s and emirs; and he was distinguished with special honors and favors. As for the emirs and *malik*s, those who on the first occasion had not been honored with *paiza*s and *yarlıgh*s now received them. [. . . was now succeeded by] his son . . . , although he was younger than his other sons, because he could write the Mongol language in the Uighur script, and that, in this present age, is the essence of learning and proficiency. . . .

The Emir Arghūn arrived in Khurasan in Ramadan of the year 656 (September, 1258), and having been witness of important affairs of Court, and experienced the subtlety thereof, and learnt the method of inquiry and investigation there practiced, he carried out a minute examination of the accounts, punishing some of the [administrative officers] and appointing as his deputy in the affairs of the Divan and the private treasury . . . , a man whose character was as pure as his name and whose competence and capacity were manifest to all mankind. . . .

(261) . . . The Emir Arghūn now set out to join Hülägü, who was in the region of Arrān. Having arrived and made his report he proceeded to Georgia, where he began to hold a census and divide the population into thousands. On the first occasion the *qopchur* had been fixed at 70 dinars per 10 persons but since the expense of levies of men, posthouses, relays and supplies for the army exceeded the estimates and could not be met by the *qopchur* as then fixed, it was so adapted that the excess requirements were assessed in proportion to the original assessment. Before the introduction of the *qopchur*, landowners and men of wealth, people for example who had interests in ten different places of widely scattered property were proportionately taxed for each separate interest, so that one person might have to pay 500 or 1,000 dinars.

But when this new tax was imposed the assessment was 10 dinars, which would have been no great burden to the rich even though it had been doubled, whereas it weighed heavily upon the poor. The Emir Arghūn had reported on this state of affairs and the order was given for the reassessment of the *qopchur* at 500 dinars for the wealthy descending proportionately to 1 dinar for the poor, in order that expenses might be met. This procedure was adopted and the census was carried out with great thoroughness.

The Emir Arghūn first went to Georgia because David Malik [King David IV, 1249–59], the son of [the Queen Rusudan] had risen in rebellion there and Hülägü had dispatched thither a large force of Mongols and Moslems. The Emir Arghūn proceeded in that direction from Tiflis with his own immediate following and some troops. The armies united from every side and slew or took prisoner a great number of Georgians. The Emir Arghūn then turned back and at the end of Ramadan, 657 (beginning of September, 1259) joined the Prince in Tabriz at the moment when he was preparing to march against Syria and reported to him on the affairs of (262) Georgia. Hülägü deputed a Mongol army for the task of levying the *tümen*s of Iraq'and the subjugated portion of Georgia. All of this army he placed under the command of the Emir Arghūn. When the latter arrived back in Tiflis, David Malik the Elder [the co-monarch David V; 1249–96] had also risen in rebellion because of demands for arrears of taxes and had shaken off the noose of allegiance.

(Juvaini, *History of the World-Conqueror*, II, 505–25 [=Part II, 242–262].)

8. Taxation in Persia under the Mongol Rule

(68) Appointment of Sa'd ad-Daulä[35] in connection with an increase in Baghdad's tax revenue:

In the year 1284/5, Tunsakai was sent to Baghdad as ruler [on behalf of the Mongol Khans of Persia]. When he arrived there, he

[35] Of Jewish extraction, he later on became the all-powerful minister. He was executed in 1291 in a popular revolt while the Khan Arghūn was on his death-bed.

appointed as his deputy and treasurer Sa'd ad-Daulä . . . of Abhar, an efficient and well-to-do man who was well informed about everything in Baghdad. Without any other patronage, merely through his ability, agility, and his knowledge, he came to be completely in charge. At that time, the governor of Baghdad was a certain Qutlugh Shāh, a trusted servant of the Minister of Finance . . . . Because of Sa'd ad-Daulä's appearance on the scene these persons had lost their authority. They went, therefore, in 1287, to the summer camp of the ruler [Arghūn, 1284–91] to . . . , where they complained about him to the emirs and beys. They said . . . Sa'd ad-Daulä was an incomparable doctor and worthy of being called to the service of the court. The courtiers made these facts known to persons of influence. Thereupon a *yarlıgh* went out calling him there, and removing him from Baghdad. In the autumn and winter of that year [the bey], Orduqaya, who was greatly respected at that time, became friendly with him. Sa'd ad-Daulä told him, that in Baghdad a lot of tax revenue could be levied. If he were to become governor there, he would assist him in this; moreover, he would provide for the state treasury better than others would. The private wealth of the bey would increase simultaneously. In the rural districts of Baghdad too a lot of [tax] arrears were due; they could also be collected.

Orduqaya presented the case to [the Khan] Arghūn, who inquired how great the tax arrears in Baghdad were. Sa'd ad-Daulä gave the figure of five hundred tomans. The ruler liked Sa'd ad-Daulä's clever report; he gave the two of them *yarlıgh* and *paiza*, and sent them to Baghdad, to collect the arrears and to demand the balance. They went there without delay, and, with the aid of floggings and tortures,[36] they collected a considerable sum. Afterward, they returned to the court camp of the ruler . . . , and presented the treasure to him. The ruler was very pleased about this, and, on 6 June 1288, he gave the administration of Baghdad to the bey Orduqaya; the posts of city governor and commissioner[37] were . . . also newly filled; Sa'd ad-Daulä became Supreme Inspector of Taxes and made his way into Baghdad at their head (69). There they went to work. . . .

[36] A very popular method of tax collection in the Orient.
[37] *Malik*, a position, the functions of which are not known precisely.

9. As a Result of the Intrigues of the Beys Whom He Had Annoyed, Bögä Is Overthrown and Executed

After the execution of [the minister] Sa'īd Shams ad-Dīn, the influence of [the bey] Bögä grew enormously. Within a short time, he amassed a considerable fortune. Due to his extraordinary pride in his wealth and his position, he overreached himself and treated the confidants of the ruler . . . with contempt. The latter were greatly angered by this and turned against him; two of them especially, . . . , took exception to his haughtiness and his boasting, and even mentioned the matter to the ruler, who, however, . . . took little notice of it. Above all, the bey Tagan who at Bögä's instigation had twice suffered floggings in accordance with the *yasa*, and had been insulted by him, was extremely angry about him. . . . On every possible occasion he described Böga's actions to Arghūn as vile and iniquitous. Similarly, the administrative officer, Aruq, carried on a life in Baghdad which was not at all approved of by the beys. He gave himself the airs of a ruler, and paid no attention to Arghūn's messengers when they called on him; neither did he hand over the tax revenue. Once, when Orduqaya and Sa'd ad-Daulä handed in five hundred tomans, which they had collected, they told the Khan, that Aruq had [equally] taken such sums annually, but had embezzled them for his own use. As a consequence, Orduqaya's faction brought about the redistribution of the administrative posts mentioned above [p. 137] and Aruq was dismissed. Soon afterward, Ṣadr ad-Dīn Zinjānī . . . , from whom Aruq demanded the tax arrears of the province of Fars (in southwest Persia), turned to the bey . . . , whose deputy he was, and said to him: 'Aruq is preparing to set himself up as ruler; in contradiction of the orders of the Khan and the advice of the beys he does just as he pleases. He uses the incoming revenue in any way he likes. All in all, one might think that Bögä, not Arghūn was the ruler. Things have gone so far, that any state messenger who comes to Tabriz with a *yarlıgh* or a *paiza* not bearing Bögä's red seal[38] is completely disregarded by the local governor, 'Alī, and has to return with his mission unfulfilled.' When such words came to the ear of Arghūn (70), he

[38] Carried by the senior state officials. It roughly corresponds to the 'countersigning' by the Chancellor.

got very angry with Bögä who as a result fell ill, and the beys mentioned above expected his death. But when he recovered, Arghūn forgave him, and installed him again in his office, though handing the administration of the domains which previously had [also] belonged to him, to the bey . . . , and the leadership of the middle army[39] to the bey. . . . Bögä was extremely vexed and his appearances at court became rarer; consequently anybody who was seen to visit him at all frequently, was suspected of special sympathies toward him. Therefore, the public largely avoided him. . . . When he became aware of the fact that he no longer enjoyed his previous esteem with public opinion he feigned another illness. Some beys who were annoyed about him let the Khan Arghūn know that he only pretended to be ill. Upon this a *yarlıgh* went out for the account books to be brought from his house; his officers and intimates were dismissed from the administration of finance, first of all ʿAlī, the tax inspector of Tabriz. Several complaints and charges were brought against Bögä. The consequence was that the *basqaqs*[40] came from Fars and handed taxes amounting to one hundred and fifty tomans to . . . , who had gone there in his place; from other provinces . . . there also came complaints. Now Bögä fell into complete disfavor with Arghūn. When he realized that the administration was slipping out of his hands he seized hold of immense sums of money and plotted with a number of beys against the Khan.

There follows an extensive report of the plot which eventually was uncovered by a ruse, and brought to the notice of Arghūn. Bögä was arrested and executed.

10. The Introduction of Paper Money and the Resulting Confusion in the State (of the Persian Mongols)[41]

(87) Ṣadr ad-Dīn[42] and some other beys repeatedly made investigations and studies of the *chao*[43] which is circulating in China, as

---

[39] The Mongol army was *permanently* organized in definite units (center, right, left wings). These names do not imply any temporary organization for battle.

[40] Tax collectors.

[41] Cf. Karl Jahn, 'Das iranische Papiergeld,' *Archiv Orientálni*, X (1938), 308–40.

[42] The chief minister.   [43] The Chinese term for paper money.

well as about its introduction and use in these regions. They submitted the results of their investigations to the ruler. Accordingly,
the Khan Gaikhātū (1291–5) made inquiries with Bolad Ching
Siang,[44] who said; '*Chao* is a paper that bears the coat of arms of
the ruler and is used all over China instead of coined money. The
gold bars . . . are kept in the Imperial state treasury.' Since
Gaikhātū was a very generous ruler who gave away a lot of money
in donations . . . , and since Ṣadr ad-Dīn wanted to make bene-
factions in a way that had not previously been done in this country,
he was very attracted by the issue of paper money. The most
prudent of the beys . . . stated, it is true, that paper money would
mean the ruin of the country, would wreck the ruler's reputation,
and would bring economic disaster to his subjects. The followers
of Ṣadr ad-Dīn declared, however, that this bey was extremely
keen on gold and for this reason opposed the introduction of paper
money. Thus a *yarlıgh* went out that it should be prepared with all
haste. On Friday,[45] 23 July 1294, several [influential persons,
among them] Ṣadr ad-Dīn, went to Tabriz, in order to put the
paper money into circulation, and they arrived there on 13 August,
1294, bringing with them the *yarlıgh* and they laid out in preparation a great quantity of paper money; on Saturday, 12 September
1294, they issued the paper money in the city of Tabriz and put it
into circulation. Orders were given that anybody who did not
accept it should be brought before the courts. From fear of the
sword, it was accepted for one week; but then, nobody would give
anything in exchange for it. Most of the citizens of Tabriz avoided
the compulsory acceptance of these bills, and removed materials
and foodstuffs from display in the bazaars,[46] so that nothing was to
be found any more. The people forced their way into the gardens
to eat fruit; the thickly crowded city was in this way completely
denuded of people. Mobs and gangs formed everywhere in the
streets. The caravan traffic was cut. The gangs lay in ambush in
the corners of the gardens; and, if some poor man had craftily
managed to get hold of a donkey-load of grain, or a basketful of
fruit to take to his home, they took it from him. If he raised any

---

[44] The permanent representative of the Great Khan and Emperor of China,
Qubilai (1259/80–94) at the court of the Ilkhan in Persia.

[45] Friday of each week is the Islamic holy day.

[46] The traditional oriental business quarters, often roofed over.

objections, they said to him: 'Sell it, and take the blessed paper money for it, and do show us where you have bought this!' Eventually the population was stripped of everything; the poor raised their hands in supplication.

One day, [the Khan], Gaikhātū, went to the bazaar, and noticed that the individual shops were empty. He inquired as to the reason, and Ṣadr ad-Dīn replied: 'The local supervisor . . . has died, and it is the custom among the people of Tabriz to mourn [the death of] an important person by withdrawing from the bazaar.' [Eventually] the masses in the great mosque persuaded Qutb ad-Dīn [a high official] to permit the sale of food for gold. But again, people were executed for this reason; trade and commerce (88) declined completely. One day, in the bazaar, a dervish[47] gripped the reins of Ṣadr ad-Dīn's horse and said: 'The call of the compassionate is everywhere; if you do not notice it, take care, for it is meant for you!'

Ṣadr ad-Dīn was so impressed by these words, that, with the agreement of his circle . . . , he obtained a *yarlıgh* which permitted again the sale of food for gold. From this, the people took heart, and did all their trading once more for coined gold. Now, everybody returned to the town which was soon thronging with people once again. The paper money could not assert itself in the long run; its circulation was abandoned; mankind was relieved of this torment.

(After Rashīd ad-Dīn, ed. Jahn, pp. 68-70, 87-8.)

B. LETTERS OF THE ILKHAN TO KING PHILIP IV OF FRANCE (CALLED 'THE FAIR'; 1285-1314)

1. Arghūn's Letter (1289)

'Through the power of eternal heaven! Under the auspices of the Emperor! [The following are] Our, Arghūn's, words: O roi de France [to the king of the Franks?]! We agree to your proposition which you had conveyed to Us last year through the mission headed

---

[47] A hermit (not necessarily a beggar) surrounded by a religious aura and connected more or less closely with mystical movements.

by Mār Bar Ṣaumā Saḥura: "If the armies of the Ilkhan go to war against Egypt, we too shall set out from here to go to war and to attack [the rear of the enemy] in a common operation." And we decided [accordingly], after reporting to heaven, to mount our horses in the last month of winter in the Year of the Tiger [1290] and to dismount outside Damascus on the 15th of the first month in spring (1291). Now, We make it known to you, that in accordance with Our honest word, We shall send Our armies [to arrive] at the [time and place] agreed, and, if by the authority of heaven, We conquer those people, We shall give you Jerusalem. If, [however], you should fail to meet the appropriate day, and thus lead our armies into an abortive action, would that be fitting? Even if you should later regret it, what use would that be to you? [You would have reason to regret it later.] Further, if you were to send an envoy carrying some message from you and were to entrust to his care rare objects from the land of the Franks, falcons and precious stones of various color, then the power of heaven and the majesty of the Emperor bear witness, We would reward you in some way. To tell you this We send the quiver bearer Müskeril.[48]

We have written Our letter on the 6th of the last decade in the first month of summer in the Year of the Cattle [1289], during Our stay in Köndelen.'

[The above translation agrees in points of fact with that by Vladislav L. Kotvič, 'Popravki k razboru mongol'skich pisem persidskich il'-chanov (Corrections to the Reading of Ilkhan Letters),' *Zapiski Kollegii Vostokovedov*, I (1925), 342–4, except for the two points in lines 8–9 and 20–1 above. These two discrepancies, however, alter the sense of the letter considerably.]

2. Öljäitü's Letter (1305)

'Our, the Sultan Öljäitü's, words:

O roi de France [To the king of the Franks?]

Since ancient times, the sultans of the peoples of all the Franks have had friendly relations with Our noble Great-Grandfather, Our noble Grandfather, Our noble Father and Our noble elder Brother, and We thought that, although you were far from Us,

---

[48] In western reports 'Biscarello' (Busquarel).

you came, as it were, [through your messages] close to us, sending as you have, your ambassadors, and your peace gifts to Us in the process of exchanging your news with Us. Why do you neglect to do this [now]? Now that, thanks to the power of heaven, We have ascended the sublime throne, we remain desirous of keeping strictly to the orders and commands of Our predecessors, Our noble forebears, Our noble Father and elder Brother, and of not allowing the agreements with the former heads of the newly ordered regions to lapse, but regarding them as sworn obligations, and of exchanging Our envoys for an even closer mutual contact. We Brothers had allowed Ourselves to be estranged in Our love, through the calumnies of evil fellows. Now, however, heaven has inspired Us with the thought that We, Temür Khāqān,[49] Tokhtogha (Tokhtu),[50] Chabar and Togha,[51] and We[52] other descendants of Chinggiz Khāqān should put an end to the vituperation which had been going on for forty-five years up to now, and now, thanks to heaven, all of Us brothers get on well together and, moreover, from the land of the Chinese where the sun rises, to the Talu Sea, we have joined Our mail lines together, in order to connect the states. We have given each other Our word, that if anyone among Us should become disloyal We would all stand together against him.

Thereafter, assuming that you, [too], wish to continue the friendly relations which have existed with Our noble forebears, noble Fathers, and Our noble elder Brother, We now send you these two [messengers]. . . . It has been reported to Us concerning you, the sultans of all the Franks, that you all get on well together. What, in truth, is better than to be on good terms! If now, there should be people among you, or among Us, who do not wish to be on good terms, then, with the power of heaven We shall all stand united against them. Of this Heaven be witness! We have written Our letter, in the year [of the Hijra] 704 (1304/5), in a Year of the Snake on the eighth day of the last decade of the first month of summer, when we were staying at Aliyan.'[53]

[49] The Great Khan and Emperor of China (1294–1307).
[50] Khan of the Golden Horde (1291–1312).
[51] Two Khans of the Central Asian portions of the empires of Ögädäi and Chaghatai.
[52] The writer who was Ilkhan in Persia (1304–16).
[53] In the Mūghān steppe, south of Baku.

[The translation agrees in points of fact with that by Kotwič, *op. cit.*, except for the point in line 19. The writer appears to be mainly interested in resuming the exchange of presents.]

(Both after E. Haenisch, 'Zu den Briefen der mongolischen Il-Khane Arġun und Öljeitü an den König Philipp den Schönen von Frankreich (1289 und 1305),' *Oriens*, II [1949], 216–35.)

C. THE LEGISLATIVE WORK OF GHĀZĀN KHAN (1295–1304)

1. The Conversion of Ghāzān Khan and His Emirs to Islam

(76, left) Since Eternal God had ordained from the earliest beginnings that he would make his servant happy and aid him in a special way, he invested him even before his birth ... with the ability for happiness. The word of the prophet [Muhammad] is an irrefutable proof confirming this idea and bearing witness to this statement. (77)

... Eventually, in order that the light of the [true] teaching might pour forth the grace of the Lord, ... led the angelic Ghāzān Khan on to the path of the true faith and the divine revelation. When [Ghāzān], in his early boyhood, was with his grandfather [Abaqa, 1265–82], the latter, being devoted to the teachings of the *bhikshu*s [Buddhist priests] and sharing their convictions, entrusted him to one or two highly respected *bhikshu*s, requesting them to teach him to the best of their abilities, and to guide him toward the acceptance of their doctrines. They were permanently with him and endeavored diligently to lead him toward their faith. Because of his sharp wit, intelligence, and insight, he quickly understood the essence and the meaning of this teaching; he made the doctrinal and liturgical profundities and subtleties of their community his own, and achieved such a perfection in them that he became an expert authority in this field.

With divine help, however, he was able, with his sharp eye and correct attitude, to see through the mysteries of these idolatrous practices. He reflected on the different faiths, and on their adherents; he became enlightened through the light of the religion of Muhammad streaming into his radiant inner being. The inclination toward this true community became stronger and stronger, within his fragrant heart. From these beginnings, he developed increasing conviction; he continued to follow this path, and showed himself in this respect solid and unshakable.

Out of a deep devotion to the [Buddhist] doctrine, he built in Khabūshān in Khurasan soaring temples, and in this way followed all the prescriptions of this faith. All the *bhikshu*s and monks were highly astonished at these mortifications and exercises of self-denial. At the same time, he strove hard to recognize the mysteries of truth and to determine the right way, until the occasion when everybody gathered around Baidu [who was Khan from March to September, 1295]. The emirs present concluded a treaty and an agreement; the Muslims swore on the Koran, the Mongols on gold. [The emir] Naurūz suggested on this occasion: 'If the Master of the World were to strengthen Islam through his own profession [of faith], how then would that be?' [Ghāzān] replied: 'For some time now I have had something like this in mind.' Upon which Naurūz produced an incomparably beautiful cut pearl, fell on his knees and said: 'Although it is not for a subject to make (79) bold and offer presents to princes, perhaps the ruler would be gracious toward his servant and accept this gift until the time comes for service by his servant.' When Naurūz and the other emirs then came back from Baidu without having achieved anything, the ruler [Ghāzān] became very angry and wondered what he should do about him. Naurūz repeated this performance yet again. After these events, there appeared the respected sheikh, Ṣadr ad-Dīn Ibrāhīm ibn Quṭb al-Aulijā Saʿd ad-Dīn Ḥamawī, . . . who devoted himself almost permanently to the service of the ruler. The latter asked him about the doctrines of the Islamic faith, as well as its details and truths. According to the divine promise . . . , the inspiration of supreme grace in his blessed heart gave strength to the light of the faith pouring into his inner being, and he was overwhelmed by the aid of divine guidance. He said: 'Islam is truly a strong and lucid religion; it contains all the rules for a religious and a worldly life. The miracles of the prophet . . . are impressive, deeply affecting, and for all of us to see; the signs of its truth can be seen clearly and unmistakably in the leaves of time. Without doubt, the permanent observance of its rules and duties, and the performing of further practical and symbolic actions will lead to God. The adoration of idols is, in contrast, completely without rhyme and reason, and far removed from all understanding and all intelligence. To lower one's head to the ground, in front of an idol [dead object], is simply heathen ignorance and stupidity, and appears to a man who has sense and reason, and also upon reflection, as absurd. From this, it follows clearly, that no mature man would agree to lower his head to the ground in front of such an [idol]. For the sake of truth, the statue of Buddha should be made into a doorstep, so that people would stride across it, and step on it with their feet. The acceptance, by the whole people, of Islam and the rejection of the worship of Buddha is no mere phantasy.'

In short: early in November, 1295, Ghāzān, with all his emirs and in the presence of the great sheikh, Ṣadr ad-Dīn Ibrāhīm Ḥamawī, professed the oneness of God [as the main dogma of Islam] and (80) everybody went over to Islam. In the same month, a feast was celebrated and people followed religious observances. [The ruler] conferred favors on all the sayyids [descendants of the prophet Muhammad], all priests and sheikhs; he gave favors and alms, and furthered with great enthusiasm the construction of mosques, religious schools, dervish monasteries, and charitable institutions. When the [fasting] month of Ramadan came, he devoted himself together with priests and sheikhs to religious exercises. To the intelligent, it became obvious that the faith of the ruler of Islam, Ghāzān Khan, sprang from sincere conviction and was free from all stains of illusion and folly. In view of the exalted position and the importance of the ruler's office, and in view of his great power, it is impossible to imagine any compulsion or coercion [in the conversion]. Since there was no necessity and no over-zealousness, there can be no thought of hypocrisy and pretence.

(Rashīd ad-Dīn: *Geschichte Ġāzān Ḫāns*, ed. K. Jahn [Leiden, 1940], pp. 76–80.)

2. The Financial Situation

(182) When Ghāzān Khan ascended the throne, the treasures of his predecessors had been spent. The treasures that Hülägü Khan had collected from Baghdad, the provinces of the heretics [the Assas-

sins,][54] from Syria, and from other places, and had stored in the castle ... had gradually been stolen by the guards. They sold gold bars and jewelery to the merchants, and once, when the tower of the castle that stood on Lake Urmia collapsed, they maintained that the gold bars and jewelery had fallen into the water, and, after this, they stole even more. The rest was spent by [the Mongol Khan] Aḥmad (1282–4), on the winning of the empire and on troops: it was said to have been not more than one hundred and fifty tomans. Arghūn Khan piled up many treasures in Sughurluq, which were partly stolen and partly squandered. Gaikhātū did not collect any treasures, and he gave to his people what was left of the treasures (183) of Arghūn, so that Ghāzān found nothing.

Ghāzān took the greatest personal interest in the welfare of the state. He sat in person from morning till (184) night, and anything written which was laid before him, he himself corrected in the draft. Due to this, the empire prospered.

The clothing manufacturers who had previously not supplied two thirds of the quota expected from them due to shortage of means, now supplied the total requirement because they received sufficient means.

(185) At the time, when he held court in ..., he had a great tent set up, and all the treasures which had been received from the provinces of the empire laid out there. Everything was sorted separately according to type, and bags of red gold and silver were filled separately, according to weight, and marked with the amount and the name of the recipient of the gift. Within ten or eleven days, he spent in this way three hundred tomans in money, and distributed twenty thousand garments, fifty belts studded with jewels, three hundred golden belts, a hundred bars of red gold, and on top of this he took even more from the treasury. Not a penny and not a single garment that he wanted to grant as a gift took the form of a draft on a province, but everything was presented in cash and kind. Equally, what the emirs and viziers laid before him was not paid for by draft but in cash.

(186) No day goes by when he does not pay out 10,000 to 20,000

[54] A fanatical Shi'ite religious party; its center Alamut to the south of the Caspian Sea had been destroyed by Hülägü, the Mongol conqueror of Persia, in 1255/6.

dinars in cash and a hundred, two hundred or even three hundred, garments from the treasury.

3. Tax Administration

(243) Previously, Mesopotamia, Azerbaijan, and the provinces where the production tax and the Divan[55] impositions were levied in the shape of qopchur and tamgha,[56] had been given to the governors as tax farms, in such a way that on each one a certain sum was imposed, and each one was allowed a certain sum for his expenditure. Such a governor would levy the qopchur from the peasants twice yearly, in some areas even up to twenty and thirty times. He made it a rule to levy qopchur sums included in his revenue, but then, if a state messenger arrived on some state business or in order to demand tax revenues or to make other requirements, he would use this as a pretext to levy the tax a further time. The more frequently such state messengers arrived and thus claimed increasingly greater sums for their expenses and demands, the better such a governor was pleased, since he collected revenue either with reference to state requirements or with reference to the expenses of board and lodging for the state messenger. Part of the money collected in this way he used for the (244) stated purpose, some part he kept for himself, and yet another part he passed on to the commandants and secretaries, so that they should make common cause with him, and bear witness to his lies. Of all the taxes that were extorted in this way from the peasants, not a single camel load went to the crown treasury; in fact the total revenue of the provinces was swallowed up in the permitted allowances and multiple drafts. In Khurasan[57] there was a backlog of four-fifths of these drafts, and as a result the state messengers and holders of drafts came to the Divan with cheques in their hands, and were told in reply that the sum was due from the province, and why had it not been paid to them there? Again a directive was written out, furnished with the state seal, to the effect that the sums were to be paid to the persons in question immediately. Then these people traveled again to the provinces and bore the traveling expenses, and the governor took this as a pretext for yet

---

[55] Roughly 'Ministry'.   [56] Cattle and excise tax.
[57] Province in north east Persia.

another tax collection, telling the peasants: 'You can see, yourselves, how many messengers are staying here, and if we do not provide for their expenses, they will start forcible collection.' Yet, he used for this purpose only one-third of the money collected, and two-thirds were shared between the governor and his accomplices, until eventually the state messengers went away without having received the tax revenue. The result was a permanent coming and going, and the cheques grew old in their hands, so that, eventually, the messengers were no longer anxious to cash them, and the cheques remained for years in the accounts offices. Instead of it being the case—as laid down in the regulations—that it should be known in the Divan what the net tax revenue of each province is, and to whom it was, or could be, assigned for collection, now nobody knew what was going on. Complying with the wishes of the creditors, drafts were written out all the time, but the viziers and secretaries were fully aware of the fact that the sums could not (245) be realized. It was enough to them that in this way time passed, and the people were grateful to them for their efforts, and took their drafts away with a joyful heart. The only result was the ruin of the provinces.

Then it came about, that the chief officer and the vizier reported to the ruler in audience, that numerous state messengers were in the provinces, and that these ought to provide a certain sum for the crown treasury. Immediately, a *yarlıgh* was made out, that nothing was to be paid to the collectors and holders of cheques, but that, first of all, this and that amount had to be sent in. This was meant for use as presents for the ministers, and for the payment of salaries to the governors. The ministers wrote to the governors, telling them that they had kept the tax collectors off their necks, and therefore the sum destined for the crown should now be sent to court, without delay. In this way, they gained possession of those sums meant for salaries, and the viziers on the one hand, and the governors on the other, thus worked hand in glove with each other. Cheques which did not bear the signature of the vizier were not cashed by the governors, and, consequently, the state messengers and finance officers went home embarrassed. The governors who knew that the vizier was on their side, accordingly became arrogant and used up two or three *qopchur* per year plus the excise tax of the cities 'for messengers' expenses', of which, in reality [as explained], they kept the greater part for themselves.

(246) In fact, not a penny from these provinces ever reached the treasury, and equally, only a fifth of the agreed expenditure that was to be counted against the net tax revenue was actually paid out. Nobody ever saw the head officer in charge of the tax administration; he regularly had either fled, or was a prisoner at the hands of the collectors who beat him up. He might also endeavor to entrust people secretly with the administration of excise tax in order to collect the fees, so that inspectors went secretly at night to the houses, and, of necessity, had to be content with getting half the rate. In this way the administration went bankrupt, since the small sums which still came in, were used up for state messengers. As far as the salaries of officials and those entitled to a fixed revenue from the provinces were concerned, and their prosperity, after all, depended on these payments [and for this very reason this expenditure was given priority in the tax collecting instructions], nobody was ever paid a penny. Early in the year, the excuse was made to those entitled to receive them, that the taxes had to be sent to the treasury first; later, it was said that payment would be made at harvest time, and then the numerous messengers were used as a pretext to avoid payment. In this way, those entitled to salaries and alms were kept waiting all through the year, and only a few of them managed to extract even a small fraction from the high officers of the governor, by giving up half or even three-quarters of the amount due them.

(247) Others were less lucky and, filled with envy, got nothing at all. If one or the other managed, eventually, to get some attention at the court, the Grand Divan would write a letter to the governor asking why he had failed to pay the sum which had, as he well knew, been demanded. The reply would be that tax collection was behind in the province, and the person entitled to the money should be given a draft, so that he could collect his money. In this way, the poor man received a draft on the outstanding revenue—when in fact everything was sucked dry, and many peasants were leaving their homes and farms, except where some local potentate or influential person resisted the collection of further levies, and managed to persuade the collectors to content themselves with half the amount of the previous levy.

All levies were entered in the books. Although *qopchur* was only to be levied once, in fact it was obvious that in some places it had been collected several times, and from this the secretaries concluded that in places where it had not been collected repeatedly, arrears were due. Since the Minister of Finance and the revenue clerks shared in the robbery through this repeated levying of the tax, they accordingly noted down, 'In such and such an area, so and so many dinars in arrears outstanding,' and certified this, and the matter took its course. Had a vizier asked, 'Are these arrears due on net revenue, or on additional levies,' he would have seen through the matter instantly. But the viziers knew in any case what was going on, and since the high officials and viziers received from the governors part of these additional levies by way of bribes, their mouths were sealed. The previous viziers had always taken action against such abuses, except Ṣadr ad-Dīn Chao'ī,[58] who was an expert in this, and had developed these embezzlements to perfection, consequently endangering the whole empire and its administration (248). During his period in office, nobody could cash a revenue draft; no person of merit received his pension or his salary. The result was a general flight from the land by the peasants. Whatever the number of state messengers sent out to lead the fugitives back to their home soil, they could not persuade a single peasant to do so. Those remaining in the towns barred their doors with stones or walls, and entered their houses by the roofs. The inhabitants fled for fear of the revenue collectors. If these came to a town district, there was always some scoundrel who showed them the way, and knew how to get to the houses; thus they dragged the people out from nooks and crannies, from under the earth, from their gardens and out of the ruins. If they could not get hold of the men, they laid their hands on the women, and drove them ahead of them like a flock of sheep, from one district to another; strung them up by their feet (249) with ropes and beat them so that the women's cries of anguish rose to high heaven. It often happened, as we have seen ourselves, that a tax collector mounted the roof, found an inhabitant there and pursued him until in his extreme helplessness he jumped to the ground, then the tax collector went to him, took pity on him and comforted

[58] As the additional name he bears says, the Minister who in 1294 introduced the paper money (cf. above, p. 139).

him. But often somebody broke a leg in the process. In Yezd,[59] for instance, the fact was that anybody walking through the villages of the province would meet no one at all from whom he could have asked the way. For the inhabitants had agreed, that, if anybody approached from afar, at some sign they would without exception hide in the irrigation ditches or in the sand. Any landowner who owned property in Yezd, and went to inspect it, found none of his tenants in any of the villages from whom he could have inquired about the position or the state of his gardens.

In most cities, people had altered the way into their houses, putting them underground and making them as twisted as possible, in order to deter the state messengers from billeting themselves on them. (250) Even so messengers and their servants took liberties in people's houses. In Yezd, in the year 695/1296, ... and his mother took lodgings in the house of an Imām and remained for four months. After their departure, the city valuers came and estimated that the house, which previously had had a value of fifty thousand dinars, now commanded a value of no more than two thousand dinars. The doors that had been particularly delightful had been used for firewood. Gardens that through many years of toil had been made to flourish were destroyed in one day by the messengers allowing their animals to graze there (251). If, by chance, a canal ran through the garden, and a donkey or horse fell into it, the owner of the garden had to pay damages, and this was also the case, if there was a breach in the wall through which the animal escaped. The attendants of the state messengers tore down the garden walls, and in winter burnt the fruit trees for firewood. If such a tree was particularly straight, the governors or potentates demanded that it be felled in order that lances be made from it.

In 1292, one of the landowners went to a large village in order to receive some of the harvest from his property there. In spite of all his efforts, he did not meet any tenant for three days; on the other hand, seventeen tax collectors sat in the middle of the village. They had strung up with ropes a field guard and two peasants whom they had seized in the field, and were beating them to make them disclose the whereabouts of the others, and to provide food. But it was to no avail. All these collectors and their servants de-

---

[59] Town in south east Persia.

manded money of all kinds, wine[60] and girls, and from this their other impositions can easily be imagined.

In view of all this, the Ilkhan Ghāzān introduced well thought out measures for the suppression of such high-handed methods, saw to it that, where necessary, punishment was severe, and laid down precisely the level of taxation.

(255) With all these measures, prosperity was restored, those who had left their homes returned of their own free will, and the finances of all provinces nowadays flow more freely than even the output of the Imperial Mint. Two or three times each year, tax revenue flows into the crown treasury without delay. Nobody has been required to pay a single penny, a load of chopped straw or grain, a ram, wine or a chicken by way of 'extras' of various kinds. The treasury is never empty, in spite of the enormous presents which Ghāzān gives to the army and the emirs within a given year, presents bigger than those handed out by previous rulers over five years. Accordingly, the (256) administration too is never short of funds. At present the administrators of finance in the high yielding provinces are still holding sums of money which they have not yet handed over [because the Divan has had no need of them]. The whole of last year's harvest is still in the granaries, and the grain need not be sold compulsorily to the people, nor is there any need to sell the grain year after year, immediately after the harvest, let alone to use the unripe corn as had often been the case before. Now the Divan has always one year's grain in store.

Ghāzān issued a *yarlgh* to all the competent authorities regarding the new tax regulations, ordering the employment of reliable officials and the compilation of tax schedules, and laying down the dates for payments. It was required that this order should be made known everywhere.

4. State Messengers

(270) There came a time when princesses, princes, courtiers, emirs of ten thousand, of a thousand and of a hundred men, the commanders of provinces, the falcon keepers, panther keepers, equerries, armorers, superintendents of the imperial kitchens and

---

[60] The enjoyment of which is, of course, forbidden to Muslims.

other groups of persons, sent *ilchi*s (state messengers) about any matter large or small to the provinces and—for any reason—even to the Mongol nomadic settlements. It had become customary for the people in the provinces to send their sons to the feudal estates, to princesses, princes, and emirs and to accept in return only small sums [of money]; the fathers usually owned land and movable chattels and were involved in much business and many lawsuits [thanks to being protected by their sons' benefactors!]. Every one of these [fathers] dragged in state messengers and in this way brought his interests to a successful outcome. When anybody died and the heirs were not satisfied with their shares, they applied for the patronage of some prominent person, and saddled each other with state messengers they sent.

(271) Their numbers increased to such an extent, that even if fifty thousand mounts had been stationed at each mail stage, they would not have been enough. All the herds of the Mongols were used for mounts. Then the messengers began quarreling among themselves; thieves exploited the situation for their own purposes, posing as messengers themselves, and waylaying those who were smaller, taking their horses and *yarlıgh*s and *paiza*s from them, and once they had these, cheerfully plundered caravans. The state messengers not only required horses and food, they also robbed the people of turbans, clothes, and other possessions. While on their travels they sold the excess from the food they had requisitioned with such skill and craftiness that they even outshone the Chinese and Indian merchants. They tormented, flogged, hanged, and tortured people in every way so that it was small wonder that cultivation declined and the peasants became preoccupied with protecting their possessions against robbery. The pretentious messengers brought themselves into disrepute with the (273) postmasters and governors, and consequently, if, once in a while, a messenger traveled on important and secret state business, he was considered to be on a par with those rascals, and therefore held in ill repute. In consequence his journey took two or three times as long as expected, since he was given thin horses or no horses at all at the stage posts etc. Even if there were as many as fifty horses assigned to a stage post, there would still not be found two well-fed ones among them for the express messenger to mount. The money intended for the posthouses was largely kept by the governors for

their own purposes, and the customs and excise which are the most free flowing sources of revenue to the state were largely used up in covering the expenses of the state messengers. Even then it was insufficient. The governors made out drafts, and then made their escape. If this was still not enough the customs and excise officials went into hiding, the messengers started fighting among themselves and the strongest of them pocketed the tax yield. The riffraff attaching themselves to the messengers numbered up to two hundred or even three hundred men on horseback, in the case of messengers traveling with simple orders; some of the more renowned ones had up to five hundred or a thousand men on horseback with them. At the end of the year all these messengers returned to court without having achieved anything but the squandering of enormous amounts in expenses.

These conditions were gradually reformed by Ghāzān.

5. Safety on the Highways

(277) At one time there were vast numbers of robbers about, Mongols, Tajiks,[61] Kurds, Lurs, and Shuls,[62] as well as escaped slaves and ruffians from the cities. Occasionally peasants and individual settlers combined with them and acted as their guides. They had spies in all the cities so that they knew in good time about any caravan due to depart. Some of these robbers were famous for their bravery (278), and if they fell into the hands of any tribe, they were spared in view of their bravery and courageousness. In the event of an ambush it used to be the rule for caravans, messengers and individual travelers to combine instantly to fight against the robbers; but now this was no longer the case. The robbers made it their principle to rob only people above a certain degree of wealth; in this way the poorer people were separated from the others who now became an easy prey. In many villages the robbers had friends among the notables, and in the cities among the merchants who sold the stolen cloths for them; occasionally the robbers stayed a month with them and together they ran through the stolen money with reckless abandon.

[61] Apparently meaning the Persians (the use of the name varies in the course of development).
[62] Three west Iranian tribes.

(279) Others confined their activity to plundering the travelers and holding up caravans on the pretext that there were thieves among them, and thus signaling their presence to the robbers. If an attack was made, they did not chase after the robbers, and generally travelers were less afraid of the robbers than of the protectors of the highways, since the former robbed them only occasionally, but the latter did so constantly, whenever they rested.

Ghāzān Khan remedied the situation by employing reliable gendarmes and displaying their numbers on public notice boards.
Further paragraphs deal with coinage, the supervision of weights and measures and the regulation of the issue of public documents.

6. Soldiers' Pay

(300) At one time, Mongol troops as a rule received neither wages nor salaries nor fief. As long as the old traditions continued among them, every year the whole army collected the *qopchur* on horses, sheep, cattle, felt, and furs for the benefit of the army camps and the soldiers without means. Later, under the Ilkhan[63] certain provisions (301) were made available to those troops near [the court], and as time went by Ghāzān Khan spent considerable sums on this. These provision quotas were drafted on the provinces, and the administrators of finance cheated the Mongols when fulfilling them. At the same time they oppressed the provinces and imposed expenses on them on the pretext of collecting provisions by demanding horses, feed and foodstuff. As a result, the peasants on whom the provision quotas were drawn were ruined, and in addition great inconvenience was caused by the collection on the part of the governors and administrators of finance. In spite of this the provisions reaching the troops were not at all plentiful, partly because the administrators of finance were malevolent, partly because the intendants were dilatory, partly because the court secretaries responsible for the provisions failed to make out the drafts in time. The troops waited in vain for the supplies to be collected, while the provisioners bought [the grain] at half the price and kept it for themselves, leaving the soldiers with the drafts on their hands. For this reason there were constant quarrels

[63] The Mongol rulers of Persia.

between them and the provisioners, and they complained to the ruler. Ghāzān Khan allowed this to go on for about four or five years. He ordered that in each province at the time of the harvest, whether summer or winter, the grain was to be put into stores which were to be made over to the commander of the province. On the delivery of the draft, issue was to be made directly from the store; the intendants were neither to exact any premium nor were they to demand any provisions or payments for themselves. This was the basis on which the drafts were issued. Some also received cash from the state treasury, so that within three or four years nobody could say that any ration of foodstuffs was outstanding with the Divan.

A decree was issued making regulations to this effect.

7. Measures against Usury

(313) At the time of Abaqa Khan (1265–82), who enjoyed widespread fame as a just ruler, the people lived in peace. He kept to the guiding rules and laws of his father Hülägü. At that time some merchants brought to Abaqa Khan from their own stocks a selection of armaments [such as armor for men and horses together with other war material], and in addition some good horses. They were paid the amount due by the armament officers and made a good profit in the process. Others, envious at seeing this, but possessing no capital of their own, borrowed some against interest. They then acquired goods, and obtained from the armament officers receipts which they presented at the Divan, receiving there drafts and then collecting on these. In this way many who previously were altogether without possessions soon acquired wealth, rode on Arab horses and mules and such like.

(314) People began to wonder about it, and made inquiries since they knew their previous status. Several thousands, Muslims and Jews, who were jobbing-tailors and hawkers by trade, that is, individuals who sold torn sacks, coriander, and haberdashery, from bags which they carried over their shoulder, together with weavers and others who had never had a penny to call their own nor enough bread to eat their fill, now borrowed money. They did not, however, use it to buy weapons and horses, but for various clothes

and similar things, and to bribe the emirs mentioned above, who issued them with false receipts, for instance, for a thousand weapons of a specific type, for so many horses and the like. They took these receipts to the secretaries, who, although they saw through all this, accepted inducements to keep silent, and issued drafts for cash and on the provinces. When some had been success- ful this way, others cheerfully indulged in the business of money- lending, and a vast number lent dirhems, dinars, gold, robes, various objects and other articles desired by the people. Beggars who previously would have been satisfied with ten tomans, that is, a hundred thousand dinars, were no longer satisfied with a hundred tomans. Criminals who now called themselves merchants and dealers in armaments went to such lengths that they were willing to take into their houses anyone who could write just a little Mongolian, so that he should write out receipts for them according to their wishes, and forge as required the signature of any emir. They took these to the secretaries at the Divan, with whom there was an understanding that for each toman so many dinars had to be paid for them to keep silent.

(315) They soon had so many receipts that their redemption would have required more than the funds of the whole world. Moreover, each one of this black fraternity had managed not only to bribe the emirs to silence, but also to ingratiate themselves with some emir or princess in such a way that there was a close under- standing between them. When eventually the matter had got completely out of hand, the Minister of Finance . . . [who had died in the meantime] endeavored to put a stop to it. He assembled the fraternity and said to them: 'The goods you demand are not avail- able in the whole world, and I have noticed that you have only covered expenses. This time I am willing to come in on your business, and for every thousand dinars at nominal value, I shall obtain from the Pādishāh[64] two hundred which we will share be- tween us.' Since for every thousand dinars they had not even had expenses of half a dinar, everybody agreed. When Jowainī[65] had obtained the approval of the emirs, he submitted to the Pādishāh that for each ten tomans [in the form of drafts] he intended to pay eight tomans from the tax revenue and draw only two tomans on the provinces and in this way to pay the debt to the moneylenders.

[64] Ruler.   [65] The minister.

The ruler greatly approved of this. (316) The Minister of Finance collected their *yarlıgh*s, gave to each of them for every ten tomans a draft for two tomans on a fertile region, and since half of this was his share, he gave them for their share goods that were worth less than a quarter, and kept the resulting cash himself. When these villains demanded new advances which they intended to pay back once their goods had been sold, the moneylenders would not lend any more, because they could entertain no hope of seeing their capital or interest back. But now that they learned that the money had arrived for the old drafts, and they heard about the deal with the Minister of Finance, they were delighted once more to lend the scoundrels money and goods against interest. The latter became impudent again and began once more to forge receipts in their own houses; they took them to the secretaries and received either *yarlıgh*s or drafts. The Minister of Finance despaired. Among this riffraff was a Jewish jobbing tailor who at the time of Hülägü had taken refuge in the Mongol camp. Now he gathered together a number of Mongols and went at their head to the Minister of Finance to demand the money for the drafts. The Minister asked the Jew how high his demand was. The Jew submitted to him *yarlıgh*s and drafts amounting to five thousand tomans. The Minister of Finance was helpless in the face of such abuse. The people, however, were ruined as a result of the borrowing.

(317) Then these scoundrels negotiated with their lending partners, arguing that they were in possession of *yarlıgh*s marked with the seal and cheques marked with the stamp [of the Divan] relating to certain taxes and cash levies on the Imperial provinces. They said they were willing to share these with the moneylenders, and proposed that each party should entrust a messenger of the Princess X or the Prince Y with the collection. The greed for money got the better of them, and the deal was clinched. But in order to equip the messenger they needed money again, and so the scoundrels sold their landed property. Most of them went with the state messengers into the provinces, but were unable to collect anything, and so they went bankrupt with large debts from borrowing. Things went on in this way under the rule of Aḥmad (1282–4), Arghūn Khan (1284–91), and Gaikhātū (1291–5), and all the time they chased after the collection of their drafts, forced themselves as messengers on the princesses, princes, and emirs,

traveled to the provinces, and ate up any returns through their expenses and salaries. The provincial governors in their greed were anxious to sell an item worth ten dinars for thirty or even forty and to receive the cash value for it from the state treasury. So they passed on to the messengers jewel-studded belts, pearls, and other precious things, priced very high. The messengers never dreamt of delivering these objects to the state treasury, however, but embezzled them, and sold them at low prices, or pawned them cheaply at a pawnshop. As a consequence of these swindles, jewelery prices dropped to such an extent that there was no longer a market for jewels. In spite of this the messengers did not manage to collect anything worth mentioning, and even that went on their keep. In the end the criminal (318) partners in the trading associations and their business partners (the moneylenders) were stricken by hunger and nakedness; the state treasure was squandered until Ghāzān took over as ruler and strictly prohibited any money-lending against interest. The nightmare of the unbacked cheques and drafts came to an end. Everybody follows his trade again, and once more there is an obvious difference between the rich and the beggars.

Another evil that had existed was this: The people who had lent money at that time were mainly Mongols and Uighurs. Since in the end the borrowers were all unable to pay, they became with their wives and children debt slaves to them. It was not until Ghāzān Khan became the ruler that this oppression of the Muslims was abolished.

Regulation of money matters; prohibition of usury.
Further paragraphs deal with the giving of dowries, public buildings, the drinking of wine and the provision of the court with food.

8. Allowances for the Princesses and the Ordus

(329) At the time of Hülägü and Abaqa (together 1255–82) the needs of the princesses and their courts were satisfied in the Mongolian manner, and expenditure and allowances were moderate. Whenever an enemy province yielded up booty (330), they received a share. Everyone owned a few estates which brought in a little money, and perhaps somebody gave presents. They also

owned a few herds which provided them with young animals and other supplies, so that they had sufficient. Toward the end of Abaqa's reign they received small allowances. Under Arghūn a certain sum was set aside for each court and drawn on the provinces. Then, when their messengers and pageboys went to collect the money, the governors, under the pretexts so often described above, gave them nothing, and they busied themselves with acquiring bonuses and 'presents'. If they did manage to collect something, the greater part got into the wrong hands on the journey and finally the administrative officers embezzled as much as they could. The provisioning of the courts can easily be imagined from all this. Under Gaikhātū (1291–5), as well, it was much the same. During the reign of Ghāzān Khan, quarrels broke out between the pages of the hordes;[66] lawsuits arose in consequence, and part of the taxes remained uncollected in the provinces and the rest was squandered by the pageboys. He therefore ordered warnings to be issued to some of them; others he dismissed.

Regulations for the provisioning of the courts.

9. Regulating the Treasury

(331) Thus far it had not been the custom to keep accounts of the treasures of the Mongol rulers with the proper recording of receipts and expenditure. Just a few treasurers had been appointed who collectively received everything added to the treasure and in the same way spent collectively. When there was nothing left, they said so. This treasure was guarded by officials, who carried around (332) their burden, picking it up and putting it down, and everything was extremely disorderly so that they did not even have a tent for the purpose, but put down the treasures in the open, and covered them with felts. This gives some idea of the whole organization. Every time a treasure was brought along, emirs and friends of the treasurers turned up and demanded a share, and the treasurers gave them something according to their rank. Minor officials came along too and everyone brought something to eat and to drink, and soon they, too, demanded something. The treasurers took counsel among themselves, and gave them something. Every

[66] Individual royal households.

guard received something as well. On top of all this, the treasurers awarded shares to one another, took counsel with one another, and everyone of them took something home. In this way, every year, eight tenths of these treasures were squandered, and only two were spent according to the instructions of the Pādishāh. Once the governors had got wind of all this, they demanded bribes in the form of receipts for twice the amounts, whenever they supplied sums to the treasury, and supplied less accordingly, and that meager amount was misappropriated in the way described. In view of this, it seemed a good idea to prevail upon the guards to keep a strict watch. Anybody stealing a garment or some other article from the treasure was to be arrested. But this happened only once every few years, since their own interests were involved.

Ghāzān introduced a new order [by setting up treasure houses which were strictly guarded; moreover bookkeeping was introduced].

Further paragraphs concern themselves with the obtaining of weapons, the state herds, and the hunting personnel.

10. Provision of Draft Animals in the Empire

(346) Earlier the finance administration of the provinces had kept on reporting that most of the provinces were devastated, the peasants were impoverished and lacked the resources to farm the land even with cattle and seeds so that a lot of land with irrigation potential was lying fallow. Nobody listened to their words or did anything about it. Furthermore, at the time of high prices, the peasants used the small quantities of grain of which the amount had been decided in former times, and which had been issued by the Divan, for making bread rather than as seed, so that the Divan as well as the peasants suffered loss.

Ghāzān Khan ordered that every governor and tax farmer should set aside from the sum total of his taxes a certain amount as purchase price for working animals, seeds and agricultural requirements, against documentary evidence [receipts?], so that in these provinces there should be draft animals for work, and farming should be encouraged. Ghāzān Khan said that no doubt the peasants would draw twice, even three times the benefit from the soil. But since through these allocations the governors would incur higher expenditure, the peasants would have to deliver a third of the harvest to them, or a quarter; the peasants should be allowed to keep whatever they produced in excess of this, so that they would make greater efforts in their farming. Once the farms [of the people concerned] had prospered for two or three years, they would have to deliver a quarter to the state treasury in repayment of the cash amounts [which had been advanced to them?]. Then this was to be inserted in the regulations regarding the collection of taxes.

(347) Now cultivation increased tremendously. In areas where it had been usual for the Divan to contribute grain as seeds, but where the administrative officers had misappropriated it and sold it, Ghāzān Khan ordered that seed corn should again be distributed from the state treasures.

The procurement of cattle and the breaking of new land.

11. Providing Accommodation for State Messengers

(356) Previously it was usual at any one time for a hundred, or even two hundred, state messengers (ilchis) to be lodged in people's houses in every city. In addition to these there were many others who on arrival in the city were compulsorily billeted in people's houses by the commander, as a favor. It was the job of the charhiyān when a messenger arrived to ride ahead in a body, and to go to the door of some house where the messenger was to be lodged, for which service they expected a consideration. They liked to take messengers to people to whom (357) they wanted to do harm, so that in future they would stand in fear of them. They requisitioned on behalf of the state messengers rugs, sleeping attire, kettles, and other implements from the houses of these people, and usually the messengers and their men kept these things, or the billeting organizers did not return them to the owners under the pretense that they had been taken away by the messengers.

Since the messengers and commanders always lodged in the best houses, nobody dared any longer to build a house well. The buildings that were erected were made to appear like mausoleums, or they were described as monastic cells or theological colleges, but still it was of no avail. Many people made their doors unusable, or hid a barely accessible entrance under the ground. The messengers used to hand their animals to the billeting organizers who sent somebody to tear down people's garden walls in order to provide for the animals there. Whenever one messenger (358) packed up, another was already approaching. In any quarter where a messenger was billeted, the inhabitants suffered injury and hardship; the servants of the messengers broke into neighboring houses by the roofs and through the doors, taking whatever they found and shooting arrows at pigeons and chickens, frequently hitting children.

Ghāzān sharply reduced the abuses of the messenger system. Ghāzān's legislation did not last beyond his death—he died in 1304 at the age of only 31 years. The old conditions, described above, soon prevailed again and a generation later brought about the complete ruin of the Mongol Empire in Persia.

(After Rashīd ad-Dīn, *Geschichte Ġāzān Ḫans*, ed. Jahn, translated into German by W. Hinz, pp. 182–358.)

IV

THE MONGOL KHANS IN CHINA

A. FROM AN ORIENTAL SOURCE

1. A Description in the Court Style of the Great Khan and Chinese Emperor, Qubilai (1259–94)

Although it is a full year's journey from the borders of this ocean [the Chinese] to the center of the empire which is the prop of heaven and to the pasture where fortune always walks with joy, namely to the residence of the just Pādishāh and Khāqān, the praises of his monuments and his laws, of his justice and his wit, of his good intentions and of the abilities with which he was so richly adorned, issuing from the mouths of trustworthy men and meritorious merchants have resounded in this country in such a way that a catalog of these glorious achievements and a small fraction of this ruler's power eclipses the monuments of the Roman Caesars and the Persian Chosroes, of the Chinese Emperors and the Arab Kings, of the Rulers of the Yemen, of the Rajahs of India, of the Sassanid and Būyid Kings, as well as those of the Seljuk Sultans. [Half verse]: *The lesser gives proof of the greater.*

Here will be summarized just a few of his characteristic habits and qualities from which may be gathered how unequaled was his bravery and how abundant was his fortune as a ruler. One thing which demonstrates his wit and intelligence is the fact that he was on intimate terms with men of merit and masters of science, that he liked their company and welcomed them more than any other set of people, that in place of the Uighur script he worked out and organized [for the Mongolian language] a new script, the shape of which is pleasing to the heart like the delicate lines of the down on the lip of a beautiful woman, which appeals to the eye and to the inner light.[1] In this script, he issued orders to all countries, and he

[1] The so-called 'Mongol square script'.

made it famous like the reputation of his justice. He had an innate sense for administering the laws of justice, and much as he was accustomed ceaselessly and constantly to the disposal of resources and the dispensing of gifts, . . . he was nevertheless loath to squander them. He wrote to the nobles in the various countries and to the assistants of majesty: How can it be reasonable to give a thousand *balish*[2] to one man while another hangs himself in despair[3] and who can approve of this? Whoever provides against all expectation more than is required, is bound to lack what is required in the event of real need. This was a retrospective allusion to Ögädäi Khāqān and his thoughtless prodigality and generosity.

With this in mind he laid down a rule which sums up the general principles of monarchical justice, which encompasses the universal order and governs the existence of the sons of men, which is approved and justified by reason as well as by tradition and adorns the latter as the light of the eye adorns the eyeball.

. . . [verse]. If an enlightened and rational man considers this sentiment, reason will tell him that money can only satisfy a few people. . . . [Arabic half verse]. Even if one possessed the treasures of Qārūn, the empire of Solomon and the life-span of Noah, even then, notwithstanding the duration of this time and the exercise of such power, such a crowd of the needy and the petitioners from all nations would come together, that most of them would be left lamenting and without comfort; and assuming the impossible, that grace could be bestowed and benefits distributed so as to reach everybody, it would still be difficult to satisfy human greed and not easy to fulfill the wishes of all who pleaded. The distribution of the different types of food has to be taken care of, because, although they have been laid down from the beginning of time, and each type of food tends to be governed by the accidents of the market and by skill, the smug rich man still flaunts the ring of the Koranic verse: *Man is ungrateful to his Lord;*[4] and the poor man with his heart in darkness drags along the fetters of the text: *Little is needed to turn poverty into faithlessness.*

But through the spread of justice which contains within itself all the benefits of religion and of the state, and which in no way

[2] A gold coin.
[3] . . . in desperation, tears his breast to shreds with his own hands.
[4] Koran 100:6 Cairo/Flügel.

fails to satisfy the needs of life and property, there shines forth suddenly in bridal splendor the rule of the world, in a phrase: *Through justice heaven and earth exist* and the blessed memory of it carries on through times to come, into eternity.

Another occasion that deserves favorable mention, and provides a wondrously rare example of the proliferation of his many good deeds, is that recorded in the following: One day in the heat of battle one of his most honored sons together with a great number of individuals was separated from the army . . . [Persian double verse]. Their way led them through a village belonging to Beshbalıgh, where he dismounted for a short while so as to let the mounts and other horses rest and take a breather. With all the prancing and dancing of the horses the fire of the craving for nourishment blazed up in flames on the hearth of the stomach, as the verse says: *The bodies we gave them could not dispense with food.*[5] He ordered that the villagers should be required to provide as refreshment a sheep for food and a vessel of wine for a drink, and that neither more nor less should be imposed on them. In the following year a few from this group, who had ridden with the prince, passed through the place which was the seat of privileged merchants, and once again demanded a sheep and a vessel of wine. The villagers, however, went straight to the just Khāqān, and reported to him in every detail how the first and the second demand for food had come about, and how, when these people returned, this unusual ritual had been repeated. 'We are afraid', they said, 'that, as the days go by, this imposition will be regarded as a traditional custom and that somebody else will turn it into an order.' The Khāqān, enraged, and with his forehead, bright as the sun, furrowed by the lines of indignation, called for the prince and scolded him with uncouth words: 'You were the first to start this objectionable practice: *The one who starts bears the greater blame; the one who follows may be judged more lightly.* When the succession to the Khanate falls to you, and it pleases the divine ruler of destiny to entrust you with the business of the Khanate, if you are already breaking the law and breaching the contract so as to give cause for complaint to your subjects who are a trust from the creator, the highest, you will steer the government along its course, and

[5] Koran 21:8 Cairo/Flügel. (R. Bell adjusted from R. Paret: 'We have not made them with bodies which could dispense with food.')

see to the provision of food for your subjects, in this same bad way. Until you have three times saved your honor with a simple [quiet] countenance in battle, and have burnished the smooth and radiant mirror of the heart clean from the rust of wickedness, you shall not glance at Our Face which is the mirror of Alexander [not appear before my eyes].' The prince asked forgiveness, and took it upon himself to pitch the tent of his body in the fight against the rebels. The just Khāqān of lofty enterprise ordered that presents be given to the offended people; in order to put their minds at rest, and to give them assurance regarding their position he handed them a letter. They used as coloring for their eyes the dust from the edge of the tent which is the refuge of the world, which is the meeting place of every new arrival and the [sheep's] pen of happiness and good fortune, and praying for the just Pādishāh's continued fortune, they returned.

(Waṣṣāf, *Geschichte Wassafs*, ed. Hammer, I, 37–40 = German trans. pp. 37–9)[6].

2. *The Conquest of the Island of Java*

Among the conquests [of Qubilai] was the island of Mol Java [= Java] in India in the year 1292 (691 H.). . . . An army . . . [Persian hemistich] moved with arms and armor, with dancing horses and with lances [Arab hemistich]: *On boats which rode the waves sailing* [across the sea]. When they had landed on the elected coast they gained possession of the island which is 200 parasangs[7] in length and 120 parasangs in breadth through spreading fear of the fury of their sword. . . . The local governor Shri Rāma hastened to show with [gifts of] precious objects and rarities his submission to the majesty. His majesty did not permit that certain death should exercise his power here, but put his [the governor's] son on the steps of the high throne. He bestowed on him a ceremonial dress

---

[6] The German translation by Joseph, Freiherr von Hammer-Purgstall (1774–1856), captures the author's characteristically flowery style to perfection. Hammer also succeeded well in his imitation of the prose rhyme frequently used in the original text. Much of this is inevitably lost in re-translation into English.

[7] Roughly 'hours of travel'.

of honor, and conferred on him much grace, and, against the payment of tribute and taxes in the shape of pearls and gold, he left the island in his hands [those of the governor's son]. In fact this place, surrounded by the sea, is full of movable and immovable wealth and blessed with treasure, and is one where it rains pearls, and gold and silver coin and goods of the most precious kind. The creative power of the Almighty has perfumed this place and its surroundings with the breath of aloe and of cloves; in the houses and in the districts the parrots cry in Arabic:

'I am a garden, whose glories and pleasures are envied by every paradise; from jealousy of my splendor the 'Omān coasts[8] weep pearls. The aloe . . . burns in the censer of my similes as wood on the altar of fire. In spring the turtledoves in their morning arbors sound recurring notes on the two-stringed lute and on the three-stringed guitar. My virtues vie with those of Eden, not just in what we obviously have in common, but in everything: The praises of my beauty are sung by the parrots as by eloquent orators. Thanks be to God for His grace; may He cover with the hem of His forgiveness the guilt of all sinners so long as books shall be rolled up and feet tread the earth.'

(Wāṣṣāf, ed. Hammer, I, 45 f. = German trans., p. 44.)

3. Peking (Khānbalıgh), the Residence of Qubilai

At other times and under other Khans the residence was Khānbalıgh [Turkish for 'Imperial City'; Marco Polo's Cambaluc]. When Qubilai's Khanate had reached the apogee of its power, at the moment when the sun stood at its noblest point, he extended this city as a residence, and built a four-walled city four parasangs square. You might have said that this number corresponded to that of his high-mindedness in the cabalistic calculating table. He called the city Taidu [Chinese for 'Great City']. He commanded that artists and craftsmen should be brought from all directions to this city. Because of the number of its inhabitants and the milling crowds, this city in a short time became a place of assembly resplendent and ornamented overall. On one side of this city he built the *qarshi*: that is what they call the throne of rule and khan-

[8] 'Om(m)ān in Arabia.

ship in their language. It was built from wood and planks, and was also square with each of its four sides four hundred paces long. This elysian structure was endowed with a cupola and windows, putting to shame the pinnacles of the celestial tabernacle, with solid pillars richly decorated and embellished with ornament. The floor was inlaid with jasper. Statues were set up and pictures painted, with both art and wit, radiating talismanic art. Archimedes would have been astonished and baffled by these delicate combinations and Euclidean inventions; the grills in front of the windows were made of gold and silver, and above the pinnacles of the canopy the moon in its three stations . . . trembles with jealousy. A quotation: 'The many-columned city of Iram, whose like has never been built in the whole land.'[9] Anybody who saw the creations in this place and the beauty of this treasure [Arabic double verse]: 'saw how Spring and the bejeweled fields, just as the hill and the mountain, bowed down.'

In this way, the business of the empire and the foundations of prosperity were organized; the opinions and thoughts of both the noble and the common people were turned toward obedience and devotion.

When his life had passed the flour-dusted ten [the sixties] and was bordering on seventy . . . [Arabic verse] he desired to raise his eldest son Jemkin even during his lifetime to the position of deputy and successor as ruler. He therefore consulted with the princes to find a place for him in the government of the various countries and to make room for him on the throne of the Khanate. . . .

(Waṣṣāf, ed. Hammer, I, 46 f; = German trans., p. 45.)

B. THROUGH EUROPEAN EYES

1. The Ruler

(167) Qubilai Khan [the Great Khan, 1259–94, who resided in China] is greater and more powerful than any of the others [the regional princes ruling at his side and under him]. For if all the

[9] Koran 89:7, 8 Cairo (=6, 7 Flügel).

other five were together they will not have so much power as this
Qubilai, for he inherited what the others had, and then obtained as
it were the rest of the world. . . . All the emperors of the world and
all the kings both of Christians and of Saracens also, if they were all
together, would not have so much power nor could they do so
much as this Qubilai Great Khan could do, who is lord of all the
Tatars of the world, both of those of the sunrising and of those of
the sunsetting, for all are his men and subject to him. And this
name Qā'ān means Emperor in our tongue. And I will show you
this his great power in its own place in this book quite clearly.

2. *Burial Customs*

All the great Khans and the great lords of the Tatars who are
descended from the line of their first Lord Chinggiz Khan are
carried for burial when they are dead to a very great mountain
which is called Altai [in Central Asia]; . . . if they die a good hundred days' marches away from that mountain, they must be carried
there to the said mountain for burial with the others, nor are they
willing to be buried in another place. . . . When the bodies of these
Great Khans of the Tatars are carried to that mountain to bury,
though they may be distant forty days' marches or more or less
(168) all the people whom they meet by the way by which the bodies
are carried are put to the edge of the sword by those who conduct
the said body. And they say thus to them when they kill them: 'Go
serve your lord in the other world!' For they have come to such
foolishness and the devil has so blinded them and surrounded
them with such madness that they believe truly that all those whom
they kill for this cause must go to accompany and to serve the
great lord [the dead Khan] in the other world. And they do the
same with the horses which they find on the road, and say that he
has so many horses in the other world. For when the lord dies
they kill all the best horses, camels and mules that are left that the
lord had. . . . When Möngkä the [fourth] Khan died more than
twenty thousand men were killed on the way, as I have told you,
all those who met the body when it was being carried by the horsemen. . . .

3. Herds

The Tatars commonly feed many flocks of cows, mares, and sheep, for which reason they never stay in one place, but retire to live in the winter in plains and hot places where they have grass in plenty . . . ; and in the summer they move themselves over to live in cold places in mountains and in valleys where they find water and woods and good pasture for keeping their beasts; and also for this cause, that where the place is cold flies are not found nor gnats and such-like creatures which annoy them and their beasts; and they go for two or three months ascending continually and grazing, for they would not have enough grass for the multitude of their beasts, feeding always in one place.

4. Dwellings

And they have their small houses like tents of rods of wood and cover them with felt; and they are round; and they always carry them with them on four-wheeled wagons wherever they go. For they have the wooden rods tied so well and orderly that they can fit them together like a pack and spread them, take them up, put them down, and carry them very easily where they please. . . . And every time that they stretch and set up their house they set it so that the door is always looking toward the south.[10]

5. Carts

They have, beside this, very beautiful carts with (169) only two wheels covered with black felt which is so good and so well pre-pared that if it rained all day on the cart water would soak nothing that was in the cart under that cover of felt. And they have them brought and drawn by horses and by oxen and sometimes by good camels. And on these carts they carry their wives and their children and all the things and food which they need. And in this way they go wherever they wish to go . . . . The Tatar ladies trade, buy, and sell, and do all the work that is needed for their lords and family and for themselves. In expense they are not burdensome to

[10] The alignment toward the south is a characteristic of the Mongols and other Central Asian peoples.

their husbands, and the reason is that they make much gain by their own work. They are also very provident in managing the family and are very careful in preparing food, and do all the other duties of the house with great diligence. And so their husbands leave all the care of the house to their wives. For the men trouble themselves with nothing at all but with hunting and with feats of battle and of war and with hawking and with falcons and with goshawks, like gentlemen [in the West], and in this they take great delight. They have the best falcons in the world, and likewise dogs. They live only on flesh and on milk and on game, the flesh of all wild animals which they take in their country, and also they eat certain little animals which are like rabbits, which with us are called Pharaoh's rats, which are there in great abundance in the midst of the plains below and everywhere. They eat even flesh of horses and of dogs and of mares and oxen and camels, provided that they are fat, and gladly drink camel and mare's milk, and in general they eat of all flesh of other animals clean and unclean.

6. Marriage

They keep themselves so that for nothing in the world would the one touch the wife of the other, for if it happen that a man were taken they hold it for an evil thing and vile exceedingly. And the loyalty of the husbands toward the wives is a wonderful thing, and a very noble thing the virtue of those women who if they are ten, or twenty, a peace and inestimable unity is among them, nor is it ever heard that they say an evil word, but all are intent and anxious [as has been said] over the trade, that is, the selling and buying, and things belonging to their occupations, the life of the house and the care of the family and of the children, who are common between them. For in my judgment they are those women who most in the world deserve to be commended by all for their very great virtue; and they are all the more worthy of very well-earned praise for virtue and chastity because the men are allowed to be able to take as many wives as they please, to the very great confusion of the Christian women (I mean in these our parts—Italy). For when one man has only one wife, in which marriages there ought to be a most singular faith and chastity, or

[else] confusion of so great a sacrament of marriage, I am ashamed (170) when I look at the unfaithfulness of the Christian women, [and call] those happy who being a hundred wives to one husband keep [their virtue] to their own most worthy praise, to the very great shame of all the other women in the world. . . . Nor would a woman be found false to her husband, and they are very hardworking women and take great pains to do the necessary duties of the household very well.

The marriages are done in this way. For each can take according to their custom as many wives as he likes, up to a hundred if he has the power to be able to maintain them; and the men give the dowries to the wives and to the mother of their wife to obtain them, nor does the wife give anything to the man for dowry when she is married. But you may know too that they always hold the first of their wives for more genuine and for better than the others, and likewise the children who are born of her. And they have more sons than all the other people in the world have because they have so many wives as I have told you, and it is a marvel how many children one man has, I mean those who have the power to keep many wives. They take their cousins[11] for wife, and what is more, if the father dies his eldest son takes to wife the wife of his father, if she is not his mother, and all the women who are left by the father except his mother and sisters. He takes also the wife of his own brother[12] if he dies. And when they take a wife they make very great weddings and great gathering of people.

7. Religion

. . . [The Mongols] say that there is the high, sublime, and heavenly God of whom every day with censer and incense they ask nothing else but good understanding and health. For they worship idols, and they have one of their gods whom they call Natigai, and they say that that is a terrestrial god or god of the land who protects and cares for their wives and their sons and their cattle and their corn. And they do him great reverence and great honor, for

[11] Which is, of course, prohibited by Canonic law; that is why Marco Polo mentions it.

[12] The levirate marriage, as was also demanded, for instance, of the ancient Jews.

each keeps him in an honorable place in his house. For they make this god of felt and of other cloth and they keep him in their houses; and they believe that this god of theirs has a wife and sons, and so they make other little images and say they are his sons. And the wife of this god they put on the left side and the sons in front, who seem to be doing him reverence. . . . And when they come to eat breakfast or supper, first they take some of the fat flesh and anoint the mouth of that god and also of his wife and of his sons; (171) and then they take some broth or water in which the flesh is cooked to wash their mouth and sprinkle it in their honor outside the door of their house or room, where that god of theirs stands, to the other spirits. And when they have done this they say that their god and his family have had their share. And after this they eat and drink the rest. . . . They drink mare's milk. But I tell you too that they have learnt to prepare it in such a way that it is like white wine; and it is very good to drink and they call it in their tongue 'qumys'.

8. Clothes

For the rich men and nobles wear cloth of gold and cloth of silk and under the outer garments rich furs of sable and ermine and vair and of fox . . . ; and all their trappings and fur-lined robes are very beautiful and of great value.

9. Weapons

Their arms are bows and arrows and very good swords and clubs studded with iron, and some lances and axes, but they avail themselves of bows more than of any other thing for they are exceedingly good archers, the best in the world, and depend much from childhood upon arrows. And on their backs they wear armor made of buffalo hide and of other animals very thick, and they are of boiled hides which are very hard and strong. They are good men and victorious in battle and mightily valiant and they are very furious, and have little care for their life, which they put to every risk without any regard. They are very cruel men . . . . When the army goes out for war . . . , more readily and bravely than the rest of the world do they submit to hardships, and often when he has need he will go or will stay a whole month without carrying any common food except that he will live on the milk of a mare and will eat of the flesh of the chase which they take with their bows. And his horse will graze on the simple grass that he shall find in the fields by the way so that he need not carry barley and other grain or hay or straw. And they are very obedient to their lord and I tell you that when there is need they stay two days and two nights on horseback without dismounting, and he stays all the night on horseback with all his arms and sleeps on horseback, and the horse will go grazing all the time on the grass wherever it may be found. And they are those people who most in the world bear work and great hardship and wish least expense, and are content with little food . . . and are for this reason suited best to conquer cities and lands and kingdoms. . . . When a lord of the Tatars (172) goes to war he takes with him an army of a hundred thousand horsemen. . . . He arranges his men in this way. He makes a chief to every ten, and to every hundred, and to every thousand, and to every ten thousand, so that the chief lord he has to take counsel with only ten men, the captains of ten thousand men, who are heads of a hundred thousand; and he who is lord of ten thousand men has only to do with ten men; and he who is lord of a thousand men has only to do with ten; and likewise he who is lord of a hundred has only to do with ten. Thus as you have heard each answers to his chief . . . [and each is answerable for ten men only].

. . . [Everybody's responsibilities are precisely defined.] . . . Each is obedient to that which is commanded them more than any people in the world. . . . (173) And when the lord with the troops goes to do anything, to get cities or kingdoms, whether they are on a plain or in mountains and valleys, they always send two hundred men or more two days marches before for spies to spy out the roads and the country, and he leaves as many also behind and at the sides, that is so that they have outposts in four directions. . . . When they go a long way to war they carry nothing of kit, especially of those things which are needed for sleeping.

10. Food

They live at most times on milk [as has been said], and of horses and mares there are about eighteen for each man, and when any horse is tired by the road another is taken in exchange. For they carry no food but one or two bags of leather in which they put their milk which they drink, and they carry each a small *pignate*, that is an earthen pot, in which they cook their meat. But if they had not this, when they find some animal they kill it and take out the belly and empty it and then fill it with water, and then put it over the fire and let it cook; and when it is cooked they eat the flesh, cauldron and all.

And they carry with them also a small tent of felt in which they stay for the rain. . . . Sometimes when there is need and the press of some enterprise requires that they go a great way in haste, they ride quite ten days' marches without eating any cooked food and without lighting fire, in case their journey may chance to be delayed by cooking of food . . . but often, for want of wine or water, they live on the blood of their horses; for each pricks the vein of his horse and puts his mouth to the vein and drinks of the blood till he is satisfied. And again they carry [dried] blood with them, and when they wish to eat they take some water and put some of it in the water and leave it to dissolve, and then they drink it. And in the same way they have their dried mare's milk too which is solid like paste. And it is dried in this way. They make the milk boil, and then the cream which floats on top is put in another vessel, and of that butter is made. . . . Then the milk is put in the sun, and so it is dried. And when they go to war they carry about ten pounds of this milk. And in the morning they take some of that milk [each man takes half a pound of it] and put it in a little leather flask . . . with water and stir it with a stick and carry it until that milk in the flask is dissolved being beaten up and made like syrup as they ride, and then they drink it when a convenient time comes, and this is their breakfast.

(174) There follow details about their tactics; mass attack; when necessary, pretense of flight. The skill of their horses; rain of arrows.

Now [i.e., toward the end of the thirteenth century] the Mongols have forsaken some of these customs, for those who frequent China keep themselves very greatly to the ways and to the manner and to the customs of the idolaters [i.e., the inhabitants in general] of those regions and have very much left their law; and those who frequent the Levant keep themselves very much (175) in the manner of Saracens and hold the faith and laws of Muhammad.

11. Justice

And they maintain justice and judgment in such a way as I shall now describe to you. For a murderer there is no ransom. Indeed if a man strikes with steel or with a sword, whether he hits or not, or threatens one, he loses his hand. He who wounds must receive a like wound from the wounded. It is true that when a man has taken some little thing for which he ought not to die, they condemn him to be beaten. There is given him by the government at least seven blows with a rod or, if he has stolen two things, seventeen blows, or if three things twenty-seven blows or thirty-seven or forty-seven, and in this way it goes up sometimes to a hundred and seven, always increasing by ten blows for each thing which is stolen, according to what he has taken and the measure of the crime. And many of them die of this beating. And if a man steals 15 oxen so that it would come to exceed 107 blows [or] a horse or other thing, for which he ought to lose life he is cut in two with a sword and killed; so, truly, that if he who steals can pay and will give nine times as much as the value of that which he has stolen he escapes from death. . . .

And the country is so secure that each lord or the other men who have animals in plenty, they have them marked with their seal stamped on the hair. . . . Then he lets them go safely to graze anywhere over the plains and over the mountains without a watchman; and if on their return they are mixed the one with the other, each man who finds them recognizes the owner's mark and immediately takes pains to inquire for him and quickly gives back his own to him whose mark is found. . . . But the flocks and small animals, the rams and the sheep and the goats they have indeed watched by men, without a stamp. Their flocks are all very large and fat and very fine beyond measure.

12. Marriages between Dead Children

. . . They make among themselves marriages of their dead children. You may know quite truly that when there are two men who,

the one having had a male child who is dead—and he may have
died as young as four years of age—and he inquires for another
man who may have had a female child suited to his son, and she
also may have died before being married, these two parents make
a marriage of these two at the age when the son would take a wife
if he were alive. For they give the dead girl to the dead boy for wife,
and they have documents made (176) about it in corroboration of
the dowry and marriage aforesaid. . . . Then a necromancer
throws this paper into the fire . . . and when they see the smoke
which goes into the air then they say that they go to their children
in the other world and announce this marriage to the dead, . . .
and that they, the dead boy and dead girl in the other world, hold
themselves as husband and wife. . . . And then they make a great
wedding feast and banquet, and of that food they scatter some of it
hither and thither . . . that the bride and bridegroom [in the other
world] may eat their share of that feast. And having made two
images, one in the form of the youth and the other in the form of
the maid, they put both of these images on a cart adorned as richly
as possible, and the carriages being drawn by horses they take
these two images with great festival and rejoicings through all the
land, and then conduct them to the fire and burn those two images,
and with great prayer and supplication to the gods that they make
that marriage known in the other world with happiness.

And again they do another thing, for they have painted and
portrayed on card men in the likeness of slaves and horses and
other animals and clothes of all sorts . . . and every kind of
furniture and many utensils, and all that they agree to give one to
the other for dowry, without being obliged to give it: and then they
have them burnt and say that their children, the dead bridegroom
and bride, will have in the other world all those things in reality
which they have had portrayed and burnt.

And when they have done it they the parents and kinsmen of the
dead count themselves as kindred and keep up their relation as
long as they live as well as if that wedding had been exactly
celebrated in reality, and as if they their dead children were
alive.

The ensuing sections contain information on the individual Mongol
tribes, about the life at the court of the Great Khan Qubilai (1259-94),

who was also Emperor of China,[13] and finally about the individual provinces of the Chinese Empire.

(Marco Polo, *The Description of the World*, ed. A. Ch. Moule and P. Pelliot, Vol. I [London, 1938].)

[13] The report deals, therefore, mainly with Chinese court ceremonial.

V

THE EMPIRE OF
THE GOLDEN HORDE
IN WHAT IS TODAY RUSSIA

A. EXTERNAL RELATIONS:
ENVOYS FROM EGYPT

[After traveling through east Roman territory and crossing the Black Sea, the envoys] (54) arrived at a mountain called Sudaq [on the Crimea]. There they were received in the village of Krim by the governor of that region which is inhabited by people of various nationality: Qıpchaq, Russians, and Alans [= Ossetians]. The journey from the coast to this village [takes] one day. From Krim [the envoys] traveled one day to the steppe, where they met the administrator of this area who commanded ten thousand horsemen. After that, they traveled for twenty days through a steppe dotted with tents and [flocks of] sheep, until they reached the river Itil [Volga]. It brings fresh water, and its width is roughly that of the Nile. It carries Russian ships; on its banks is the camp of the Khan Berke (1257–67). By means of it, food and sheep are brought to them. When [the envoys] approached the horde, they were received by the vizier . . . ; subsequently they were granted an audience by the Khan Berke. They had already acquainted themselves with the etiquette to be observed in his presence. According to this they had to enter from the left side, and after their message had been received [by the ruler] to step to the right and go down on both knees. Nobody enters his tent with a sword, a knife, or any other weapon; nor is anybody permitted to step on the threshold of his tent. Everybody lays down his weapons to the left only; the bow must neither be left in its case nor bent. Nor must the quiver be filled with arrows. It is forbidden to eat snow or to wash one's garments in the horde.

[The Khan] was in a large tent which could have held [five?] hundred people. The tent was covered in white felt and was lined on the inside with silks, Chinese materials, precious stones, and pearls. [The ruler] sat on a throne, next to him his chief wife, and around him fifty or sixty beys and notables on the seats of the tent. When [the envoys] had entered, he called on (55) his vizier to read out the letter, then made them step from the left side to the right, questioned them about the Nile and said: 'I am told that spanning the Nile is a human bone by which the people cross over.' [The envoys] replied: 'We have not seen anything of this kind.' ... The Chief Judge who was standing close by, explained the letter and handed the document to the Khan; for the benefit of the [dignitaries] around Berke, the letter from the [Egyptian] Sultan was read out in Turkish. This pleased [the Tatars]. [Berke] gave the envoys his reply and dismissed them attaching to them his [own] messengers.

Every bey [emir] in the ruler's circle, equally each of his wives, has a muezzin and a priest [Imām]. The children read the sublime Koran at school.

The envoys returned via east Roman territory and, on 4 September, 1264, reviewed the armies in their [full] array after their reported victory. The messengers [from the Golden Horde] were constantly invited to Court and took part in the ball games. ... They resided in [the Cairo quarter of] al-Lūq.

(Ibn 'Abd az̧-Z̧āhir in Woldemar, Freiherr von Tiesenhausen, *Sbornik materialov otnosjaščikhsya k istorii Zolotoi Ordy* ('Collection of Material Bearing on the History of the Golden Horde') [St. Petersburg, 1884], I, 54 ff.)

B. THE LIFE OF THE TATARS IN THE GOLDEN HORDE

Ibn Baṭṭūṭa (1304–69), from whose writings the following texts were taken, was one of the most important writers of travel accounts in Arabic literature. He was born in Tangier in Morocco. Between 1325 and 1353 he undertook journeys that took him by way of Asia Minor and Eastern Europe to India, Ceylon, and China and later via the Malayan Archipelago and Arabia to Timbuktu.

1. Horse Breeding

(371) ... The horses in this country [the Volga steppe] are exceedingly numerous and their price is negligible. A good horse costs fifty or sixty of their dirhems, (372) which equals one dinar of our money or thereabouts. These are the horses known in Egypt as *akādīsh* and it is from [the raising of] them that they make their living, horses in their country being like sheep in ours, or even more numerous, so that a single Turk [Tatar] will possess thousands of them. It is the custom of the Turks who live in this country and who raise horses to attach a piece of felt, a span in length, to a thin rod, a cubit in length, for every thousand horses [possessed by each man]. These rods are put on the wagons ['*arabas*] in which their women ride, each being fixed to a corner of the wagon, and I have seen some of them who have ten pieces [of felt] and some with less than that. These horses are exported to India [in droves], each one numbering six thousand or more or less. Each trader has one or two hundred horses or less or more. For every fifty of them he hires (373) a drover, who looks after them and their pasturage, like sheep; and this man is called by them *alqashī*. He rides on one of them, carrying in his hand a long stick with a rope on it, and when he wishes to catch any horse among them he gets opposite to it on the horse that he is riding, throws the rope over its neck and draws it to him, mounts it and sets the other free to pasture.

When they reach the land of Sind with their horses, they feed them with forage, because the vegetation of the land of Sind does not take the place of barley, and the greater part of the horses die or are stolen. They are taxed on them in the land of Sind [at the rate of] seven silver dinars a horse, at a place called Shashnaqār, and pay a further tax at Multan, the capital of the land of Sind. In former times they paid in duty the quarter of what they imported, but the king of [the Muslim part of] India, the Sultan Muḥammad, abolished this [practice] and ordered that there should be exacted from the Muslim traders [374] the *zakāt* [alms tax required by Islamic law] and from the infidel traders the tenth. In spite of this, there remains a handsome profit for the traders in these horses, for they sell the cheapest of them in the land of India for a hundred silver dinars [the exchange value of which in Moroccan gold is twenty-five dinars], and often sell them for twice or three times as much. The good horses are worth five hundred [silver] dinars or more. The people of India do not buy them for [their qualities in] running or racing, because they themselves wear coats of mail in battle and they cover their horses with armor, and what they prize in these horses is strength and length of pace. The horses that they want for racing are brought to them from al-Yaman [Yemen], Oman, and Fars, and each of these horses is sold at from one to four thousand dinars. . . .

(377) I witnessed in this country a remarkable thing, namely the respect in which women are held by them, indeed they are higher in dignity than the men. As for the wives of the emirs, the first occasion on which I saw them was when, on my departure from al-Qiram [Old Krim, in the Crimean peninsula], I saw the Khatun, the wife of the emir Salṭīya, in a wagon of hers. The entire wagon was covered with rich blue woolen cloth, the windows and doors of the tent were open, and there were in attendance on her four girls of excelling beauty and exquisitely dressed. Behind her were a number of wagons in which were girls belonging to her suite. When she came near the encampment of the emir, she descended from the wagon to the ground and with her alighted (378) about thirty of the girls to carry her train. Her robes were furnished with loops of which each girl would take one, and altogether they would lift the skirts clear of the ground on every side.

She walked thus in a stately manner until she reached the emir, when he rose before her, saluted her, and sat her beside him, while her maidens stood around her. Skins of *qumys* were brought and she, having poured some of it into a bowl, went down on her knees before the emir and handed the bowl to him. After he had drunk, she poured out for his brother, and the emir poured out for her. The food was then served and she ate with him, he gave her a robe and she withdrew. Such is the style of the wives of the emirs, and we shall describe [that of] the wives of the king later on (cf. p. 188). .

As for the wives of the traders and commonalty, I have seen them, when one of them would be in a wagon, being drawn by horses, and in attendance on her three or four girls to carry her train, (379) wearing on her head a *boghtaq*, which is a conical head-dress decorated with precious stones and surmounted by peacock feathers. The windows of the tent would be open and her face would be visible, for the womenfolk of the Turks do not veil themselves. One such woman will come [to the bazaar] in this style, accompanied by her male slaves with sheep and milk, and will sell them for spicewares. Sometimes one of the women will be in the company of her husband and anyone seeing him would take him to be one of her servants; he wears no garment other than a sheepskin cloak and on his head a high cap to match it, which they call [in Persian] a *kulah*.

We made preparations to travel from the city of Majār [in the northern approaches to the Caucasus] to the sultan's camp, which was four days' march from Majār at a place called Bish Dagh (Beshdagh). *Bish* in their language means 'five' and *dagh* means 'mountain' [probably the modern Pyatigorsk, where the Russian has the same meaning]. In these Five Mountains there is a hot spring (380) in which the Turks bathe, and they claim that anyone who bathes in it will not be attacked by disease. We set out for the site of the *maḥalla* and reached it on the first day of Ramadan (734 H. = 6 May, 1334), but found that the *maḥalla* had left, so we returned to the place from which we started because the *maḥalla* was encamping in its vicinity. I set up my tent on a low hill thereabouts, fixed my flag in front of the tent, and drew up my horses and wagons behind. Then the *maḥalla* came up—they call it the *ordu* (meaning 'camp'; thus 'horde')—and we saw a vast city on the move with its inhabitants, with mosques and bazaars in it, the smoke of the kitchens rising in the air [for they cook while on the march], and horse-drawn wagons transporting the people. On reaching the camping place they took down the tents from the wagons and set them on the ground, for they are light to carry, and so likewise they did with the mosques (381) and shops. The sultan's khatuns passed by us, each one separately with her retinue. The fourth of them [she was the daughter of the emir 'Īsā Beg, and we shall speak of her presently], as she passed saw the tent on top of the hill with the flag in front of it as the sign of a new arrival, so she sent pages and girls who saluted me and conveyed her salutations to me while she halted to wait for them. I sent her a gift by one of my companions and the remembrancer of the emir Tuluk-tumūr (Toloktemür). She accepted it as a token of blessing, and gave orders that I should be taken under her protection, then went on. [Afterward] the sultan came up and encamped separately in his *maḥalla*.

His name is Muhammad Özbeg and Khan in their language means 'sultan'. This sultan is mighty in sovereignty, exceedingly (382) powerful, great in dignity, lofty in station, victor over the enemies of God, the people of Constantinople the Great, and diligent in the *jihād* against them. His territories are vast and his cities great; they include al-Kafā [today Feodosiya], al-Qiram [Old Krim], al-Māchar [Majār], Azāq [Azov], Surdāq [Sudaq, in the Crimea] and Khwārizm [Chōrizm, today Khiva], and his capital is al-Sarā [Sarai, on the lower Volga]. He is one of the seven kings who are the great and mighty kings of the world. . . . This sultan when he is on the march, travels in a separate *maḥalla*, accompanied by his *mamlūks* (slaves of the royal household) and his officers of state, and each one of (383) his khatuns travels separately in her own *maḥalla*. When he wishes to be with any of them, he sends to her to inform her of this, and she prepares to receive him. He observes, in his [public] sittings, his journeys, and his affairs in general, a marvelous and magnificent ceremonial.

It is his custom to sit every Friday, after the prayers, in a pavilion, magnificently decorated, called the Gold Pavilion. It is constructed of wooden rods covered with plaques of gold, and in the center of it is a wooden couch covered with plaques of silver gilt, its legs of pure silver and their bases encrusted with precious stones. The sultan sits on the throne, having on his right hand the khatun Taidoghlı and next to her the khatun Kebek, and on his left the khatun Bayaluṅ and next to her the khatun Orduja. Below the throne, to his right, stands the sultan's son Tinibeg (Tīna Bak), and to his left his second son Jānībeg (Jāni Bak), and in front of him sits his daughter It Küchüjük (Ît Kujujuk) (cf. below p. 191). As each of the khatuns comes in the sultan rises before her, (384) and takes her by the hand until she mounts to the couch. As for Taidoghlı who is the queen and the one of them most favored by him, he advances to the entrance of the pavilion to meet her, salutes her, takes her by the hand, and only after she has mounted the couch and taken her seat does the sultan himself sit down. All this is done in full view of those present, without any use of veils. Afterward the great emirs come and their chairs are placed for them to right and left, each man of them, as he comes to the sultan's audience, being accompanied by a page carrying his chair. In front of the sultan stand the scions of the royal house, that is, his nephews, brothers, and relatives, and parallel to them, at the entrance to the pavilion, stand the sons of the great emirs, with the senior officers of the troops standing behind them. Then the [rest of the] people are admitted to make their salute, in their degrees of precedence and three at a time, and after saluting (385) they retire and sit at a distance.

After the hour of afternoon prayer the queen-khatun withdraws, whereupon the rest of them also withdraw and follow her to her *mahalla*. When she has entered it, each of them retires to her own *mahalla*, riding in her wagon, each one accompanied by about fifty girls, mounted on horses. In front of the wagon there are about twenty elderly women riding on horses between the pages and the wagon. Behind the whole cortege there are about a hundred young *mamlūks*, and in front of the pages about a hundred adult *mamlūks* on horseback and an equal number on foot carrying staves in their hands and swords girt on their waists, who walk between the horsemen and the pages. Such is the ceremonial of each of the khatuns both on her withdrawal and on her arrival.

My camping place was in the *mahalla*, in the vicinity of the sultan's son Jānībeg, of whom an account will be given later (p. 191). On the morrow of (386) the day of my arrival I made my entrance to the sultan after the afternoon prayer. He had assembled the sheiks, *qāḍīs* [judges], jurists, *sharīfs* [descendants[1] of the Prophet] and poor brethren and prepared a great banquet, and we broke our fast[2] in his presence. The *sayyid* and *sharīf*, the Marshall of the Sharīfs, Ibn 'Abd al-Ḥamīd, and the *qāḍī* Ḥamza spoke favorably about me and made recommendations to the sultan to show honor to me. These Turks do not know the practice of giving hospitable lodging to the visitor or of supplying him with money for his needs. What they do is to send him sheep and horses for slaughtering and skins of *qumys* and this is their [manner of] honorable treatment. Some days after this I prayed the afternoon prayer in the sultan's company and when I was about to withdraw he bade me be seated. They brought in dishes of the various soups,

---

[1] Genuine or imaginary.

[2] During the month of Ramadan no food or drink must be taken before sunset.

like that made from *dūqī*, then roasted fleshmeat, both of sheep and of horses. It was on that night that I presented to the sultan (387) a plate of sweetmeats, when he did no more than touch it with his finger and put that to his mouth.

2. Account of the Khatuns and Their Ceremonial

Each of the khatuns rides in a wagon, the tent that she occupies being distinguished by a cupola of silver ornamented with gold or of wood encrusted with precious stones. The horses that draw her wagon are caparisoned with cloths of silk gilt, and the conductor of the wagon who rides on one of the horses is a pageboy . . . . The khatun, as she sits in her wagon, has on her right hand an elderly woman called Ulugh Khatun, which means 'Great Lady' = 'lady vizier', and on her left another elderly woman called Kütchük Khatun which means 'Little Lady' = 'lady chamberlain'. In front of her are six young slave girls called 'girls', of surpassing beauty and the utmost perfection, and behind her two more like them, on whom she leans. On (388) the khatun's head is a *boghtaq* which resembles a small 'crown' decorated with jewels and surmounted by peacock feathers. And she wears robes of silk encrusted with jewels, like the mantles worn by the Greeks. On the head of the lady vizier and the lady chamberlain is a silk veil embroidered with gold and jewels at the edges, and on the head of each of the girls is a *kulāh* [cap], which is like an *aqrūf* [fez] with a circlet of gold encrusted with jewels round the upper end, and peacock feathers above this, and each one wears a robe of silk gilt. . . . In front of [the wagon of] the khatun are ten or fifteen pages, Greeks and Indians, who are dressed in robes of silk gilt, encrusted with jewels, and each of whom carries in his hand a mace of gold or silver, or maybe of wood veneered with them.

Behind the khatun's wagon there are about a hundred wagons, in each of which there are four (389) slave girls, full grown and young, wearing robes of silk and with the *kulāh* on their heads. Behind these wagons [again] are about three hundred wagons, drawn by camels and oxen, carrying the khatun's chests, moneys, robes, furnishings, and food. With each wagon is a slave boy who has the care of it and is married to one of the slave girls that we have mentioned, for it is the custom that none of the slaves may set

foot among the girls except one who has a wife among their number. Every khatun enjoys the honor of this style, and we shall now
describe each one of them separately.

3. Account of the Principal Khatun

The principal khatun is the queen, the mother of the sultan's two
sons Jānībeg and Tinibeg (cf. below, p. 191). She is not the mother
of his daughter It Küchüjük; her mother was the queen before this
one. This khatun's name is Taidoghlı (390) and she is the favorite
of this sultan, with whom he spends most of his nights. The people
hold her in great honor because of his honoring her; otherwise, she
is the most close-fisted of the khatuns. I was told for a fact by one
in whom I have confidence, a person well acquainted with matters
relating to this queen, that the sultan is enamored of her because of
a peculiar property in her, namely that he finds her every night just
like a virgin. Another person related to me that she is of the lineage
of that queen on whose account, it is said, the kingdom was withdrawn from Solomon (on whom be peace), and whom, when his
kingdom was restored to him, he commanded to be placed in an
uninhabited desert, so she was deposited in the desert of Qıpchaq[3]
[that is, the region north and northeast of the Black Sea]. . . .

(391) On the day after my meeting with the sultan, I visited this
khatun. She was sitting in the midst of ten elderly women, who
seemed to be attendants waiting on her, and in front of her were
about fifty young slave girls, whom the Turks call 'girls', and
before whom there were gold and silver salvers filled with cherries
which they were cleaning. In front of the khatun also there was
a golden tray filled with cherries, and she was cleaning them.
We saluted her, and among my companions there was a Koran-
reader who recited the Koran according to the method of the
Egyptians, (392) in a pleasing manner and agreeable voice, and he
gave a recitation. She then ordered *qumys* to be served, and it was
brought in light and elegant silver bowls, whereupon she took a
bowl in her hand and offered it to me. This is the highest of honors
in their estimation. I had never drunk *qumys* before, but there was
nothing for me to do but to accept it. I tasted it and [finding] it
disagreeable passed it on to one of my companions. She asked me

[3] This refers to one of the numerous Muslim legends about Solomon.

many questions concerning our journey, and after answering her we withdrew. We went to visit her first because of the great position she has with the king.

4. Account of the Second Khatun, Who Comes after the Queen

Her name is Kebek Khatun [this means 'Swarthy Lady', literally 'bran' lady.] She is the daughter of the emir Naghatai, and her father is still living, [but] suffering from gout, and I (393) saw him. On the day following our visit to the queen we visited this khatun, and found her sitting on a divan, reading in the Holy Book. In front of her were about ten elderly women and about twenty girls embroidering pieces of cloth. We saluted her, and she gave us gracious salutations and speech. Our Koran-reader recited and she commended his recital, then ordered *qumys*, and when it was brought she offered me a bowl with her own hand, just as the queen had done and we took leave of her.

5. Account of the Third Khatun

Her name is Bayalūn, and she is the daughter of the king of Constantinople the Great, the Sultan Takfūr [Takfur is the Arab term for the Byzantine emperor, not a personal name; the emperor referred to is Andronicus III, r. 1328–41]. When we visited this khatun, she was sitting on an inlaid couch with silver legs; before her were (394) about a hundred slave girls, Greek, Turkish, and Nubian, some standing and some sitting, and pages were [standing] behind her and chamberlains in front of her, men of the Greeks. She asked about us and our journey hither and the distance of our native lands, and she wept in pity and compassion and wiped her face with a handkerchief that lay before her. She then called for food, which was brought, and we ate before her, while she looked on at us. When we made to withdraw, she said 'Do not stay away from us, but come to us and inform us of your needs.' She showed herself to be of a generous nature, and sent after us food, a great quantity of bread, ghee, sheep, money, a fine robe, three horses of good breed and ten of ordinary stock. It was with this khatun that my journey to Constantinople the Great was made, as we shall relate below.

6. Account of the Fourth Khatun

(395) The visit took the same course as the previous visits.

7. Account of the Daughter of the Exalted Sultan Özbeg

Her name is It Küchüjük, which means 'little dog', for *it* means 'dog' and *küchüjük* means 'little'. We have mentioned above that the Turks give names by chance of omens, as do the Arabs. We went to visit this khatun, the sultan's daughter, who was in a separate *maḥalla* about six miles from that of her father. She gave orders to summon the jurists, the judges [*qāḍi*s], the descendant of the Prophet [the *sayyid* and *sharif*] . . . , the body of students of religion, the sheikhs and poor brethren [*fakir*s]. Her husband, the emir 'Īsā, whose daughter[4] was the sultan's wife, was present, and sat with her on the same rug. He was suffering from gout, and was unable for this reason to go about on his feet or to ride a horse, and so used to ride only in a wagon. When he wished to present himself before the sultan, his servants lifted him down and carried him into the audience-hall. (397) In the same state too, I saw the emir Naghatai, who was the father of the second khatun, and this disease is widespread among the Turks. By this khatun, the sultan's daughter, we were shown such generosity and good qualities as we had seen in no other, and she loaded us with surpassing favors— may God reward her with good.

8. Account of the Sultan's Two Sons

They are uterine brothers, the mother of both being the queen Taidoghlï, whom we have mentioned above. The elder is named Tinibeg, *beg* meaning 'emir' and *tin* [Persian *tän*] meaning 'body', so that he is called, as it were, 'emir of the body'. His brother is named Jānībeg, and as *jān* means [Persian] 'spirit', he is called, as it were 'emir of the spirit'. Each one of them has his own separate *maḥalla*. Tinibeg was one of the most beautiful of God's creatures (398) in form, and his father had designated him [to succeed him] in the kingship, and gave him the preference and superior honor. But God willed otherwise, for when his father died (1341) he ruled

[4] Of course by another woman!

for a brief space and was then killed for certain disgraceful things that happened to him, and his brother Jānībeg, who was better and worthier than he, succeeded to the rule. The *sayyid* and *sharīf* Ibn 'Abd al-Ḥamīd was the tutor who had supervised the education of Jānībeg. . . .

There follows a partly invented description of the region of the Volga Bulgars around present-day Kazan.

9. *Account of Their Ceremonial on the Festival (of Breaking the Fast[5])*

(402) On the morning of the day of the festival the sultan rode out on horseback among his huge bodies of troops, and each khatun rode in her wagon, accompanied by (403) her troops. The sultan's daughter rode with a crown on her head, since she is the queen in reality, having inherited the kingdom [rank] from her mother. The sultan's sons rode, each one with his troops. The Grand Qāḍī Shihāb ad-Dīn as-Sā'ilī had come to attend the festival, having with him a body of legists and sheikhs, and they rode, as did also the *qāḍī* Ḥamza, the *imām* [prayer leader] . . . and the *sharīf* [descendant of the Prophet]. . . . These doctors of the law rode in the procession with Tinibeg, the designated heir of the sultan, accompanied by drums and standards. The *qāḍī* Shihāb ad-Dīn then led them in the [festival] prayers and delivered a most excellent *khuṭba* [sermon].

The sultan mounted [again] and [rode until he] arrived at a wooden pavilion, which is called by them a *kushk* (whence our 'kiosk'), in which he took his seat, accompanied by his khatuns. A second pavilion was erected beside it, in which sat his heir and daughter, the lady of the crown. (404) Two [other] pavilions were erected beside these two, to right and left of them, in which were the sons and relatives of the sultan. Chairs (which they call *ṣandalīya*) were placed for the emirs and the scions of the royal house to the right and left of the [sultan's] pavilion, and each one of them sat on his own chair. Then archery butts were set up, a special butt for each *emir ṭūmān*. An *emir ṭūmān* in their usage is a

---

[5] After the month of fasting during Ramadan has ended, the first three days of the following month of Shawwāl are one of the two main Muslim festivals.

commander under whose orders there ride ten thousand [horsemen] and there were present seventeen of such emirs, leading one hundred and seventy thousand, yet the sultan's army is even larger than this. There was set up for each emir a kind of pulpit and he sat on this while his soldiers engaged in archery exercises before him. They continued thus for a time, after which robes of honor were brought; each emir was invested with a robe (khil'a; from this probably Spanish gala),[6] and as he put it on he would come to the bottom of the sultan's pavilion and do homage. His manner of doing homage is to touch the ground with his right knee and to extend his leg (405) underneath it while the other leg remains upright. After this a horse is brought, saddled, and bridled, and its hoof is lifted; the emir kisses this, then leads it himself to his chair and there mounts it and remains in his station with his troops. Each emir among them performs the same act.

The sultan then descends from the pavilion and mounts a horse, having on his right his son, the heir designate, and next to him his daughter, the queen It Küchüjük, and on his left his second son. In front of him are the four khatuns in wagons covered with silk fabrics gilded, and the horses that draw them are also caparisoned with silk gilded. The whole body of emirs, great and small, scions of the royal house, viziers, chamberlains, and officers of state alight and walk on foot in front of the sultan until he comes to the otaq [wiṭāq], which is an āfrāg [his great tent]. At his place there has been erected a huge bārgāh, a bārgāh [Persian] in their language being a large tent supported by four (406) wooden columns covered with plaques of silver coated with gold, each column having at its top a capital of silver gilt that gleams and flashes. This bārgāh, seen from a distance, looks like a hummock. To right and left of it are awnings of cotton and linen cloth, and the whole of this is carpeted with silken rugs. In the center of the bārgāh is set up an immense couch which they call the takht [Persian], made of inlaid wood, the planks of which are covered with a large rug. In the center of this immense couch is a cushion, on which sit the sultan and the principal khatun. To the sultan's right is a cushion, on which his daughter It Küchüjük took her seat and with her the khatun Orduja, and to his left a cushion on which sat the khatun Bayalūn and with her the khatun Kebek. To

---

[6] Corresponds to the conferring of medals.

the right of the couch was placed a chair, on which sat Tinibeg, the sultan's son, and to the left of it a chair, on which sat Jānībeg, his second son. (407) Other chairs were placed to right and left on which sat the scions of the royal house and the great emirs, then after them the lesser emirs such as [those called] emir *hezārā* [Persian] who are those who lead a thousand men.

The food was then brought in on tables of gold and silver, each table being carried by four men or more. Their food consists of boiled horsemeat and mutton, and a table is set down in front of each emir. The *bavurjı*, that is, the carver of the meat, comes, wearing silken robes on top of which is tied a silken apron, and carrying in his belt a number of knives in their sheaths. For each emir there is a *bavurjı*, and when the table is presented he sits down in front of his emir; a small platter of gold or silver is brought, in which there is salt dissolved in water, and the *bavurjı* cuts the meat up into small pieces. They have in this matter a special art of cutting up the meat together with the bones, for the Turks do not eat any meat unless the bones are mixed with it.

(408) After this, drinking vessels of gold and silver are brought. The beverage they make most use of is fermented liquor of honey [*nabīdh al-ʿasal*], since, being of the Ḥanafite[7] school of law, they hold fermented liquor to be lawful. When the sultan wishes to drink, his daughter takes the bowl in her hand, pays homage with her leg, and then presents the bowl to him. When he has drunk she takes another bowl and presents it to the chief khatun, who drinks from it, after which she presents it to the other khatuns in their order of precedence. The sultan's heir then takes the bowl, pays homage, and presents it to his father, then, when he has drunk, presents it to the khatuns and to his sister after them, paying homage to them all. The second son rises, takes the bowl and gives it to his brother to drink paying homage to him. Thereafter the great emirs rise, and each one of them gives the cup to the sultan's heir and pays homage to him, after which the [other] members of the royal house rise and each one of them gives the cup to this second son, paying homage to him. The lesser emirs then

---

[7] The Ḥanafites are followers of the legal school founded by Abū Ḥanīfa (who died in 767) and to which belong today almost all the Turkish peoples (with the exception of part of the Azerbaijanis). This legal school, one of the four great schools of Sunni Islam (which recognize one another as following the true faith), is considered to be relatively tolerant on many questions.

rise and give the sons of the kings to drink. During all this [cere-mony], they sing (409) [songs resembling the] chants sung by oarsmen.

A large pavilion had been erected also alongside the mosque for the *qāḍī*, the *khaṭīb* [preacher], the *sharīf*, and all the other legists and sheikhs, including myself. We were brought tables of gold and silver, each one carried by four of the leading men of the Turks, for no one is employed in the sultan's presence on that day except the principal men, and he commands them to take up such of the tables as he wishes [and carry them] to whomsoever he wishes. There were some of the legists who ate and some who abstained from eating [out of scruples at doing so] on tables of silver and gold.[8] To the limit of vision both right and left I saw wagons laden with skins of *qumys*, and in due course the sultan ordered them to be distributed among those present. They brought one wagon to me, but I gave it to my Turkish neighbors.

After this we went into the mosque to await the Friday prayers. The sultan was late in coming, and some said that he would not come because (410) drunkenness had got the better of him, and others said that he would not fail to attend the Friday service. When it was well past the time he arrived, swaying, and greeted the *sayyid sharīf* [descendant of the Prophet], smiled to him, and kept addressing him as *ata*, which means 'father' in the Turkish language. We then prayed the Friday prayers and the people withdrew to their residences. The sultan went back to the *bārgāh* and continued as before until the afternoon prayers, when all those present withdrew, [except that] his khatuns and his daughter remained with the king that night.

After this, when the festival had ended, we set out in company with the sultan and the *maḥalla* and came to the city of al-Ḥajj Tarkhān [Astrakhan]. Tarkhān in their usage means 'a place [more correctly: such a person] exempted from taxes'. The person after whom this city is named was a Turkish pilgrim, a saintly man, who made his residence at its site and for whom the sultan gave exemption to that place.[9] (411) So it became a village, then grew in size and became a city, and it is one of the finest of cities,

---

[8] A Koranic commandment forbids eating and drinking from vessels made of precious metals.

[9] An etiological legend.

with great bazaars, built on the river Itil (Volga), which is one of the great rivers of the world. It is there that the sultan resides until the cold grows severe and this river freezes over, as well as the waters connected with it. The sultan gives orders to the people of that land, and they bring thousands of loads of straw, which they spread over the ice congealed upon the river. Straw is not eaten by the animals in those parts, because it is injurious to them, and the same applies in the land of India; they eat nothing but green herbage, because of the fertility of the country. The inhabitants travel in wagons over this river and the adjacent waters for a space of three days' journey, and sometimes caravans cross over it at the end of the winter season and perish by drowning.

When we reached the city of al-Ḥājj Tarkhān, the khatun Bayalūn, the daughter of the king of the Greeks, begged (412) of the sultan to permit her to visit her father, that she might give birth to her child at the latter's residence, and then return to him. When he gave permission I too begged of him to allow me to go in her company to see Constantinople the Great for myself. He forbade me, out of fear for my safety, but I solicited him tactfully and said to him, 'It is under your protection and patronage that I shall visit it, so I shall have nothing to fear from anyone.' He then gave permission, and when we took leave of him he presented me with 1,500 dinars, a robe, and a large number of horses, and each of the khatuns gave me ingots of silver [which they call ṣaum, the singular being ṣauma]. The sultan's daughter gave me more than they did, along with a robe and a horse, and altogether I had a large collection of horses, robes, and furs of miniver and sable.

C. ACCOUNT OF JOURNEY TO CONSTANTINOPLE WITH A TATAR PRINCESS

We set out on the tenth of Shawwāl [734 H. = 14 June 1334] (413) in the company of the khatun Bayalūn and under her protection. The sultan came out to escort her for one stage, then returned, he and the queen and his heir designate; the other khatuns traveled in her company for a second stage and then they returned. The emir Baidara, with five thousand of his troops, traveled along with her, and the khatun's own troops numbered about five hundred, some two hundred of whom were slaves and Greeks in attendance on her, and the remainder Turks (Tatars). She had with her about two hundred slave girls, most of them Greeks, and about four hundred wagons with about two thousand horses to draw them and for riding, as well as some three hundred oxen and two hundred camels to draw them. She also had ten Greek pages with her, and the same number of Indian pages, whose leader in chief was named Sumbul the Indian; the leader of the Greeks was named Michael (the Turks used to call him Lu'lu'),[10] and was a man of (414) great bravery. She left most of her slave girls and most of her baggage in the sultan's *mahalla*, since she had set out with the intention [only] of paying a visit and of giving birth to her child.

Subsequently Ibn Baṭṭūṭa describes his journey via Ukek to Sudaq and further via Baba Saltuq to the Byzantine Empire. There follows a description of Constantinople. Continuing his journey to Central Asia, Ibn Baṭṭūṭa visits (New) Sarai, then the capital of the Tatar empire of the Golden Horde.

(447) The city of Sarai is one of the finest of cities, of boundless size, situated in a plain, choked with the throng of its inhabitants, and possessing good bazaars and broad streets. We rode out one day with one of its principal men, intending to make a circuit of the city and find out its extent. Our lodging place was at one end of it and we set out from it in the early morning, and it was after midday when we reached the other end. We then prayed the noon prayer and ate some food, and we did not get back to our lodging until the hour of the sunset prayer. One day we went on foot across the breadth of the town, going and returning, in half a day, this too through a continuous line of houses, among which there were no ruins and no gardens. The city has (448) thirteen mosques for the holding of Friday prayers,[11] . . . as for the other mosques, they are exceedingly numerous.

There are various groups of people among its inhabitants; these include the Mongols, who are the dwellers in this country and its

[10] Lu'lu' = the pearl; in Islam one of the typical names for slaves.
[11] Only certain larger mosques which must be a certain distance away from each other are allowed to celebrate the midday service on Fridays.

sultans, and some of whom are Muslims, then the Ossetians [Ās],[12] who are Muslims, the Cumans [Qıpchaq; Russian: Polovtsy], the Jarkas [Circassians], the Rūs [Russians], and the Rūm [Greeks]—[all of] these are Christians.[13] Each group lives in a separate quarter with its own bazaars. Merchants and strangers from the two Iraqs,[14] Egypt, Syria, and elsewhere, live in a quarter which is surrounded by a wall for the protection of the properties of the merchants. The sultan's palace in it is called Alṭūn Tāsh, alṭūn meaning 'gold' and ṭāsh 'stone'.

There follow details about Islamic lawyers and hermits in the city.

(449) The sultan Özbeg comes to visit him [a local priest and prayer leader] every Friday; but the sheikh will not go out to meet him nor rise before him. The sultan sits in front of him, addresses him in the most courteous manner, and humbles himself to him, whereas the sheikh's conduct is the opposite of this. But in his dealings with poor brethren, with the needy and with wayfaring visitors, his demeanor is the antithesis of that which he adopts toward the sultan, for he humbles himself (450) to them, speaks to them in the kindest way, and shows them honor. He received me honorably (God reward him well) and presented me with a Turkish slave boy. I was witness, too, to an example of his endowment with blessed power.

There follows a—banal—story of a 'miracle'.—Volume 2 of Ibn Baṭṭūṭa ends here.

(The Travels of Ibn Baṭṭūṭa, ed. Sir Hamilton Gibb [Cambridge, 1958, 1962], II, 241–517 passim [=371–450 passim].)

Volume 3 of Ibn Baṭṭūṭa begins here.

(2) From there [i.e., from Saraichıq on the mouth of the Ural river] we traveled by forced marches for thirty days. We rested only two hours a day, one hour in the morning and one at sunset. The stops

[12] Only a few, of (eastern) Iranian origin, remain today living in Caucasia.
[13] The Jarkas went over to Islam in the sixteenth/seventeenth century.
[14] The Arab and Persian.

were only long enough for cooking a porridge of millet [it is boiled up only once] and for eating it. The local population carries dried meat which they add to the dish; they pour milk on top.

During the journey everybody eats and sleeps in the cart. I had three women servants in my cart. The journey through this region is speeded up because of the small amount of grass growing there. Most of the camels used for this die; those that survive are not used again until the following year, when they have once more been fattened. (3) Water is to be found at intervals of two or three days' journeys in certain places; it is rain or well water.

Having passed this region we reached Khwārizm. It is one of the largest, most imposing, most beautiful and most extensive cities of the Turks, and has beautiful bazaars, broad streets, numerous buildings, and remarkable sights. It might be said to be vibrating with the multitude of its inhabitants, and it is in motion like the sea. I rode about in it for a day, and, in the course of this, came to the bazaar. In the center of it, I got into such a dense crowd . . . , that I could not get any further because of the bustle; nor was it possible, in view of the thronging people, to turn back. I was, therefore, in difficulty, and only after intense effort did I manage to squeeze through. I was told (4) that on Fridays the bazaar was much less crowded, since on that day the main bazaar [ḳaisārīya][15] and other sales areas were closed.

On Friday, I rode out again, and turned toward the main mosque and the theological college (madrasa). The city is subject to the Khan [of the Golden Horde] Özbeg. He has there a governor, Qutlugh Demür. It was he who built this mudrasa and its ancillary buildings. The mosque had been endowed by his wife, the pious lady Törä Beg. Furthermore, there is a hospital at Khwārizm with a Syrian doctor, named as-Ṣihjauni after the city Ṣihjaun in Syria.[16]

Nowhere on earth have I seen more beautiful people than the inhabitants of Khwārizm, nor any of more noble mind or more hospitable toward the stranger. With regard to prayer, they have a commendable custom which I have not seen anywhere else, and which requires that the muezzin regularly (5) visit the houses in

[15] The principal bazaar is so named after the large stores for goods which were set up in many cities of the Middle East by the Roman Emperors, perhaps (according to Ernst Herzfeld) after that in Antioch; cf. also *Encyclopaedia of Islam*, Vol. II (Leiden and Leipzig, 1927), pp. 660 ff.

[16] Near Ḥimṣ.

the neighborhood of the mosque, asking the inhabitants to attend the service. Anybody missing the Friday service is beaten in the presence of the congregation by the prayer leader. For this purpose a horse whip hangs in every mosque. Moreover, the laggard has to pay five dinars [gold pieces] for the benefit of the mosque, money that may also be used for feeding the poor and the needy. This custom is said to have existed here for ages.

The river Oxus, one of the four rivers of paradise, flows past Khwārizm. During the cold season, it freezes over, just like the river Volga. During that time the people walk on it; the ice cover stays for five months. Frequently reckless people have stepped on the ice when it has started to thaw, and have perished. During the summer, ships travel on the river as far as Tirmidh, and corn and barley are imported from there. Down river, the journey takes five days.

(9) *The governor of Khwārizm* is the great bey, Qutlugh Demür, which means 'Fortunate Iron'. On his mother's side, he is a cousin of the Khan Muhammad Özbeg and the supreme bey and governor of Khurasan [more precisely: Transoxiania]. His son Hārūn is married to the above-mentioned (p. 191) daughter of the Khan, whose mother was the Queen Taidoghlı, also mentioned before (p. 189). His wife, the lady Törä Beg, made a name for herself by pious endowments. And when the judge came to me to bid me welcome . . . , he told me: 'The bey has heard of your arrival, but an illness prevents him from coming to see you.' So I rode with the judge to see him. We arrived at his house and entered a large reception building whose rooms were mainly made of wood. Its walls were covered with multicolored carpets; the ceiling was lined with silk interwoven with gold. The bey sat on his own silken carpet; because of the gout from which he was suffering his feet were covered (it is a disease very widespread among the Turks).

I greeted him, and he made me sit next to him; the judge and the theologians also sat down. The bey asked me about his lord, the Khan Muhammad Özbeg, and about the Lady Bayalūn and her father and his city of Constantinople. I told him about them. Now tables with food were brought in: roast chicken, cranes, young pigeons, bread fried in butter (11) called [in Persian] *kulijä*, drinks and sweetmeats. Afterward other tables with fruit were brought in:

pomegranates in gold and silver vessels with golden spoons; some of them were in Mesopotamian glass dishes with wooden spoons. There were also grapes and excellent melons.

The bey adheres to the following custom: the judge appears daily in his audience chamber and is present at the audience; he is accompanied by his theologians and his secretaries. Opposite them one of the grand emirs with eight of his Turkish peers and nobles, called *yarguchi* [civil judges], takes his seat. Then the people arrive to submit their legal affairs. Anything falling within the jurisdiction of the spiritual judges is settled by the spiritual judge (*qāḍī*): the rest is judged by the beys. They are precise and just in their judgment; they avoid any bias toward one party and do not accept any (12) presents.

After we had returned from the audience with the bey, to the theological college, he sent us rice, flour, mutton, butter, and spices, as well as loads of firewood. In all these areas charcoal is unknown, the same applies to India, Khurasan, and Persia. In China they burn stones that ignite the same way as charcoal. When they have burnt to ashes they are mixed with water and placed into the sun to dry. Thereafter they are used [once more] for burning on the hearth until they are completely used up.

(14) The Lady Jije Agha, the wife of the judge, sent me a hundred dinars in silver. Her sister Törä Beg, the wife of the bey, gave a dinner for me in the hermitage which she had founded. She invited to this the theologians and the dignitaries of the city. They distribute there food to the passing travelers. Furthermore, she sent me a sable coat and a fine horse. She is a splendid, pious and charitable woman; may God reward her with good things!

When I left the party which this lady had given for me, and left the hermitage, I noticed at the door a woman in dirty clothes, her head veiled. She was accompanied by other women the exact number of whom I cannot now recall. She greeted me, and I returned the greeting without stopping or turning toward her. When I was (15) finally outside, somebody from the crowd came after me and said: 'The woman who greeted you is the Lady [of the bey].' I was now ashamed and wanted to go back to her; but I noticed that she had gone away already. Through one of my servants I expressed to her my respect and made my apology, saying that I had not recognized her. . . .

D. THE KHAN OF TRANSOXIANA

(31) It is the honorable sultan[17] 'Alā ad-Dīn Tarmashīrīn [which is the subject of what follows]. He is an influential ruler with a large army and a mighty kingdom; his rule is just. His state extends between the territories of four powerful rulers: the Emperor of China, the Indian Sultan, the ruler of Iraq,[18] and the Khan Özbeg. All four rulers give him presents, and honor and esteem him. He followed his brother Eljigidai to the throne. Eljigidai had been an infidel, and in his turn had succeeded his elder brother, Kebek (1309/10 and 1318–26), also a non-Muslim. Even so he was a just ruler who took action against the violent and treated the Muslims with respect.

(32) It is said that one day Kebek talked to the theologian and preacher Badr ad-Dīn al-Maidānī and said to him: 'You maintain that God has mentioned everything in His sublime book [the Koran].' He replied: 'Yes.' Then the ruler said: 'Where then is my name given in it?' To this the theologian replied: 'It is contained in his words [chapter 2, verse 8 according to the count of the official Cairo edition of the Koran]: "He created [rakkabak(a)] you in the way that pleased him."'[19] The Khan liked this and exclaimed 'Yakhshɪ', which in Turkish means 'excellent', and he treated him with great distinction. His respect for the Muslims was increased by this even more.

One of the judgments given by Kebek is reported as follows: A woman complained to him about one of the beys, pointing out that she was poor and the mother of several children. She sold milk to earn a living. The bey had taken it from her and drunk it. The Khan said to her: 'I shall have the bey halved; if (33) the milk flows from his stomach he has met his just punishment. Otherwise I shall have you cut in two halves after him.' The woman replied:

[17] as-Sulṭān al-mu'aẓẓam: one of the official titles of the Mongol Khans at that time.

[18] This certainly refers to the dynasty of the Ilkhanids which after the disintegration of the Mongol (Ilkhan) Empire in Persia after 1335 soon became established in Mesopotamia.

[19] The last part of the word Rakkabak(a), vulgarly pronounced 'Rakkebek', is here connected with the ruler's proper name Kebek; a typical trick of the Muslim theologians who due to their authoritative knowledge of the Koran are extremely quick-witted in this way.

'I forgive him and do not want anything from him.' [In spite of this] he had the bey cut in half; and the milk appeared in his belly.

Now to return to Khan Tarmashīrīn. After I had been staying for some time in the camp, for which the Turkish word is *ordu*, I went one day to the mosque for early prayer, as was my custom. While I was praying, one of the people present told me that the Khan was in the mosque. When [after his prayers] he had risen from his prayer mat, I stepped forward to greet him. A sheikh and a theologian told him of me, and of my arrival a few days earlier. He asked me in Turkish: 'Khosh mısın? Yakhshı mısın? Qutlu eyüsin?' which means 'Are you well? Do you feel well? Are you satisfied and comfortable?'[20] On that occasion, the Khan (34) wore a sleeved gown of [material from] Jerusalem colored green, together with a matching hat. Afterward, he returned on foot to his audience hall, and on the way his subjects submitted their complaints. He stopped for each plaintiff, short or tall, man or woman. Then he sent for me. When I entered he was sitting in a tent; his entourage stood in front of or behind him. The beys sat on chairs; their escorts stood in front of or behind them. The other soldiers had sat down in individual rows; each of them had his weapon before him. They were on guard, and sat here until halfway through the afternoon; then, they were relieved by others who remained until the end of the night. Cotton awnings had been put up, under which they sat [so as to be protected from the sun].

When I entered the tent, I found the Khan sitting on a chair which resembled the pulpit [in a mosque] and was covered with silk interwoven with gold. (35) On the outside, the tent was also covered with silken material, interwoven with gold. A yard above the head of the ruler a coronet encrusted with precious stones and hyacinths was suspended. The grand beys sat on chairs to his right and his left; in front of him stood princes with fly whisks. At the door of the tent the Chancellor, the Vizier, the Chamberlain, and the Keeper of the Seal, had positioned themselves. (The seal is [al-]tamgha in Turkish.) All four rose as I entered, and accompanied me into the tent. I greeted the ruler; he asked me—and the Keeper of the Seal acted as interpreter—about Mecca, Medina, Jerusalem, Hebron, Damascus, Egypt and

[20] Here Ibn Baṭṭūṭa's Arab translation does not give the meaning of the Turkish original precisely and has been adjusted accordingly.

their ruler, al-Malik an-Nāṣir (1293–1340), about the two Iraqs
and their ruler (Abū Sa'īd, 1316–35), and about the Persian lands.

At that point, the muezzin called for the midday service. (36)
We went there, and in the presence of the Khan participated in
the prayers. There reigned a bitter, deadly cold. [In spite of this]
the Khan did not fail to perform the morning and evening prayers
together with the congregation. He sat down in order to call to
God in the Turkish language from the end of the morning prayer
until sunrise. All the visitors of the mosque came to him, and
pressed his hand. The same thing happened at the afternoon
prayers. If he was given as presents raisins or dates (which in these
parts are very rare, but highly appreciated), he shook hands with
everybody in the mosque.

Among the noble acts of the ruler is the following: One day,
when I was attending afternoon prayers, the Khan was not present,
but one of his pages appeared with a prayer mat which he put down
in front of the prayer niche[21] in the place where the ruler usually
prayed. Then, he said to the prayer leader[22] . . . : (37) 'Our Lord
[His Majesty] would like you to delay the prayers a little while,
until he has finished his ablutions [which the religious law requires
before each prayer].' At this the prayer leader mentioned rose and
said: 'Is the prayer for God or for Tarmashīrīn?' He, then, ordered
the muezzin to pronounce the second prayer call [at which those
who are praying form up in rows]. The Khan did not arrive
until the holy service was half finished. He took part in praying
the last two *rak'a*s [prostrations], and did so near the gate of the
mosque, where people usually leave their sandals.[23] Then, he
performed the prostrations he had missed. Afterward he rose,
went up to the prayer leader to greet him, laughed, and sat down
in front of the prayer niche. The sheikh and prayer leader sat down
at his side; I sat beside him. The Khan said to me: 'When you
return home,[24] you may report there, that an ordinary poor
Persian [*faqīr*] is allowed to treat the Turkish Khan in this way.'

This sheikh preached every Friday in front of the people, and
admonished the Khan to act in accordance with the law, and to

[21] The prayer niche (*miḥrāb*) serves to indicate the direction of Mecca as
required for prayer.
[22] The prayer leader (*imām*) leads community prayer in the mosque.
[23] In the mosque the faithful have to remove their shoes.
[24] Ibn Baṭṭūṭa came from Tangier in Morocco.

avoid doing forbidden things. (38) He seriously took him to task; the Khan wept and was silent. The sheikh did not accept any of the presents given by the ruler, nor did he accept his invitations to meals, or wear any of the clothes [presented] by him. . . .

When I decided to continue my journey, after (39) a stay of fifty-four days, the Khan gave me seven hundred silver dinars and a sable fur worth a hundred dinars, for which I had asked him because of the cold. When I had talked to him about it, he had taken me by the sleeve and, personally, given me what I had asked for, thus showing humility, nobility, and strength of character. In addition, he gave me two horses and two camels. When I went to take my leave of him, I found him on the point of departure for his hunting grounds. It was very cold that day, and due to the severe frost I could literally not utter a single word.[25] He laughed and gave me his hand, and I went on my way.

Two years after my arrival in India, I learned that the leading nobles and the beys had banded together in the farthest region of the empire, which borders on China, and where most of the garrisons are stationed. There, they had paid homage to his cousin Buzun Oghly (40) [all princes have *Oghly*, which is Turkish for *son*, added to their names] who was a Muslim, but cared little for religion and led a dissolute life. The reason why they paid homage to him, and turned away from Tarmashīrīn, was that the latter no longer kept the laws of their accursed[26] ancestor Chinggiz Khan, who had conquered the Muslim countries. . . . He had produced a book containing his laws, called (*yasa(q)*).[27] It is the accepted code among these people, that anybody who contravenes this law must be deposed. One of these laws requires them to assemble once a year. That day is called *toi* which means the day of festive gathering. On this occasion, the descendants of Chinggiz Khan and the beys arrive from all regions of the empire; the 'ladies' and the generals are also present. If any of their Khans has changed anything with regard to the precepts of this law, the notables go up to him and say: 'You have changed this and that, and done this and (41)

---

[25] As the native of a southern country Ibn Baṭṭūṭa was naturally particularly sensitive to the cold.

[26] A term frequently applied by Muslim writers to the external enemies of Islam.

[27] This book of laws has not been preserved but its contents can be reconstructed.

that.' They take him by the hand, and lead him down from the throne, and put some other descendant of Chinggiz Khan in his place.[28] If one of the grand emirs has been guilty of an offense in his district, they judge him according to his deeds.[29]

The Khan Tarmashīrīn had on that day quashed the sentences, and abolished this procedure. His subjects opposed this most vehemently, and, moreover, reproached him for having stayed for four years exclusively in that part of the empire which borders on Khurasan and not having come to the frontier region near China. It had been customary for the ruler to travel there annually, and inspect the army stationed there, since the ruling house originated from there, and the city, Almalyq, was [the proper] residence.

After Buzun had accepted their homage, he set off with a big army. Tarmashīrīn became frightened of his beys, and did not trust them any more, and rode with only fifteen companions (42) toward Ghazna which was part of his empire. Its governor was his bey-in-chief and trusted friend Buruntai who was friendly toward Islam and the Muslims. In his province he had ordered to be built about forty hermitages where passing travelers were looked after. He had considerable fighting forces at his command. I have never seen anywhere a man physically so big and strong as him.

When Tarmashīrīn had crossed the Oxus, and was on his way to Balkh, he was seen by a Turk who was one of the followers of Yangı, the son of his brother Kebek. Tarmashīrīn had killed this brother of his [in 1326?]; the son Yangı had remained in Balkh. When the Turk told him of Tarmashīrīn's approach, Yangı concluded that Tarmashīrīn could only have fled because of some emergency which had arisen, rode out with his men to meet him, and took him prisoner.

In the meantime Buzun had pushed on as far as Samarkand and Bukhara, where homage was paid to him. Now (43) Yangı brought Tarmashīrīn to him. It is said that he was executed at Nesef near Samarkand, and also buried there. . . . According to others he was not killed.[30] [After Buzun's victory Tarmashīrīn's family fled to

[28] But only weak rulers of later periods put up with this!

[29] In the long run Islamic law did prevail over the *yasa.*

[30] Ibn Baṭṭūṭa's statements here contradict those of the historians. The facts can no longer be ascertained: in any case Tarmashīrīn's rule came to an end in 1334.

India, where they were well received. Later a false Tarmashīrīn appeared there.]

Before long Buzun was overthrown and strangled. Ibn Baṭṭūṭa then continued his journey, visiting Samarkand and eastern Persia and passing through present day Afghanistan to India.

(After Ibn Baṭṭūṭa, *Voyages*, ed. and trans. Charles Defrémery and Benjamin Raphael Sanguinetti, Vols. II and III [2nd ed.; Paris, 1877], III, 2–43.)

CHRONOLOGY

1206   Temujin (b. 1155, 1162 or 1167) is accorded the title of 'Chinggiz Khan' (ocean-like Khan?).

1215   The Mongols invade northern China and destroy the empire of the Kin dynasty (Jurchens).

1218–21 Central Asia, Transoxiana, the northern (present-day) Afghanistan and northern Persia are overrun by the Mongols: collapse of the empire of the Khwārizm-Shāhs.

1223   Russians and Cumans are defeated on the Kalka river.

1227   Chinggiz Khan dies during the siege of the capital of the Tanguts.

1229–41 Ögädäi, his son, rules as Great Khan with his brother Chaghatai by his side as preserver of the Mongol tradition.

1237–41 The greater part of Russia subjugated by the Mongols: beginning of the 'Tatar Yoke'—1240 fall of Kiev.

1241   (April 9) The Battle near Liegnitz; an army composed of German Knights and Poles is defeated, Duke Henry II of Silesia (son of St. Hedwig) is killed.

1241   (April 11) The Hungarian King Andrew IV suffers a crushing defeat in the plain of Mohi.

Golden Horde

1240–55 Batu, a grandson of Chinggiz Khan, ruler of the Golden Horde.

1256–67 Berke, his brother, becomes a Muslim; friendship with the Mamluks in Egypt, discord with the Ilkhan, for religious reasons, among others.

1267–80 Möngkä Temür returns to Shamanism.

1280–99 Rise and fall of Prince Nogai (Nokhai 'dog'); the Nogai are named after him.

1299–1313 Tokhtu (Tokhtagha) puts the state on a firm footing again; attempts to annex Caucasia fail.

1313–41 Özbeg, his nephew, adopts the Islamic faith; the Özbegs (Uzbegs) are named after him. Establishment of Islamic culture and civilization in the capital New Sarai. The differences with the Russians are exacerbated by the religious antagonism; but it prevents the Tatars from being absorbed into the Russian people—Relations with Egypt become gradually cooler.

1333 The traveler Ibn Baṭṭūṭa from Tangier visits the Golden Horde.

1341–58 Özbeg's son Jānībeg sees the collapse of the Ilkhan empire in Iran; vain attempt to salvage Azerbaijan from the remnants and add it to the Golden Horde.

1359ff. Disintegration of the Golden Horde in the course of civil wars.

1362 Defeated on the 'Blue Waters' (present-day Sinyukha) by the Grand Principality of Lithuania which is growing in power.

1376–1405 Tokhtamish unites the Golden Horde for the last time; he is defeated twice by Tīmūr (see below p. 211).

1399 Victory over the Russians on the Vorskla river.

1419 Death of the chamberlain Edigü, the last influential politician.

1438 Beginning of the dissolution of the state into the Khanates of Crimea, Kazan, Astrakhan, and 'Great Horde'.

1475 The Khan of Crimea subjects himself to the Osman Sultan.

1480 The Grand Duke of Moscow stops paying tribute.

1502 The last remnants of the 'Golden Horde' are defeated and dispersed.

1552 The Russians conquer the Khanate of Kazan.

1557 The Russians conquer the Khanate of Astrakhan.

1783 The Khanate of Crimea is incorporated into the Russian Empire.

The Ilkhans in Iran

1256–9 Hülägü, a grandson of Chinggiz Khan, conquers Transoxiana, Iran, and Iraq.

1258 Demise of the Abbasid Caliphate in Baghdad—1260 defeated by the Mamluks of Egypt at the Spring of Goliath (north of Jerusalem).

1265 Hülägü dies, a Shamanist with Buddhist tendencies; his chief wife was a Nestorian Christian.

1265–82 Abaqa, his son, fights against the Golden Horde and the Mamluks.

1284–91 Arghūn, his son, attempts to establish Buddhism in Iran. Financial pressure. The Ilkhan dies during a people's revolt.

1294 Attempted introduction of paper money.

1295–1304 Ghāzān, his son, establishes law and order again. Renewed economic prosperity. The great program of reforms worked out by his minister, the physician, and historian Rashīd ad-Dīn, is not carried on after his early death—Futile wars in Syria and Caucasia.

1295 Ghāzān becomes a Sunni Muslim; in this way the Ilkhans become the national dynasty of Iran—The ties binding them to the Mongol Great Khans of China disappear.

1304–16 Öljäitü, Ghāzān's brother, builds in 1307 the new capital Soltaniyä. He adopts Shi'ism in 1310.

1316–35 Abū Sa'īd, another Sunni, succeeds in infancy; Chamberlain (until 1327) Choban.

1335–54 The state of the Ilkhan disintegrates in civil wars.

1360 Tīmūr, starting from Samarkand, begins to assert himself. He conquers large areas, among others Iran and Mesopotamia, and invades the Golden Horde (1375, 1379), northern India (1398), and Turkey (battle of Angora 1402).

1405 Tīmūr dies in Otrār on the Jaxartes river during a campaign against China.

Central Asia/Transoxiana

1251–59 Möngkä, a brother of Hülägü (cf. above, p. 210), Great Khan in Karakorum; tolerant Shamanist.

1253–6 William of Rubruck, a lower-German Franciscan, as envoy of the Pope and of St. Louis of France at the Great Khan's court in Karakorum.

1260–94 Qubilai, Möngkä's brother, in 1279/80 conquers China south of the Yangtze Kiang; end of the Sung dynasty. The Mongol Yüan dynasty which is to rule China until 1368 is founded.

1260–1309 In Central Asia fighting occurred between the Khans descended from Ögädäi and Chaghatai. Attacks made by the Ilkhan and the Golden Horde.

1326–34 The Khan Tarmashīrīn (that is, the Buddhist Dharma Shri or Dharmaśīla) goes over to Sunna Islam which spreads rapidly in Central Asia.

1334–60 Central Asia splits into a western half (Transoxiana) with a predominantly feudal structure founded on Islam, and an eastern part, 'Mogholistān', under monarchic rule where Islam has little influence.

1360 Tīmūr (born 1335) starting from Samarkand, begins to assert himself. He makes Samarkand the capital of his vast empire

and adorns it with magnificent buildings, which to a large
extent are still standing today.

1405   Tīmūr dies.

1405–1507 The Tīmūrids, his descendants, soon embrace Iranian
culture. The spiritual life of the country benefits greatly from
rulers who generally seek peace and who, in addition, have
literary interests. The Mongol-Turkish power gives way
before the Iranian spirit and is in this way ennobled.

INDEX

INDEX

[Page references given in italics refer to sources.]